EVOLUTION FROM CREATION TO NEW CREATION

"Evolution from Creation to New Creation is like a scorecard to help you tell one player from another in a lively cultural contest. The science of evolution often 'comes shrink-wrapped in an ideology that appears to be an anti-Christian religion of its own.' Peters and Hewlett abhor the 'ontological materialism' (read: atheism) blatant in many social applications of Darwinism. They deal critically but respectfully and separately with creationism and Intelligent Design, then focus on the broad middle ground of theistic evolution, within which they stake out their own position. They offer what amounts to a cladistic taxonomy of theistic responses to evolution based on five credential branch-points: deep time, natural selection, common descent, divine action, and theodicy. The book's title hints at the importance of eschatology to their own schema. Recommended as a thoughtful, theologically oriented approach to an issue that divides the church as well as society."

Walter R. Hearn, Professor of Christianity & Science,
New College Berkeley; author of *Being a Christian in Science.*

D0067934

"This is a wonderful book—informed, punchy, comprehensive, fun. . . . This should be on the reading list of all who care about these issues, and indeed on the reading list of those who do not yet (but should) care about these issues."

Michael Ruse,
Lucyle T. Werkmeister Professor of Philosophy, Florida State University

---

"Peters and Hewlett provide a most welcome guide for those seeking to understand current debates over the possible relationships of religious faith and biological evolution. One of the strengths of their presentation is that it is truly interdisciplinary, but it is also sensitive to the nuances of the debates. It not only clearly distinguishes the Intelligent Design movement from Young Earth Creationism, but also provides the best overview available of the different emphases within the Intelligent Design camp. There is a similar discerning survey of various advocates of theistic evolution. Most important, Peters and Hewlett push beyond mere description of alternatives, advancing their own constructive proposal by emphasizing the eschatological dimension of theistic belief. This is an important contribution to the Science and Religion dialogue."

Randy L. Maddox,
Paul T. Walls Professor of Wesleyan Theology, Seattle Pacific University

---

"In the dialogue between science and theology, too often one is master and the other slave. I commend this book for giving science and theology each their proper due, especially against the backdrop of so contested an issue as biological evolution. Written by a scientist and a theologian, this book is refreshing for its balance, honesty, and thoughtfulness."

William A. Dembski,
author of *The Design Inference* and *No Free Lunch*

"Several factors make *Evolution from Creation to New Creation* a unique and highly valuable book on evolution and Christian theology. It provides a careful and balanced comparative analysis of a wide spectrum of views in 'theistic evolution,' and, remarkably, it adds to this a thoughtful analysis of both ultra-conservative approaches such as creation science and Intelligent Design as well as naturalistic and atheistic views. Most important, the authors exemplify the kind of interdisciplinary and ecumenical scholarship so needed today—both possess theological and scientific expertise and together represent Roman Catholic and Lutheran traditions—and out of this they offer their own constructive and original theological vision that seeks to solve the problems besetting these approaches and point the discussion forward in new directions."

Robert John Russell,
Founder and Director, The Center for Theology and the Natural Sciences,
Professor of Theology and Science in Residence, the Graduate Theological Union, Berkeley

EVOLUTION FROM CREATION TO NEW CREATION

CONFLICT, CONVERSATION, AND CONVERGENCE

TED PETERS
AND
MARTINEZ HEWLETT

Abingdon Press
Nashville

EVOLUTION FROM CREATION TO NEW CREATION
CONFLICT, CONVERSATION, AND CONVERGENCE

Copyright © 2003 by Abingdon Press

This book is printed on recycled, acid-free, elemental-chlorine–free paper.

Library of Congress Cataloging-in-Publication Data

Peters, Ted, 1941-
   Evolution from creation to new creation: conflict, conversation, and convergence / Ted Peters
and Martinez Hewlett.
      p. cm.
Includes bibliographical references and index.
   ISBN 0-687-02374-2 (pbk. : alk. paper)
   1. Evolution (Biology)—Religious aspects—Christianity. 2. Creationism. 3. Intelligent design
(Teleology) I. Hewlett, Martinez. II. Title.

   BS659.P48 2003
   231.7'652—dc21

                                                              2003009087

03 04 05 06 07 08 09 10 11 12—10 9 8 7 6 5 4 3 2 1

MANUFACTURED IN THE UNITED STATES OF AMERICA

CONTENTS

FOREWORD

The specter of Charles Darwin now hovers over science and culture more imposingly than ever. Not only biology, but also psychology, sociology, medicine, engineering, cosmology, ethics and even religious studies increasingly feel the impact of Darwin's surprising picture of life. Instead of undergoing the eclipse for which anti-evolutionists have so ardently longed, the modest nineteenth-century naturalist's ideas are now firmly entrenched. They continue to mold intellectual life and, directly or indirectly, the consciousness of people all over the world.

Why, then, have Christian theology and religious education virtually evaded, when they have not actively tried to suppress, a close encounter of faith with the Darwinian science of evolution? One reason is that during the modern period Christian thought, with some significant exceptions, has been content to grant to science alone the task of understanding the natural world. For itself theology has typically reserved the job of interpreting and shaping spiritually the inner world of the individual person and the domain of social interaction among humans. By and large theology has allowed the natural world to slip from its grasp, a most ironic development in light of the biblical tradition's robust teachings about creation. Our seminaries and religious institutions still generally abide by the neat modern separation of the world of nature from that of persons and human society.

However, as theology is now beginning to notice, Darwin and his scientific descendants have joined together the worlds of nature and humanity in a seamless narrative of becoming. Features of our humanity, of course, still make us unique within the larger community of life, but to ignore the larger story of evolution is also to ignore ourselves. The tidy theological detachment of human existence from the rest of the universe, as the present book demonstrates, will no longer work.

Another reason for the Christian world's neglect and even scorn of evolution is that theologians and religious educators have too often simply identified

Darwinism with atheistic materialism. They are not always to blame for this unfortunate mix-up, since numerous scientific experts and popularisers of evolution have themselves complacently indulged the very same conflation. But there is really no good reason to equate evolutionary biology with materialism, even if some very influential scientific thinkers and philosophers have done so.

It is now quite clear that, in spite of his own personal religious misgivings, Darwin himself had no intention of making his discoveries a vehicle for materialist philosophy. Indeed, Darwin remained until his death sensitive to the religious anxieties his ideas engendered. He was deeply troubled that they offended some readers of his works. Therefore, Christians today do the man and his thought no justice if they lazily allow scientists and other intellectuals to perpetuate the notion that biological evolution goes best with materialism. The authors of this book (a skilled Roman Catholic scientist and a highly respected Lutheran theologian) adroitly steer us away from such an unfounded association: "To hold a valid scientific position based upon an analysis of the data explained according to the model of natural selection is one thing. To turn this into a philosophy, however, is quite another thing." "In fact," as they go on to point out, "it is likely that the ideological inferences that go far beyond the biological science have generated most of the controversy that evolution has precipitated."

A third, and more substantive, reason why we have turned our gaze from evolution is that, at least at first sight, it may seem to make the world much too wicked to be interpreted as God's creation. Perhaps it would be better not to look too closely at the suffering and struggle in the evolutionary story of life lest this tempt us to change our thoughts about God in ways that deviate too much from tradition. To the authors of this book, however, the evasion of evolution is a lost opportunity for Christian faith and theology. A mature religious response to evolution has nothing to lose and everything to gain from an engagement with science after Darwin. A faith-filled look at evolution, in fact, permits theology to recover in a fresh way some of the most fundamental insights of biblical religion.

Of course, the big fear for many Christians today, is that evolution rules out divine intelligent design in nature. In an even larger sense, it seems to place in question beliefs about the possible directionality of life and purpose in the universe. Hence, the clarification of terms such as "design," "direction," and "purpose" is absolutely essential in the current debates, and it is one of the many merits of this nicely organized and clearly written book to define such terms in a manner that readers from all backgrounds will find enlightening. Going beyond clarification of terms, however, the authors of the present work set forth a theologically adventurous, yet solidly biblical, way of reconciling the apparent aimlessness of evolution on the one hand, with Christian trust in a providential and saving God on the other. Their proposal will deservedly spark worthwhile discussion of its own.

I will not reveal here the main argument of the book, but instead encourage readers to follow closely and critically the authors' layout of the relevant positions in the fevered debates about God and evolution as the book moves swiftly toward a proposed theological resolution in chapter 7. There I hope readers will find, as I do, that shifting the entire issue of "God and evolution" into the context of biblical faith's orientation toward the eschatological future makes all the difference in the world as far as our making theological sense of evolution is concerned. Readers may not agree with every facet of the creative proposal mapped out in the book's finale. However, it will be hard for them to contest its claim that any truly Christian theology of nature must be shaped fundamentally by the biblical motif of promise and hope for new creation. I am happy to recommend this book not only as an introduction to the contemporary discussion of evolution and Christian faith, but also as a fresh contribution to theology after Darwin.

John F. Haught
Georgetown University

PREFACE

It has been nearly a century and a half since Charles Darwin published the first edition of *The Origin of Species by Means of Natural Selection*. In that time the conceptual model of evolution that he proposed for all living forms, descent with modification from a common ancestor by means of natural selection, has risen to the status of one of the major intellectual achievements of Western thought. It has captured the scientific imagination, embedded itself in our culture, and inflamed critics of many sorts. Most important, the concept of evolution has lit the fuse on an apparent conflict between religious believers and practicing scientists. We emphasize here that it is an "apparent conflict," since it is our conviction that Darwinian science and belief in God are not mutually exclusive.

We present to you our analysis of the current situation. We are a complementary team of a scientist (MH) and a theologian (TP). We are both committed Christians, Roman Catholic (MH) and Lutheran (TP). Our collective experiences in our individual disciplines and in our faith journeys are brought to bear on this collaborative approach to the issues surrounding evolutionary theory, its critics, and its reconciliation with theism.

We begin with the question: Are faith and science at war? To this we answer no. A war is raging, to be sure; but it is not a war of faith *against* science. It is a chaotic war with many combatants, all trying to secure scientific territory for themselves. In our thematic introduction (chapter 1) we identify the warriors and set down the parameters of our approach. We then proceed to a description of the science in Darwinian evolutionary theory (chapter 2), followed by a discussion of social applications of this theory, particularly social Darwinism, sociobiology, and evolutionary psychology (chapter 3). What we say about Darwinian science is brief; yet we explain it in terms that are readily accessible so as to clarify just what is theologically at stake. We turn at that point to those who oppose the Darwinian model: the scientific creationists (chapter 4) and the Intelligent Design theorists (chapter 5). It may surprise the reader to see how these critics of Darwinian evolution so positively embrace science; by no means do they oppose science on the grounds of faith. Rather, they seek to improve science, from their point of view. Next we analyze those who occupy the middle ground, namely, the theistic evolutionists who develop theories showing how God uses evolutionary processes for creative purposes (chapter 6). In each of these chapters we attempt to present the various positions as fairly as possible and then provide a critique of these positions. Our own reflection leads us to support theistic evolution, offering a constructive model that integrates evolutionary change with God's transformatory promises for redemption. Our constructive proposal will be presented at the book's end (chapter 7).

Our purpose in writing this book is to explore the features of this controversy that continue to engage the scientific, educational, and religious communities within our society. The confrontation that was brought to the public consciousness with the Scopes trial in 1925 has been raised again and again with court cases and meetings of boards of education. We want to offer an analysis that will provide some perspective from the middle looking toward the extremes—a book that might be a useful tool for clarifying the positions within this great debate.

For whom have we written this book? Well, for everyone engaged in the debate, really. However, there are some readers who might benefit more immediately from it. We would like our analysis and reflection to be read by theologians, by scientists, and by those whom they instruct.

We the authors are educators, and we would hope that our book would serve as a teaching tool in colleges, universities, and seminaries. Since so much of what we discuss has direct application for congregations of believers, we suggest that this volume should be read by those preparing for pastoral leadership in seminaries, regardless of denomination, and by pastors already in the ministry. The book could be used as part of course material not only in the seminary or theological graduate school, but also as a text for religious education programs in the parish setting.

Science instructors of parochial high schools or Christian day schools can use what we have written here as background material or in some cases as direct reading assignments for their students. In the classroom setting, a work such as this can provide a valuable addition to the teaching of biology and the Darwinian model. Rather than ignoring the religious ramifications of evolution out of trepidation, we would hope that this book will bring confidence that the various religious positions can be understood sympathetically and discussed openly. We trust this book will also be of value to the growing numbers of parents engaged in home schooling, for whom a thoughtful consideration of these issues is so important.

We sincerely hope research scientists will find our scholarship of value. Frequently, scientists understandably walk on egg shells, trying to avoid arousing religious ire. Sometimes, in self-defense, scientists along with journalists paint caricatures of their perceived enemies as religious buffoons. This helps calm fears temporarily, but it fails to bring lasting peace and cooperation. Too often, we believe, the caricatures that are painted in the popular press of the protagonists in this controversy do not accurately reflect the positions being held. In this book we try to represent those positions as carefully and accurately as we can, while still offering substantive critiques of them.

Finally we think the interested lay public will find this volume to be a fresh approach to the discussion. We have tried to strike a middle ground, all too frequently left untrammeled in the polemics that surround the Darwinian model. On the one hand, we accept and celebrate the advances of science that support the Darwinian model of evolution, but we do so without embracing the philosophical postures and social ideologies that some have attempted to attach to it. On the other hand, we employ the four sources of theology—scripture, tradition, experience, and reason—in establishing a solid foundation on which to construct a meaningful integration of science with faith. We hope that our readers will find our efforts informative if not edifying.

ACKNOWLEDGMENTS

Each of us wishes to acknowledge the other and thank the other. Like combining peanut butter and jelly to make the single taste of a delicious sandwich, each has contributed something distinctive to what has become a thoroughly blended entrée. To this recipe Gail Hewlett has added steady encouragement and creative suggestions that have enhanced the presentation.

The Center for Theology and the Natural Sciences (CTNS) at the Graduate Theological Union (GTU) in Berkeley, California, has helped provide an indispensable network of communication with scientists and theologians worldwide. The mission of CTNS is to facilitate the creative mutual interaction between natural science and theological reflection. We thank CTNS and its supporters for paving the path we have followed in this book.

Because of the wide scope of subject matter and the professional tensions aroused by the public controversy, we the authors found ourselves needing advanced critical review of our work to help ensure accuracy and sensitivity. We have asked veteran scholars in the field as well as experienced educators plus our doctoral students to read portions of the manuscript and offer constructive suggestions for revision. Many individuals have generously given us their time and energy to aid in the development of our manuscript. We would like to offer our gratitude especially to Francisco J. Ayala, William Dembski, John Haught, Walter Hearn, Susan Jagoda, Thomas Lindell, Marty Maddox, Randy Maddox, Joshua Moritz, Nancey Murphy, Michael Ruse, Robert John Russell, Jeffrey Schloss, Eugenie Scott, and Howard J. van Till. We also thank Whitney Bauman at CTNS for manuscript preparation and Kathy Armistead at Abingdon Press for her editorial guidance.

Ted Peters
Martinez Hewlett
Easter, April 20, 2003

CHAPTER ONE

WAR? REALLY?

W e've put 450 pages into this earth history book and not once did we use the E word," said Susan Jagoda during our meeting at the Lawrence Hall of Science on the University of California campus in Berkeley. Susan had invited a handful of us from the Center for Theology and the Natural Sciences to meet with her colleagues. They were preparing a teacher's guide for middle school science instructors.

"What E word are you talking about?" we asked, initially puzzled.

"Why, 'Evolution,' of course. Eliminating the word 'evolution' and focusing on the fossil evidence that suggests change over time gets rid of one of the red flags teachers face in the classroom when introducing the concept of evolution."

"But you can't teach earth history without the theory of evolution, can you?" we protested.

"Well, now you're seeing the difficulty we're facing," they responded with knowing smiles.

High school science classrooms have become battlegrounds, and some teachers and even their textbook writers are in retreat. If only one or two students a day, heavily armed with anti-evolution arguments, speak up, the contentious atmosphere is discomfortable for instructors. The argumentative students come from families angry that their religious rights are being violated when tax-supported educational institutions teach a science along with an accompanying materialist philosophy that undermines their faith in God. Local school boards in virtually every state are being challenged by nationally organized religious lobbies to include creationism in their science curricula; and defenders of the policy of teaching evolution alone find legal support coming from counter-creationist national lobbies.

Is this a war between science and religion? No. It may look like it. Indeed, a battle is taking place. Yet, it would be a mistake to describe it as a battle between natural science and the Christian faith. To discern just what kind of battle is raging is the task this book sets out to accomplish.

This book is coauthored by a scientist and a theologian. For us, science and faith are like lunch and dinner; we don't want to go through a day without some of each. Both nourish a healthy mind. Both tantalize our taste buds for curiosity. And both build the brain "muscles" we need to exercise our thought processes about reality. Why would anyone want to diet and dine on one or the other rather than both? Intellectual malnutrition would result.

Why Fight?

We are by no means alone. Christians in the past, both scientists and theologians, relied on the "Two Books" metaphor. Each book reveals something about God. The Book of Nature tells us about God's rationality and ingenuity in creation; and the Bible tells us about God's story of redemption. In his *Advancement of Learning*, Francis Bacon admonishes us to read both of the books. We cannot "search too far or be too well-studied in the book of God's word, or in the book of God's works, divinity or philosophy; but rather let men endeavor an endless progress or proficiency in both."[1]

Although the U.S. National Academy of Sciences reads only one book, the Book of Nature, it does not censor the other book, the Bible. Nor does it forbid reading the great literature of other religious traditions:

> At the root of the apparent conflict between some religions and evolution is a misunderstanding of the critical difference between religious and scientific ways of knowing. Religions and science answer different questions about the world. Whether there is a purpose to the universe or a purpose for human existence are not questions for science. Religious and scientific ways of knowing have played, and will continue to play, significant roles in human history.[2]

As we can see, the National Academy of Sciences would like to bring peace to the battlefield.

Such a peace mission is the mission of the Center for Theology and the Natural Sciences (CTNS) at the Graduate Theological Union in Berkeley, California. Founded by physicist and theologian Robert John Russell in 1982, CTNS fosters the creative mutual interaction between natural science and Christian faith. Note the word "interaction" here. What the National Academy of Sciences above recommends is that science and religion should speak different languages—that is, they should ask different questions and thereby coexist without interaction in the nonoverlapping magesteria (NOMA) model of

Stephen Jay Gould. We want more. The authors of this book look for actual interaction between evolutionary biology and the Christian understanding of creation. Still more, in addition to creation we want to include the Christian understanding of redemption as well.

Who Started the Fight?

Like kids in a brawl on the playground, those seeking justice ask: Who started it? In the battle over evolution, almost every finger points at the creationists. The scientific creationists started the whole mess. Yet, if you ask the creationists who started it, they will point their finger at the Darwinists. "They hit me first," we could expect to hear. The creationists are right on this point; and noncreationist theologians need to acknowledge it.

The question of who threw the first punch arises for us because the science of evolution comes shrink-wrapped in an ideology that appears to be an anti-Christian religion of its own. The serious theologian reveres genuine science, of course. The nondefensive and curious theologian would like to investigate possible crossovers and consonance between what scientists tell us about the natural world and what Christians understand about creation and humanity. This is made difficult, however, because the science must first be extracted from its ideological wrapping.

Now, one would ordinarily think that what comes first is the pure science. Later, then, the pure science becomes colored by ideological packaging. Unfortunately, the reverse is the case. What we receive as the tradition of evolutionary thought is a complex package of ideology within which the pure science lies buried; but we have to extract it to appreciate it. The concrete situation in which we find ourselves is a battle of ideologies from which we need to abstract the scientific component, not the other way around. This by no means makes the situation impossible, just a bit more difficult.

When our small band of CTNS professors and graduate students in Berkeley trundled down to San Diego to visit the Institute for Creation Research (ICR) in October 2002, Duane Gish announced he had some news. Michael Ruse has converted, he told us. Now, philosopher Michael Ruse is widely known as a sharp critic of creationism and a staunch defender of Darwinism. Just what kind of conversion could this be? we wondered out loud. Gish provided us with an unpublished paper written by Ruse, "Evolution as Religion." In this paper, Ruse reports how Gish had convinced him to look at the history of evolutionary thought as itself a religious phenomenon. "I now think the Creationists like Gish are absolutely right in their complaint! Evolution is promoted by its practitioners as more than mere science. . . . Evolution is a religion. This was true of evolution in the beginning and it is true of evolution still today."[3]

Just what could this mean? Charles Darwin's grandfather, Erasmus Darwin, was quite instrumental in making evolutionary thought a cocktail conversation topic in England and America. Erasmus was a deist who flaunted his religion in the face of traditional Christian theism; and he interpreted progress—progress in both nature and society—according to laws laid down by a noninterventionist deity. Just as society progresses from small villages to big cities, the senior Darwin believed nature progresses from undifferentiated blobs of life called monads into an apotheosis of human complexity. Salvation comes through progress, not providence; it comes through nature, not divine grace. This in-your-face naturalism is what young Charles Darwin inherited as he began his own scientific research.

In contrast to his grandfather, young Charles sought to make his science less ideological. Yes, Charles secularized biology. Yet, he did not try to build deism, let alone atheism, into the biology. "My views are not at all necessarily atheistical," he wrote.[4] Nevertheless, Charles Darwin's own contemporaries such as Thomas Huxley saw the secularizing implications and sought to herald a materialist philosophy that would allegedly liberate modern society from the chains of Christianity's anachronistic traditions. The famous debate between Huxley and Samuel Wilberforce, Bishop of Oxford, is remembered as a victory for intellectual freedom over religious ignorance. Allegedly, the Oxford bishop asked the scientist who claimed human beings are descended from primates whether a monkey would be found on Huxley's mother's side or his father's side. Huxley response was, in effect, that he would rather be descended from an ape than from a bishop of the Church of England. Here are Huxley's words: "I asserted, and I repeat, that a man has no reason to be ashamed of having an ape for a grandfather. If there were an ancestor whom I should feel shame in recalling, it would rather be a man, a man of restless and versatile intellect, who, not content with an equivocal success in his own sphere of activity, plunges into scientific questions with which he had no real acquaintance, only to obscure them by an aimless rhetoric, and distract the attention of his hearers from the real point at issue by eloquent digressions and skilled appeals to religious prejudice."[5] This story has become a verbal icon in the new church of science as it tries to replace the supposed atavism and dogmatism of the traditional church.

Thomas Huxley's grandson, Julian Huxley, expanded the evolutionist credo in a 1959 address at the one hundredth anniversary of the publication of Darwin's *Origin of Species*. No longer can modern people who believe in evolution take refuge in a heavenly father figure who watches providentially over us, his children. Once we have evolved to a higher level of maturity, we should give up refuge under the umbrella of divine authority. The concept of evolution explains all of reality: flowers, fish, human society, and social values. "The evolutionary vision is enabling us to discern, however incompletely, the lineaments of the new religion."[6] Evolution provides the necessary tenets, according to the Huxley tradition.

Another of Darwin's contemporaries, Herbert Spencer, transmuted Darwin's science into an evolutionary metaphysics and social ethic. Spencer coined the phrase "survival of the fittest" in 1864 in the first volume of his work, *Principles of Biology*, which Charles Darwin then equated with "natural selection." Earlier, Spencer had published *Social Statics* (1851), and from the combination of the Darwinian model with Spencer's social program came social Darwinism. This proposed a naturalistic ethic that applied the animal struggle to survive to economic and political values, meaning the state should stay out of protecting the poor in society. The weak should simply fall and make way for the strong. The unfit deserve their fate. Spencer's social Darwinism is not just a suffix to evolutionary Darwinism, however. A prefix was present, too. Darwin himself, according to Stephen Jay Gould, had already gleaned from Adam Smith's economic theory the structure he then superimposed on biology: "Darwin transferred the paradoxical argument of Adam Smith's economics into biology."[7] The road from biology by way of economics to ethics is not straight; it is circular. It's like a racetrack; and science is but one pit stop.

Nineteenth-century Darwinian piety still flourishes among its early–twenty-first-century neo-Darwinian disciples. Harvard founder of sociobiology, Edward O. Wilson, wants the epic of evolution to provide the single comprehensive story of nature that includes and explains all human culture, including religion and ethics. This evolutionary epic will eliminate transcendental factors. Tipping toward deism, Wilson places his religious vision within his evolutionary vision: "We can be proud as a species because, having discovered that we are alone, we owe the gods very little."[8]

Michael Ruse advises us to be tolerant. If such people want to make a religion out of evolution, they should be permitted to do so. Religious liberty should apply to evolutionary religion just as it does to traditional religion.

However, our point here is a different one. Our point is that it is difficult for us today to discriminate between evolution as a scientific research program and evolution as a religious ideology. The two come together in a single package, the science wrapped in the ideology. What we think of as pure science is, in some sense, an abstraction. We must dissect it from the complex cultural phenomenon in which it is embedded.

Now, we might ask: Is there a "there" there? Is Darwinism merely an ideology that parades as a science? No. Genuine science is present and available. Darwinian evolutionary biology qualifies as solid science because it generates progressive research—that is, hypotheses based upon its assumptions lead eventually to new knowledge about the natural world. Biologist Kenneth Miller puts it this way: "In the real world of science, in the hard-bitten realities of lab bench and field station, the intellectual triumph of Darwin's great idea is total. The paradigm of evolution succeeds every day as a hardworking theory that explains new data and new ideas from scores of fields."[9] Darwinism is explanatorily adequate.

As explanatorily adequate, both the scientist and the theologian as well must take it seriously.

We might still ask: Is it worth the effort to extract the science from its ideological wrappings? Yes, indeed. We certainly believe it is worth the effort. When theology is not at war, theology is curious. Learning about the natural world indirectly enhances learning about God's work in the creation. Science provides a window through which we can perceive nature's intricacies and beauties. Whether the window be a microscope or a telescope, explaining nature's mysteries opens up knowledge while expanding our awareness of where we lack knowledge. The God whom Christians believe is the architect and engineer of our world has left footprints in reality's sand, and the scientist can help us follow those prints to wherever they lead.

What science has to offer by way of growth in knowledge is of intrinsic value. It needs no added value. Still, there is more. Alister McGrath reminds us: "This is a major theme of Christian theology—that the natural world, while wonderful in itself, offers a way to begin to discern the glory of God."[10] For the indirect discernment of God's glory, careful assay of the gold within the dross is called for. Like gold streaks in a stream rock, the theologian needs to engage initially in a smelting process to extract what is valuable. The seemingly impenetrable rock that is evolution can actually be refined, and the precious scientific metal can be separated from the dross for the theologian's artful craft.

Creationism, Intelligent Design, and Theistic Evolution

Most would say that the creationists have thrown the first punch, even if the creationists would complain that they were provoked by the scientific evolutionists. Others have jumped into the fray. The Intelligent Design (ID) gang has jumped on the Darwinists, provoked by the same conflation of biology and ideology. The theistic evolutionists to date have sat on the sidelines, biting their fingernails, rooting meekly for the scientific evolutionists. Once in a while they'll shout an invective against both the creationists and ID scrappers, but to date they have not wanted their own eyes blackened or their school clothes soiled by a brawl. We find the most merit in the position taken by theistic evolutionists, even though badges of courage deserve to be pinned on the T-shirts of those more involved in the mayhem.

The mantle we want to shoulder is that of theistic evolution. In responding to the call of theistic evolution, we are painfully aware that the prophet's road becomes one filled with intellectual landmines. We need to be cautious as we travel this road. The doctrine of creation leads the theological convoy; but the delicate question of teleology within evolutionary development could explode fundamental Christian commitments. Christian faith cannot get along without purpose for nature. Nature is God's creation. Nature is valuable because it is the object of God's love; and people of faith value nature because it sings hymns to God's glory. To concede to our scientific friends that evolutionary processes are without internal direction or without inherent purpose places fundamental Christian commitments about creation in a danger zone. Yet, we plan to enter this danger zone.

Even more explosive threats lie in wait. The most troublesome is the theodicy problem, the problem of evil. By *evil* here we mean not only human sinning, but also what we find in the natural world, namely, violence, suffering, and death. If a theologian is willing to affirm that evolution as Charles Darwin described it—governed by natural selection and survival of the fittest—is the divinely appointed method by which God has brought creation to its present threshold in natural history, does God then become the one responsible for the untold suffering of countless sentient beings over eons of time? Why would a God whom Christians believe to be loving and compassionate employ a method of creation that leaves such wanton carnage and such obscene debris of death?

Theologians are not alone in posing the theodicy problem. Darwin himself did:

> I had no intention to write atheistically. But I own that I cannot see as plainly as others do, and as I should wish to do, evidence of design and beneficence on all sides of us. There seems to me too much misery in the world. I cannot persuade myself that a beneficent and omnipotent God would have designedly created the Ichneumonidae [insects whose larvae are usually internal parasites of other insect larvae] with the express intention of their feeding within the living bodies of caterpillars, or that a cat should play with mice.[11]

Darwin was a sensitive person. His innate compassion was assaulted by what he observed in the natural world: laws by which the predator devoured the prey, and a history in which 98 percent of all species had become extinct before the modern era. Such waste, Darwin thought, could not be reconciled with a God of purpose or design or compassion. Without positively advocating atheism, Darwin could not ascribe the creation of this biological world to a divine designer. So, in concert with the science of his day, he expelled ideas of direction or design or *telos* from his evolutionary scheme.

Biologist and theologian Celia E. Deane-Drummond warns us of the dangers to theistic evolution lurking in the theodicy problem. If one tries to avoid the Scylla of Darwin's implicit materialism by attributing natural selection and survival of the fittest to God's active work, then God must be defined as "cruel and insensitive." If one tries to avoid this Charybdis by attributing passivity to God, by saying God self-constricts so as to leave autonomous nature to its own devices, then God ceases to be a genuine "Creator of the world" we live in. "Such problems of how to explain the apparent immorality in the natural world are a permanent aggravation for those seeking to reinstate any kind of natural theology today in a post-Darwinian world."[12]

What this means for the theistic evolutionist is that simply to relabel evolution as God's plan is to sacrifice the very qualities of God that Christian faith so reveres. Darwin could see this. Theistic evolutionists dare not be blind to it.

Creation and Providence

In what Christians call the "doctrine of creation," theologians assert that God is responsible for the very existence of the world, the entire world of nature and history. In classical theism, God is said to create from nothing (*creatio ex nihilo*), meaning that God is not dependent upon anything external to God. God does not need preexisting stuff or material to mold and shape; God creates the stuff from nothing. This means the created world had a beginning, a moment in which time and space began. The flip side of *creatio ex nihilo*, according to theists, is that God is *a se*—that is, *aseity* means God is totally independent, complete in Godself. God was not compelled by any inner or outer force to create a world. God has brought creatures into existence out of love for creatures who are other than God.

This concept of creation from nothing applies primarily to the existence of the universe in its entirety. However, it does have another application in the history of theology, a curious application. Some Christian thinkers hold that God creates each individual soul from nothing. At some point in human development, God creates an immortal soul and imparts it to a mortal body; and this establishes human personhood. Pope John Paul II, for example, is convicted by this view. The Roman pontiff intends to say that the scientist can explain the origin of our physical bodies through evolution, but only the theologian can explain the origin of our immortal souls.[13] This doctrine is known as "creationism." However, care needs to be taken here, because the one word "creationism" can refer to two quite different things. On the one hand, it can refer to the idea that each soul is created *ex nihilo*; while, on the other hand, it can refer to the school of thought that opposes Darwinian evolution. Unless otherwise indicated, the second of these two meanings will be the one employed in this book.

In addition to *creatio ex nihilo*, theologians are also accustomed to think of *creatio continua*, continuing creation. For theological schools of thought such as Whiteheadian or process panentheism, the idea of creation from nothing is repudiated, and continuing creation is put in its place. Accordingly, the universe is said to lack a beginning; the cosmos is said to exist everlastingly without beginning or end. Contemporary Christian theists, in contrast to process panentheists, affirm a beginning to the existence of the world and also affirm God's continuing creative activity—that is, they affirm both *creatio ex nihilo* and *creatio continua*. Accordingly, for both theists and process panentheists, creation at the beginning was not a once and for all time event; rather, God continues to create and we witness this by observing transformation in the ongoing natural and historical processes. God's continuing creative action is necessary for a doctrine of redemption, for trusting in God's promise to redeem the world from decay and death.

Closely allied to the concept of continuing creation is the doctrine of providence. From the Latin *providere*, to see ahead, "providence" refers to God's care for us by looking ahead toward our future with a beneficent eye. The concept of abiding providence or care distinguishes deists from theists. For a deist, God creates the world and then takes a vacation, leaving the world to baby-sit for itself. For a theist, God creates the world, sustains the world, and then, like a loving parent, nourishes it devotedly.

Creatio ex nihilo alone will give us deism. *Creatio continua* alone will give us panentheism. *Creatio ex nihilo* plus *creatio continua* plus providence will give us theism, the affirmation that God acts to bring the world into existence, acts to transform and redeem it, and acts to provide meaning and purpose and direction within the world processes. Most but not all Christian theologians involved in the controversy over evolutionary theory are theists. Our constructive proposal for a theistic evolutionary approach will follow this theistic path.

The Problem of Purpose

The central problem faced by advocates of a theistic interpretation of evolution is not one of reconciling science with a literal reading of Genesis. Nor is the problem one of transformation of one species into another. Nor is it a problem raised by gradual change over long periods of deep time. Rather, it is the problem of purpose.

Questions of purpose surround evolutionary biology like a husk surrounds an ear of corn. Is the course of evolutionary history guided by some inherent purpose? Does evolutionary change have a direction? Can we measure evolution's progress? Can we speak of human beings as a higher form of nature because we are further developed? Can we speak of the human race as nature becoming conscious of itself; and can we consider humanity as evolution's achievement? Can we discern a purpose in nature that establishes a moral guide for society?

Why is purpose a problem? Can we not think of nature progressing through evolution just as the design of automobiles is progressing through engineering? After all, we speak of technology "evolving," so is it not appropriate to equate evolution with advance? Evolution makes things better, right? The early Darwin would lead us to believe in progress. He concludes the second edition of *Origin* by prognosticating, "Hence we may look with some confidence to a secure future of great length. And as natural selection works solely by and for the good of each being, all corporeal and mental endowments will tend to progress towards perfection."[14]

This cultural interpretation of natural selection leads us to say: yes, evolution is a form of progress. As a doctrine of progress, evolution becomes one more modern Western ideology among others. As a doctrine of progress it is a philosophy, a value system, an ideology, maybe even a materialistic religion.

However, if we seek what is narrowly scientific and treat evolution strictly as a theory to explain biological change, then we must expunge all references to an overall divine purpose. Local adaptive purpose such as fins for swimming or wings for flying is obvious. So also local purpose belonging to parts of an organism contributing to the function of the whole—such as the cornea of the eye contributing to seeing—can be discerned scientifically, to be sure. Yet, no overarching direction or doctrine of evolutionary progress can be considered scientific. The expunging of a grand design is a principle of scientific research that is dogmatic to today's evolutionary biologists. They appeal to Charles Darwin himself for having set the precedent by relying upon chance variation. Natural selection, suggested Darwin, is not a secular form of divine providence, despite what he said about progress and perfection in the flourish cited above. Natural selection favors the fit, to be sure; but what determines fitness has nothing to do with an overall purpose or direction in nature. Fitness is the result of blind chance. "I am inclined to look at everything as resulting from designed laws," wrote Darwin, assigning "the details, whether good or bad, left to the working out of what we may call chance."[15] Chance, not a divinely imparted design or purpose, has become dogmatic to evolutionary biologists when conscious that they are pursuing pure scientific research.

As we shift from nineteenth-century Darwinism to twentieth-century neo-Darwinism and mix in genetic variation as the mechanism of natural selection, we still find that purpose is expunged. Genetic variation is due to random mutations in our DNA, say neo-Darwinists. It must be emphasized that mutations are random—that is, contingent events, chance events. They are not necessary. They are not guided by some inner *telos* or entelechy embedded in nature. Philosopher of science Michael Ruse drives this point home with force:

> Surely Darwinian evolution is nondirected or nonprogressive in such a way that there is simply no guarantee that humans or anything else would have evolved. . . . Darwinism is evolution through natural selection working on random mutations. Nondirectionality comes first from the randomness of mutations. They are not random in the sense of being uncaused, but they are random in the sense of not appearing on demand according to need.[16]

This expunging of purpose from nature gives nightmares to theologians. How can we speak of a creation without purpose? How can we speak of redemption without a goal toward which the creation aspires? The book of Genesis reports God saying that the creation is "very good." By what criterion is God measuring it? The book of Revelation presents a vision of the heavenly Jerusalem with the original Garden of Eden in its downtown central park. Just what constitutes eschatological harmony between civilization (city) and nature (garden) here?

On the one hand, people of faith simply cannot conceive of the natural world without purpose or at least value. To be sure, theologians have no investment in the secular doctrine of progress; nor do they feel obligated to use the language of "evolution" to indicate advancement toward a better and better world. Dropping the idea of progress from the long story of nature is no loss, theologically speaking. Yet, on the other hand, giving up totally on purpose merely to satisfy the scientific method seems like a high price to pay. A purposeless creation would not be a creation at all.

So, alas, what's a theologian to do? One option would be to throw in the towel and become a deist. No purpose within nature is discernible because, according to this option, it simply is not there. The deistic theologian could affirm that God created the initial conditions of law and chance that made evolution possible; and then God left the natural world to run itself ever since. Whatever design we find in nature is then the result of nature's self-organization. If such deism is unsatisfying, a second option would be to mix in a divine plot to the scientist's story of nature. The theologian could rewrite the Epic of Evolution by expanding on the story told by scientists. The theologian could declare that this evolutionary story has had an invisible plot all along. When God created the world in the beginning, according to this option, God placed a potential into the creation, which now through evolution is becoming actualized. God preprogrammed progressive evolution. A third option would be to treat creation eschatologically—that is, to locate the world's purpose in God rather than in nature. The problem for theologians as posed by scientists is that no purpose can be seen *within nature*. According to this option, nature's purpose is not inherent within nature itself; rather, its value or direction belongs to the relationship of nature with God. God's redemptive vision becomes the source of the divine declaration that nature is "very good."

This third option helps clarify why divine purpose present to nature is invisible to scientific method. Although God's purpose is not inherent in nature, it is present to nature while nature unfolds. Purpose is relationally present—that is, rather than belonging to nature as autonomous, it belongs to the ongoing relationship between God and nature.

As a method of investigation, science finds purposeful systems in nature and organisms designed to survive in their respective environments; yet science looks for strictly natural explanations rather than supernatural explanations. It does not search for nature's relationship to God. This is a methodological commitment. It is not a required metaphysical commitment. Such a research method is simply not attuned to an eschatological or redemptive ontology, thereby rendering divine activity within nature invisible. But absence of evidence for divine involvement is not evidence for absence of divine purpose. Evolutionary theists affirm divine action oriented toward divine purpose in, with, and under natural processes.

New Creation Transforms Old Creation

The eschatological option is the one we elect in this book. The natural world of which we are so much a part is not the only reality. There is more. Transformation is coming. In a certain sense, the power of that future transformation is affecting the processes of nature every day. Nature is not static. It is relentlessly changing. Along with calling nature "God's creation," we anticipate God's promised "new creation." This anticipated change will constitute a transformation. The transformation brought by the new creation will redefine the old creation; it will reorient the present history of evolution. At the advent of the new creation the purpose and value and direction of the grand sweep of nature's previous history will become visible. Now we see in a "mirror dimly," writes Paul, "but then we will see face to face" (1 Cor. 13:12).

We will take as our point of departure the Darwinian assumption that nature is devoid of inherent *telos*, or, more precisely, that science is not in the business of spinning out a teleology. In our version of theistic evolution, we will avoid locating purpose or direction or even value *within nature*; yet, we will affirm a divine purpose *for nature*. God's purpose for the long history of the cosmos and life on earth will be revealed retroactively at the eschatological advent of the new creation.

In addition to genesis or creation, we affirm epigenesis or new creation. If genesis connotes *creatio ex nihilo*, then epigenesis connotes *creatio continua* as anticipatory of eschatological transformation. Epigenesis also implies the possibility, though not the necessity, of emergence. Our concern here is the emergence of new wholes. We advocate understanding some phenomena in nature in terms of holism, according to which the whole is greater than the sum of the parts. Evolutionary history testifies to the emergence of living creatures, which as organisms constitute wholes that reorganize and give new meaning to the chemical parts that make them up. The emergence of new wholes transforms past parts. We can observe how integration into new more comprehensive unities preserves while renewing what had come before. Some associate such emergence with complexity; and some even posit that complexity amounts to a hidden principle within evolution. We do not need to embed complexification into evolution; we only need to tag it as an observable epigenetic possibility.

Emergent new wholes of reality that retroactively reconfigure past realities provide for us an anticipation of how an eschatological new creation might reconfigure this previous history of nature, preserving continuity while transforming it. This transformative power renders redemption possible and understandable as a natural phenomenon. We apply, by analogy, what we have observed in emergent holism to God's promise of a new creation.

The eschatological approach shares with deism the advantage of opening up nature as an arena to be understood on its own terms, according to its own principles, free of premature ideological commitments. Yet, it also shares with theism the advantage of a coherent understanding of a God who acts in our world, cares for us creatures, and promises redemption from the vicissitudes of life's struggle. As faith and science interact with each other, we would like to see further explorations into the implications of new creation for present creation.

In the meantime, we wish to treat with honest curiosity the research pursued by natural scientists who rely upon the theory of evolution. We wish to treat with respect and support those teachers of science in our public schools and parochial schools whose task it is to raise our young people to appreciate and even love the natural world around and in us. The joy of learning can easily be sidetracked when education takes place in an ideological war zone. We would like to contribute to bringing peace to the classroom.

The Divine Action Spectrum

While the battle is raging, we, like war correspondents, would like to file a report about the combatants. Who is fighting about what? We see two conceptual battlegrounds: (1) the degree of divine action in the natural world; and (2) causal explanations that connect or disconnect divine action with natural processes.

On our "divine action" spectrum, we measure the degree of reliance on evolutionary theory. We locate the scientific creationists on one end and the ontological materialists on the other end. The creationists affirm divine action in creation and deny evolution entirely, while the materialists embrace evolution and deny divine action entirely. Those in between see various combinations of divine action and natural selection in the evolutionary world.

The creationists rely exclusively on God's action. Like other traditional theists, they affirm that God is active in the world, both supplying foundational laws for nature as well as intervening on occasion to perform miracles. We call this the *interventionist divine action* position, something creationists share with other theists. What places creationists at the extreme end of the spectrum is their total denial of speciation according to natural processes. Evolution plays no role in their vision of reality.

Jumping to the other end, those we refer to as ontological materialists rely exclusively on natural selection. They construct an entire worldview based upon evolution. They begin by declaring nature to be exhaustively self-sufficient. They appeal to no factors beyond physical nature. No divine action occurs in the natural world because there is no God to take any action. Materialism supports tacit if not overt atheism. When overt, atheistic evolutionism takes the form of aggressive naturalism or secular humanism. A comprehensive metanarrative based upon science replaces religious visions of reality.

In between and closest to the creationists on the divine action spectrum we locate Intelligent Design, or ID. The ID position affirms divine intervention within natural processes. In fact, saltations or episodic jumps coming from a transcendent designer are necessary to explain macroevolutionary leaps to new species and new levels of complexity.

Moving into the spectrum's middle we find theistic evolution, which comes in many varieties. Although some theistic evolutionists deny miracles while others affirm them, overall this group prefers a *noninterventionist divine action* position. They want to affirm both divine action as well as a divine-hands-off understanding of the dialectic of law and chance in natural selection. Theistic evolutionists are still theists in that they believe God is active; so they support the concept of secondary causation. Sometimes called *concursus*, God is the primary cause, while nature's causal nexus appears independent to our eyes because it is secondary. In addition to secondary causation, many also affirm what we will call the "free-will defense." According to this group within the larger group of theistic evolutionists, God acts to self-limit or restrict divine action so as to permit nature to function autonomously. Autonomous nature, then, becomes responsible for introducing into the world competition, violence, suffering, and death. In chapter 6, we will offer a subspectrum within the divine action spectrum for theistic evolutionists, ranking them from the least degree of reliance upon evolution to the most comprehensive convergence of creation theology with evolutionary science.

As we near the far end of the spectrum beyond the theistic evolutionists, we come to deism. For the deists, God acts once and only once, at the beginning, to provide the structure of law and chance; then God goes on holiday. The law of natural selection, or descent with modification, takes over completely. No further appeal to divine action is made. Nature runs on its own. In this *uniformitarian* understanding of divine action, special acts of God that alter the course of nature are removed. After the removal of divine action within nature, it takes only two small steps to advance from deism to ontological materialism.

We have placed the science of evolutionary biology in this noninterventionist location on the spectrum, right between deism and ontological materialism. This is for methodological reasons. Research science does not require an ontological commitment. We believe that, methodologically, the scientific researcher need not be looking for explanations of natural phenomena that appeal to special acts of God or even to a divinely imparted design at the beginning. What the scientist is viewing is the nexus of secondary causation, not God's act as primary cause. When looking through a microscope or a telescope, we presume that a scientist of faith and one who is an atheist will see the same natural phenomenon.

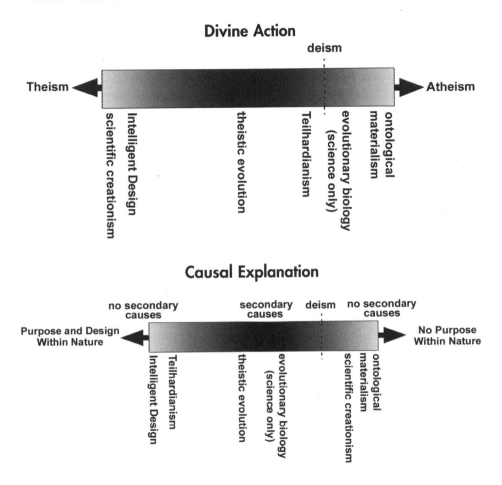

The Causal Explanation Spectrum

On the "causal explanation" spectrum—which measures degree of divine influence within the history of evolutionary advance—we see that the soldiers line up in a different configuration. On the one end we place those for whom divinely sponsored purpose and design within nature is decisive. On the other end we place those who specifically expunge divinity from natural processes, consigning what we perceive as purpose and design to either chance developments or subjective superimpositions from human consciousness. According to this criterion, Intelligent Design occupies the most extreme position. ID places design within nature because God designs specific advances in complex organisms at various points in evolutionary history. ID holds a punctuated design view. The designs we perceive within nature point to a transcendent designer beyond nature.

Next to ID we could place certain theistic evolutionists. Teilhard de Chardin, for example, could be located here. For Teilhard, God's purpose is built right into the directionality guiding evolution. Christogenesis is taking place within the natural realm, leading to a future consummation. Teilhardianism is somewhat more gradualist than ID; yet both find divine design embedded within nature. Even though Teilhard's scheme is also punctuated by thresholds crossed in evolutionary history, they arise from the inner Christification principle rather than result from transcendent interventions or saltations.

Most theistic evolutionists will find themselves in the middle of the spectrum on causal explanation, as close comrades with the evolutionary biologists. The doctrine of secondary causation accounts for this. God is the primary cause. Nature works according to secondary causes discernible through empirical research. No divine causal joint, so to speak, is discernible in test tube chemical reactions or in mathematical formulae. Science is free to follow its nose, to acknowledge local purpose when it becomes visible, or to ignore the question of purpose when focusing on specific research questions. God has a purpose *for nature*, to be sure; but that purpose is not directly perceivable *in nature*.

Most theistic evolutionists today are noninterventionists. They hold that God acts in the world, but God does not intervene to break the laws of nature, at least not when it comes to evolutionary processes. Rather, God works through the same natural processes that scientists investigate. This is why divine action becomes invisible to scientific research.

By locating ID and Teilhard toward the end that maximizes design within nature, and by placing garden variety theistic evolution and evolutionary biology in the middle, curiously enough, this places scientific creationism toward the spectrum's far end, where no purpose within evolution can be scientifically discerned. Purpose cannot be discerned because it is not there. The creationists attribute divine purpose to the creation of the natural world in the beginning, to be sure. God was the initial cause of all reality. But what happened at the beginning is not what is happening now. God's creative action *ex nihilo* involved principles no longer operative in the world. This means God's design is not responsible for subsequent natural events, for either saltations or inner teleology. The creation is now fallen, say the creationists; so what we see in natural developments such as microevolution and the second law of thermodynamics is the deterioration of nature rather than the working out of God's design. God's purpose can be seen at the beginning, not in what has come subsequently.

At the spectrum's extreme far end, then, we find once again ontological materialism. Not only do materialists expunge all purpose from within nature, they have no room for a doctrine such as secondary causation. Having ruled out divine design in nature, they also rule out divine design for nature. Atheism has become an ideology in this extreme position.

War? Really?

That a battle is raging over evolution is obvious. But, we might ask, is it a battle between science and faith? In the popular notion, the answer may seem to be yes. But we have a different answer: no. No, it is not a battle between science and faith. Evolutionary biology can be embraced both by persons of faith in God and by those who repudiate belief in God.

It is a tragedy that science educators in our public schools, parochial schools, and Christian day schools should find themselves treading on egg shells when treating the subject matter of evolutionary biology. There is so much to learn about God's fascinating world with all of its intricacies and dramas and mysteries; and how sad it is that the war-zone atmosphere of our classrooms risks snuffing out curiosity before it can be born.

Australian historian of science Kirsten Birkett sees the canon smoke on the battlefield and then waves a theological white flag of peace. There is no reason to fight, she contends. Defending "biblical Christianity," which might even include literalism where biblical interpretation warrants it, she argues that the God who created this world is a God of order. This order imparted to nature makes scientific research possible. She applauds science for investigating nature and providing descriptions of processes that avoid purpose or meaning or value. What science studies is the realm of physical causation, secondary causation. Invisible to science is primary causation, the work of God in creation. Hence, no war between science and Christianity is appropriate because they are not defending the same territory. "Science and Christianity are not in conflict," she emphasizes.[17]

This Book

In the pages that follow, our task will be both descriptive and prescriptive. Descriptively, we will offer expositions and analyses of the various positions taken by responsible theologians and scientists in the academic and public debate over evolution. We will set them side by side, comparing them with each other. Prescriptively, we will offer our own position as one among others. We will offer a constructive proposal within the larger camp of theistic evolutionism that ties together God's creation with the promise of new creation.

When it comes to the worldwide dialogue now taking place between scientists of all disciplines and religious scholars of all major religious traditions, we would like to locate ourselves. One of us is a Roman Catholic. The other is a Reformation Protestant. Although we draw on resources peculiar to each of these traditions, what we inherit in common with the comprehensive Christian tradition is much more decisive in shaping our shared point of view. One of us is a virologist. The other is a systematic theologian. Both of us have been engaged in the dialogue between science and religion for decades. We celebrate the Two Books, the Book of Nature and the Book of Revelation. Both together tell of the glory of God the creator and of the love of God the redeemer.

With regard to methodology, on the one hand, we support the statement of the National Academy of Sciences cited earlier in this chapter. Religion and science speak different languages; therefore, no conflict need break out. We can avoid conflict if each respects the domain of the other field. One of the reasons for the present war over evolution, quite obviously, is a shattering loss of respect for those with whom various parties disagree. Retrieving respect through com-plementarity is an effort well worth pursuing. We call this the *two language* or *independence* model for understanding the relationship of science and religion.

Yet, this division into separate languages is less than fully satisfactory to us. The *dialogue* and *interaction* models attract us too. There is but one reality, we presume. There is but one world. The world studied in laboratories and in the field is the very world that the biblical God is creating. So, we ask for science and faith to speak to each other, even if at first the separate languages lead to ambi-guities and misunderstandings. Such dialogue is worth the gamble, we believe, because we can expect sooner or later to arrive at some level of consonance. As creative interaction advances, we can expect to find crossovers and comple-ments and perhaps even agreements. We may not be at that point yet; but healthy dialogue between evolutionary biology and doctrinal theology we hope will eventually lead to an interaction that will provide a merged horizon of understanding.

CHAPTER TWO

DARWIN, DARWINISM, AND THE NEO-DARWINIAN SYNTHESIS

That Charles Darwin was one of the major figures of Western thought is hardly arguable as we look back over the nearly century and a half since the publication of *On the Origin of Species by Means of Natural Selection*.[1] Indeed, the late and lamented scion of evolutionary biology, Stephen Jay Gould, writes that "Darwin . . . continues to bestride our world like a colossus."[2] This allusion to one of the seven wonders of the ancient world is certainly apt. The reach of the evolutionary model of Darwin is such that all who enter the harbor of the Western academy, no matter in which disciplinary vessel they sail, must pass beneath the scrutiny of this giant.

In his seminal book, *The Structure of Scientific Revolutions*, the philosopher of science, Thomas Kuhn, analyzes the process by which changes take place within scientific disciplines.[3] Using as a model the shift from the Ptolemaic geocentric to the Copernican heliocentric cosmology, he describes the way in which the existing paradigms in a field are challenged when they fail to model observations adequately. It can be argued that such paradigmatic changes ripple throughout society at large in ways that can fundamentally alter the philosophical assumptions of that society. The end of the nineteenth century witnessed such shifts in two disciplines: physics and biology.

The failure of classical Newtonian physics to explain adequately certain observations led to the proposal by Max Planck that energy exists in discrete packets called quanta. In Kuhn's view, such shifts take place under the pressure of explanatory problems with the existing paradigm. The result for physics was to make the Newtonian model of the natural world a special case of the quantum mechanical model that now dominates.

In the case of biology, however, such observational problems did not exist. In fact, biology at the beginning of the nineteenth century did not have a theoretical basis and was, in the main, a historical science. However, explanatory models did exist to account for the features of the living world. These models were the direct targets of Darwin's proposal, and, as a result, the paradigm shift that he catalyzed led to a new view. It is that view that we wish to explore, both in its original as well as in its contemporary formulation.

Biology Before Darwin

The vast complexity of the living world is apparent to anyone who has walked through a forest or along a seashore. Even without formal training in any biological discipline, the observer is confronted with an awesome variety of animals and plants that are apparent to the naked eye. With the aid of a microscope an even more dizzying menagerie is presented, as Leeuwenhoek learned when he placed a drop of pond water under the lens of his instrument.

Aristotle was more of a zoologist than a physicist or philosopher, if one judges by his writings on the subject of animals.[4] It is true that other Greek thinkers had considered the problem of explaining the biosphere and even proposed the idea that living things might have evolved over time.[5] However, it is the categorical classifications of Aristotle that had the most influence on the development of biology as a scientific enterprise within the Western academy.

One reason for this may well have been the reintroduction of Aristotelian philosophy and science into the medieval intellectual environment in Europe. The works of "the philosopher," as Thomas Aquinas called Aristotle, had been lost to the West but had been preserved and commented on by the great Islamic scholars. While Thomas melded Christian theology with the philosophical arguments of Aristotle, his mentor, Albert the Great, expanded on the biological writings of the Greek philosopher.[6] As a result, the medieval system of the university was based, in large part, on the structure of thought laid down by Aristotle some fifteen hundred years earlier.

It is important to realize that Aristotle's notion of the universe was of an eternally existing reality. The Jewish and Christian idea of a beginning to creation, when added to the biological classification system proposed in the writings of the Greek master, led to the conclusion that all existing living things were created essentially in the form in which we see them. Aristotle did not specifically address the idea of preformation, and, in fact, he was aware of developmental stages in the formation of specific organismal structures. Nonetheless, at the dawn of the Enlightenment it was assumed that the record of Genesis was historically accurate and that all living creatures in existence had been preformed as such by the Creator.

The observations of Galileo and Kepler and the theoretical formulations of Newton led to a complete revision of the Aristotelian ideas of motion. Thus, by the beginning of the seventeenth century, Newton's *Principia* had supplanted Aristotle's *Physica* as the text of choice for understanding the interactions of bodies on this planet as well as throughout the cosmos.

However, the model combining the Bible with Aristotle persisted until publication of Darwin's revolutionary text. As a result, biological advances before Darwin involved more and more detailed descriptive work. The culmination of this line of work resulted in the eighteenth-century classification system developed by Karl von Linné (Carolus Linnaeus in his publications written in Latin) that remains in use today. This hierarchical arrangement of the biosphere with the human being at the top was a direct reflection of the accepted preformatarian Great Chain of Being that was formulated during the high Middle Ages. The Linnean system employed the binomial nomenclature of *genus* and *species* but did not question whether the organisms existed as such from the beginning or had developed from earlier, now extinct forms.

Though it is clear from the writings of late–eighteenth-century scientists such as George LeClerc (the Count of Buffon) and Erasmus Darwin (grandfather of Charles) that the idea of the "fixity" of species was being challenged, the first major rift came with the publication of *Philosophie Zoologique* by Jean Baptiste Lamarck in 1809.[7] Lamarck was an influential biologist, even though his idea about how organisms change over time was shown to be completely wrong. On the positive side, he is credited with the first use of the term "biology," as well as coining the word "invertebrates" to describe the grouping of animals without backbones. On the negative side, his theory of evolution, in which acquired characteristics were inherited by succeeding generations, was thoroughly discredited. Lamarck himself suffered terribly at the hands of his contemporaries, including his countryman, the biologist (naturalist) Georges Cuvier, as well as the geologist Charles Lyell. In fact, it was through the writings of Lyell that Charles Darwin was introduced to the ideas of Lamarck that he, Darwin, would ultimately argue against.

Lamarck's proposal that organisms change as a result of environmental adaptations that are inherited was easily countered. After all, a person who loses an extremity through accident or surgery does not pass on this loss to his or her children. However, Lamarck must be recognized as being one of the first evolutionists in modern science. It is clear that he must be counted among the influences on the work of Charles Darwin.

The Darwin of Darwinism

In 1802, the Reverend William Paley published *Natural Theology: Or Evidences of the Existence and Attributes of the Deity, Collected from the Appearances of Nature*.[8] Seven years later, on February 12, 1809, in Shrewsbury, England, Charles Robert Darwin was born to Robert and Susannah Darwin. Paley's book would come to be one of the most influential texts of the early nineteenth century. More will be said about the influence of Paley's work on nineteenth-century theology and science and on Charles Darwin (below), as well as on the ideas of the modern Intelligent Design movement (chapter 5).

In spite of an early interest in natural history, or what we now call biology, Charles Darwin was eventually shunted into a medical education in Edinburgh. Of course, his father and his grandfather (Erasmus Darwin) were both physicians. In spite of this familial influence, he came to dislike his studies and moved to Cambridge to begin theological training for entry into the clergy. However, his interest in biological studies persisted, and his interest in theology and the clergy were eventually abandoned. His botany professor and advisor, the Reverend John Henslow, saw to it that, after graduation, Charles secured a position as an expedition naturalist on what would be a five-year voyage of HMS *Beagle*.

A prevailing myth about Darwin is that his lonely reflections during this voyage, cut off from the civilization in which he had been educated, allowed him to formulate his revolutionary theory. Gould has recently reviewed the evidence and found that this was not the case.[9] As Gould recounts, "Darwin returned to England with the tools of conversion, but still as a creationist, however suffused with doubts and questions."[10] It was within the intellectual climate of London that some of these questions were asked and that Darwin began to derive answers that would influence his thinking.

Darwin had returned from his voyage in 1836, and by 1838, his notebooks reveal that the theory of evolutionary change under the force of natural selection had taken initial form. He expanded this into first a short paper (thirty-five pages) in 1842 and then a longer one (230 pages) in 1844. Neither of these was published, however.

In 1839, Darwin married Emma Wedgwood, a cousin, and in 1842, they left London for the quiet country village of Downe in Kent. Darwin would spend the rest of his life at Down House, traveling infrequently and never leaving England. He had begun his scientific publishing with a journal of his voyage, followed by reports on the geology of volcanic islands and of South America. Then, for several years, he concentrated on his studies of barnacles, producing a series of monographs on existing and fossil forms of these organisms. He lived the life of a country gentleman and scholar, supported by family wealth that derived from his father's medical practice as well as the Wedgwood china fortune from his wife's family.

In 1858, Darwin was sent an essay by Alfred Russell Wallace. A young naturalist who had been working in the Malay Archipelago, Wallace had constructed a theory that contained the essential ingredients present in Darwin's own. Darwin and Wallace each prepared papers, which were read at the same time at a meeting of the Linnean Society. Darwin then proceeded to finish his major work, *On the Origin of Species by Natural Selection,* which was published in November 1859. The first printing of fifteen hundred copies sold out immediately. And the rest, as the saying goes, is history.

Why did Darwin wait twenty years to finish the complete explication of his theory? In one sense, the voyage on the *Beagle* itself can be held to blame. It turns out that while in South America, he likely had been bitten by a reduviid bug and had contracted Chagas's disease. This malady would plague him throughout his life. Its symptoms would dominate his daily routine. In addition, he had to cope with the deaths of three of his ten children. These severe distractions may have understandably delayed his task.

Darwin's publication of *Origin* met with immediate reaction, both positive and negative. Over the course of the author's lifetime the book would see six editions. The controversy precipitated by Darwin's revolutionary theory would be felt almost immediately upon its publication. We will have more to say about this below.

Darwin lived out his days in Down House, engaging in his meditative strolls around the sandwalk, a wooded oval that he used for contemplative time. He died in the presence of his family on April 19, 1882. He was seventy-three years old.

The Essence of and Evidence for the Darwinian Model

In contrast to the preformation ideas that predated him, Darwin proposed that all living creatures descended from a common ancestor. This position, called *descent with modification* and elucidated below, is an essential feature of the theory that distinguishes it from the earlier models based upon a strict reading of Genesis. However, Darwinian evolution is much more detailed than common descent. Darwin introduced the force of natural selection that drives the observed variation into species that constitute the historical (fossil) and present-day biosphere. John Maynard Smith has succinctly described the essence of the Darwinian evolutionary model:

1. There exists a population of entities (units of evolution) with three properties:
   - multiplication (one can give rise to two);
   - variation (not all entities are alike);
   - heredity (like usually begets like during multiplication).

2. Differences between entities will influence the likelihood of surviving and reproducing. That is, the differences will influence their fitness.

3. The population will change over time (evolve) in the presence of selective forces.

4. The entities will come to possess traits that increase their fitness.[11]

The notion of "survival of the fittest" suggests a warring kind of relationship between competing entities. However, the survival in this case is with respect to the reproductive success that a particular variant enjoys in a particular environment. In fact, cooperative relationships do exist. Witness the idea of coevolution, in which two species change in response to each other. The reciprocal evolution model that this represents is an interesting adjunct to the original model.

Darwin, in the only figure included in *Origin*, tried to diagram his vision of descent with modification from a common ancestor. This figure is reproduced here.

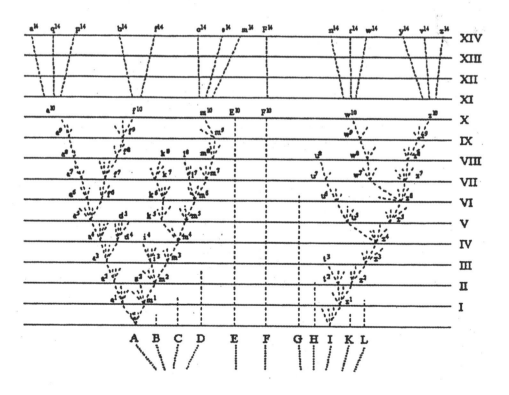

Without examining the notational details of the graph, we can see the general tenor of the theory expressed in a visual way. Beginning at the bottom we have what has become the typical branching representation of descent, with variations progressing along the various paths. Darwin proposed both extinctions (lineages that come to an end) as well as forms that survive to the present day. Speciation, in this graphic representation, occurs when variants diverge sufficiently to be no longer capable of interbreeding. Darwin's theoretical representation in this figure correlates quite well with evidence from the fossil record, when such records are complete and transitional forms have been located.[12]

Darwin also proposed that the variations or differences between individuals within a population arise over time by the accumulation of small changes. This is called gradualism, and the definition of this feature of the model has been a source of much misunderstanding. Contrast this with the concept of saltation, in which new forms arise by major steps or large-scale transformations. In fact, Darwin was so committed to this idea that in chapter 6 of *Origin*, after discussing the ways in which such slight variations might occur, he wrote: "If it could be demonstrated that any complex organ existed, which could not possibly have been formed by numerous, successive, slight modifications, my theory would absolutely break down."[13]

We will come back to this point when we discuss punctuated equilibrium and, in a later chapter, when we consider Intelligent Design.

Did Darwin create this model out of whole cloth? What were the predecessors and influences that guided his creative work?

We have already mentioned the evolutionary theory of Jean Baptiste Lamarck. His ideas attracted the attention of the geologist Charles Lyell. In his major work, *The Principles of Geology*, he argued vigorously that the earth was very old and had been formed by gradual processes and was subjected to natural forces that could be explained in terms of known scientific mechanisms in operation in the present.[14] These ideas contrasted sharply with the catastrophism that was proposed by earlier geologists, in which the earth's formation was a result of catastrophic events such as floods and earthquakes.

In addition, Lyell challenged the model of evolutionary change proposed by Lamarck. It was reading Lyell's text that introduced Darwin to ideas of gradual change and to the deficiencies of the Lamarckian position. It is evident from Darwin's letters to his close associates that Lyell's work had a major effect on the development of his biological model.

Darwin had returned from the *Beagle* voyage with a virtual treasure trove of fossil specimens. However, he was not a trained paleontologist. It was Lyell who introduced Darwin to the anatomist Richard Owen. And it was then Owen's identification of the fossils that opened the way for Darwin to formulate his theory.

The evidence that mounted for Darwin was historical, in the sense that a review of the fossil record from his voyage, as well as the data from other geographic locales, suggested strongly that ancestor-descendant relationships existed. Any number of examples can be cited from the materials that Darwin returned to England, and excellent published works recount many of these.[15] What Darwin accomplished was to draw inferences from this historical record. He was able to construct a scenario by which such descent happened. And, in contradiction to the preformationist tone of previous generations, his model assumed only natural forces at work in the process. Thus, descent with modification driven by natural selection is both a conclusion inferred from the data as well as proposal for verification by standard research methods. We will have more to say below about how modern biology uses the evidence from comparisons of present-day organisms to bolster the strength of the Darwinian model.

Another seminal influence on Darwin was from an unlikely source. As we mentioned earlier, the Reverend William Paley's text *Natural Theology* had been published seven years before Darwin's birth. In a letter to his neighbor, John Lubbock, written in 1859 just prior to the publication of *Origin*, Darwin wrote: "I do not think I hardly ever admired a book more than Paley's *Natural Theology*. I could almost formerly have said it by heart."[16] Paley's grand exposition of the manner in which the evidence of the natural world not only points to the existence of God, but also reveals much about the character of God was one of the major theological works of the nineteenth century. Paley was, at heart, an adaptationist. "Adaptation" means that an object or system is designed or suited for a particular function.[17] Paley's take on adaptation was that the complexity of living systems was evidence of design for function by the Creator. Darwin used the same evidence of objects that have been adapted to function. However, he proposed a completely different explanation—descent with modification driven by natural selection. Throughout his work it is clear, according to Gould, that Darwin is consciously critiquing the work of Paley as he lays the foundations for his theory.[18] Darwin is not writing a refutation of theism as much as he is writing a scientifically testable explanation for the same observed world that Paley considers.

Darwinism from the End of the Nineteenth Century to the Present

The publication of *Origin* was a critical success in many ways. The book unleashed a cascade of reactions from all sides.[19] Champions of the theory arose, as well as severe critics. The debate was over scientific as well as philosophical and theological issues that the theory raised. We will leave a discussion of the social implications of Darwinian evolution to chapter 3. In like manner, we will address, in the remainder of the book, the theological questions that Darwinism has produced. For now, we will consider some of the scientific debate that has characterized Darwinism from the end of the century of its inception to the present.

A common early objection was that natural selection and gradualism could not account for speciation—the development of new species from existing species. A species is defined as a reproductively isolated group of individuals who can interbreed and produce viable and fertile offspring.[20] This objection was addressed by Thomas Huxley and has been raised by critics continuously. This presumed failure to account for speciation is presented as a failure of the Darwinian model by those espousing both scientific creationism and Intelligent Design. We will address the stance of creationism in chapter 4 and discuss the case of Intelligent Design in chapter 5. With regard to evidence for speciation itself, reference to examples is given below.

The Darwinian model for biology itself stalled in acceptance at the beginning of the twentieth century for lack of solid mechanisms to explain some of the central features, such as the inheritability of traits and the target for the force of natural selection. As we shall develop shortly, the neo-Darwinian synthesis, more often called the modern synthesis, provided the necessary features that shored up the model and brought it into its present shape.

It has also been argued that the Darwinian model of natural selection is flawed because it is a circular argument or tautology.[21] Of course those that survive are the fittest, by the very fact that they survived. This is circular reasoning. However, as Michael Ruse argues, this is not sufficient for a valid objection.[22] He points out that selection depends upon the fact that more offspring are produced than could survive. Second, there are observable differences (traits) between those that do survive and those that do not, and these traits lead to success. Finally, there is a systematic feature to the observed selection, in that successful differences can be shown empirically to produce like results in like situations.

Stephen Jay Gould and Richard Lewontin[23] have argued that a too-powerful application of the Darwinian paradigm leads to a set of "just-so" stories about the world. In their objection, they raise the specter of a Panglossian pseudo-scientific picture of a world in which natural selection produces everything for the greatest good. This is perhaps the most active area of current debate within evolutionary biology.

There is another proposal by Gould and Eldredge[24] called punctuated equilibrium, in which the gaps in the fossil record are accepted as evidence that evolution has progressed by periods of no change separated by times of very rapid change. Although this does not argue that evolution did not happen, it does challenge the view that everything proceeded by a smooth, gradual pathway with the accumulation of small changes. These competing mechanisms are being argued among biologists, but in no way should this be understood as a failure of the overall theoretical framework. In fact, Gould and Eldredge are not calling for a return to a saltation model. Rather, they press the case that there were periods of intense variation within populations, although these variations occurred by the mechanism of mutational change as envisioned in the modern synthesis (see below).

Late–Nineteenth-Century Biology: Setting the Stage

Biology was, until the advent of the major advances of the twentieth century, a historical discipline. With the acceptance of Darwin's conceptual model, biology finally gained a theoretical base, although one which would not be formalized for nearly one hundred years. This formalization also has it roots within the nineteenth century. Within ten years of the publication of *Origin*, two other scientific events would take place. In 1868, an Augustinian monk, trained in the quantitative sciences, would propose a mechanism by which heredity would work. Gregor Mendel, in 1868, presented his work on the rules guiding the formation of hybrid pea plants. The Mendelian "laws" of inheritance would be ignored by a scientific community that was not yet ready to accept them. Mendel would be rediscovered at the beginning of the twentieth century by Hugo deVries and others. As a result, genetics would become one of the cornerstones of modern biology.

One year later, in 1869, the chemist Fredrich Meischer would report the isolation of a substance from white blood cells. He named this material "nuclein." Today we know it as deoxyribonucleic acid, or by its common acronym, DNA. The importance of this molecule would not become apparent until the birth of molecular biology in the 1940s.

As the nineteenth century closed, biology had been given a new direction. The effect of this in the sciences as well as in society in general was just beginning to be felt.

The Neo-Darwinian or Modern Synthesis

Of course, the force of natural selection was essential to the Darwinian model. However, in comparison to known physical forces such as gravity and magnetism, this force was rather nebulous. On what does the force of natural selection act? How could this theoretical formulation be given a sound scientific basis?

By the middle of the twentieth century, biology had come to a crossroads, at which the various disciplines that were at work defining the living world would join or continue to diverge. Julian Huxley, the grandson of Darwin's great promoter, published a book entitled *Evolution: The Modern Synthesis*.[25] Within the intellectual milieu of logical positivism that was in its heyday by 1940, the concept of synthesis was well met. Huxley explains how this idea affects the progress of biological sciences:

> Biology in the last twenty years, after a period in which new disciplines were taken up in turn and worked out in comparative isolation, has become a more unified science. It has embarked upon a period of synthesis, until today it no

longer presents the spectacle of a number of semi-independent and largely con-
tradictory sub-sciences, but is coming to rival the unity of older sciences like
physics, in which advance in any one branch leads almost at once to advance
in all other fields, and theory and experiment march hand-in-hand. As one
chief result, there has been a rebirth of Darwinism.[26]

The elements of the modern synthesis, also called the neo-Darwinian synthesis, include the Darwinian model, Mendelian genetics, and molecular biology.
Let us look at how this melding created what is now the central paradigm of
biology.

The nineteenth-century achievement for Gregor Mendel provided the quantitative mechanism that explains how inheritance operates. Recall that a central
tenet of the Darwinian model is that variations that exist in populations can be
passed on to succeeding generations—that is, the traits can be inherited. Prior to
Mendel, the prevailing model for how this operated was a qualitative one that
imagined a blending of parental traits. Mendel employed the essence of the
experimental method to derive a series of statements that argued for the quantitative nature of inheritance and, most important, for the particulate nature of
the heritable principle—what came to be called the gene. Mendel's work fell on
deaf scientific ears until the beginning of the twentieth century when Hugo
deVries recognized that his experimental results matched those published some
forty years earlier. The importance of this to the modern synthesis resides in the
need for a mechanism to explain the transmission of traits from one generation
to the next, and Mendelian genetics provided just the necessary model.

Once the concept of the gene had become established within the biological
mind-set, it only followed that inquiries into the nature of the gene would take
place. The first advance was the realization by Thomas Hunt Morgan and his
colleagues at Columbia University that genes were physical locations on chromosomes, the rope-like structures within the nucleus of cells whose presence
became known due to advances in the resolving power of microscopes. The
search was on for the identification of which cellular component constituted the
gene.

Enter the DNA discovered by Meischer in 1869. Chromosomes consist of two
molecular components: protein and DNA. In 1942, Oswald Avery and his col-
laborators at Rockefeller University published an experiment that argued for
DNA as the chemical substance of the gene. Their results were confirmed a
decade later as the new field of molecular biology was being born.

Max Delbrück and Salvador Luria were among the leaders of this new discipline. Working together at the California Institute of Technology in Pasadena,
California, during the academic year and the Cold Spring Harbor Laboratory on
Long Island, New York, during the summers, Luria and Delbrück were able to
demonstrate the nature of mutations. Variations in individual organisms were
then accepted as differences in the sequences of the four nitrogen-containing

bases that make up the molecule of DNA in the nucleus of the cell. A change in this sequence is called a mutation, and, in some cases, mutations result in observable changes in the physical appearance or performance of the organism. Luria and Delbrück showed that such changes occur in DNA in a random manner. That is, which one of the bases in a particular DNA molecule that changes as a result of environmental or experimental conditions is a chance event.

The addition of the concept of DNA and mutational variation gives the Darwinian model two important structural supports. First, a mechanism for the production of variations in the population could be imagined. Second, the fact that such variations take place one DNA base at a time gives definition to the principle of gradualism that is also a critical part of the theory.

However, the notion that randomness is also involved in the evolutionary process was not something framed within the original model by Darwin. Note that above we used the terms "randomness" and "chance" as though they were interchangeable. This is not the case within science, and much confusion has resulted from this lack of clarity. Gould attempts to distinguish between the mathematical notion of randomness as a statistical concept with the use of the same term in evolution to mean that "variation is not inherently directed towards adaptation, not that all mutational changes are equally likely."[27]

The modern synthesis, the grand melding of Darwinian evolution, Mendelian genetics, and molecular biology, has been "hardened," in Gould's terminology, into the fabric of biological thought. His concern is that the neo-Darwinian synthesis has moved into orthodoxy with a restriction that prevents the investigation of dissenting positions.[28] Nonetheless, the modern synthesis now represents the central paradigm of modern biology.

Though the fossil record was essential to Darwin and has been of paramount importance in establishing the solidity of the Darwinian model, current biological evidence for evolution relies heavily on the neo-Darwinian paradigm. When the sequence of the DNA that constitutes the genomes of many different organisms is compared, relationships are revealed that can be best explained by using the concept of descent with modification from a common ancestor. Publications in comparative genomics have become more numerous as the size of the DNA sequence database increases. In addition, experimental verification of common functions can be carried out, using easily manipulated systems in the laboratory. Thus, one result of the modern synthesis is to add additional shoring to the structure of the Darwinian paradigm.

An offshoot of this work is the idea that variations within a population of organisms (that is, within a species) that are measured by genomic differences are really only small evolutionary changes, so-called microevolutionary changes. This raises a much-debated set of terms: *microevolution* and *macroevolution*. A simple definition of these two terms revolves around the idea of species, which we defined above. In this sense then, microevolution refers to genetic changes within a species, whereas macroevolution refers to genetic changes that are above the level of species.

Critics of the Darwinian model argue that speciation, the generation of a new species from an existing one, requires macroevolutionary changes that cannot be explained by the mechanisms of the model. However, there is ample evidence that speciation can be observed in both plants and animals.[29] Arguments over the level of change required to count as macroevolution often devolve into mere semantics.

Darwinian Science and Darwinian Philosophy

The facts of biology that support the Darwinian model have accumulated since the voyage of the *Beagle*. As it currently stands, the hierarchy of biological disciplines assumes this general paradigm. Of course, in Thomas Kuhn's perspective, such paradigms are always subject to challenge and ultimate revision or even overthrow. Nevertheless, we see no reasonable *scientific* objection to Darwinian evolutionary theory.

We stress the word *scientific* because this particular model generates a progressive research program—that is, it leads scientists in directions that produce new knowledge. The problem in the evolution controversy is not biological science per se. Rather, the philosophical or ideological inferences labeled "Darwinian" that go far beyond the biological science are responsible for generating most of the controversy that evolutionary theory has precipitated.

To hold a valid scientific position based upon an analysis of the data explained according to the model of natural selection is one thing. To turn this into a philosophy, however, is quite another thing. To leap from what is physical to the metaphysical, or leap from biological nature to human nature, is to jump from solid soil into midair. To observe descent with modification in biological history and then to draw from this justification for social values and moral philosophy is a fallacious move. We call it the "naturalistic fallacy."

In the case of Darwinian evolution, such metaphysical and moral extrapolations have been a part of the debate since the very beginning. The legend of the debate between Thomas Huxley and Bishop Wilberforce, with all of its apocryphal addendums, stands as the archetype of one such philosophical division.

Where we find ourselves today is in a whirlwind with many things torn from their moorings and being tossed about: biological research, philosophical speculations on human nature, moral values, and educational goals. The science of evolution confronts us within a storm of questions about the philosophy of evolution. We have no choice but to ask philosophical questions, especially if we are dissatisfied with the philosophical positions taken by others.

Defining "Purpose"

As we mentioned in chapter 1, a central philosophical question we intend to ask in this book has to do with design or purpose, especially as it relates to the process of natural selection. Paul Davies's description of natural selection shows why the question of purpose would arise:

> There is only nature red in tooth and claw, applying a simple and brutal rule: if it works, keep it; if it doesn't, kill it. And "works" here is defined by one criterion and one criterion only, which is replication efficiency. If the mistake results in more copies made, then, by definition, without any further considerations, it works.[30]

The brute rule of natural selection seems to preclude a long-range *telos* within nature that is directing the course of evolution progressively toward any kind of perfection. Later we will discuss in more detail the concept of *telos* in nature or for nature. For now, let us begin with some definitions.

Throughout this book and certainly in the literature surrounding evolution on all sides, concepts such as design, purpose, direction, and progress will be found. To set the stage for our discussions, we wish now to deal with these terms with respect to both their scientific as well as philosophical meanings.

Design and *purpose* are the two terms that engender the most heated debates. Can one discern design or purpose in the biological world? The answer is both yes and no, depending on how one defines these words. Design can simply mean the assembly of parts that go to make up a particular structure. In this definition, design does not imply any kind of intelligent agent. So, the word *design* in and of itself is not so much at issue. Darwin was observing design in this very sense and ascribing it to the action of natural laws that include descent with modification. That is why, as we shall see in chapter 5, the use of the words "intelligent design" are so important to Michael Behe and William Dembski.[31]

Purpose, on the other hand, is a more difficult term to reconcile with the scientific method that Darwin espoused. Again, it can have different philosophical flavors. For instance, *purpose* can be synonymous with *function* for some interpreters. In this sense, it carries a modicum, but not a lot, of philosophical baggage. On the other hand, when observable purpose is said to imply an intelligent agent, a completely different philosophical issue is raised.

The word *teleology* is based on the Greek root *telos*, meaning a goal or an end point. As we shall see in chapter 5, this was a critical part of the Aristotelian classification system of the natural world. And it was this idea, the concept of purpose, that yielded Thomas Aquinas's fifth way of coming to the existence of God: the so-called argument from design or purpose.

The modern scientific method, with its emphasis on material explanation, eschews the idea of purpose as derived from an agent. As a result, another term is used to describe what one observes in the biological world: *teleonomy*. The dictionary definition of teleonomy is "the quality of apparent purposefulness in living organisms that derives from their evolutionary adaptation."[32] Here we see the way out of the Aristotelian/Thomistic inference for the scientist. The purpose is only apparent and really is a result of chance in the process of natural selection.

This brings us to the question of *direction* and *progress*. Certainly Darwin, in his cultural setting of Victorian England, was prepared to revere the idea of humankind as the epitome of the natural world. So, in early editions of *Origin*, Darwin saw, in the process of evolution directionality, with the arrow of time pointing toward successively improved structures, culminating naturally in the human species. We will come in the next chapter to the social implications of this model. For now, we wish to emphasize that Darwin's notions of "perfection" and "progress" that he discusses in the last chapter of *Origin of Species* were not based on the conclusion that some transcendent intelligence was at work. Indeed, although he mentions the Deity and the Creator in the last chapter of the book, he by no means argues that the direction or progress to improved forms has any divine guidance. In fact, his argument is just the opposite—gradual small steps produce variants that, by natural selection, result in improved and therefore more fit forms. Chance, not providence, explains evolutionary history.

It is the advent of the neo-Darwinian synthesis, with its emphasis on the random or chance nature of mutations, that has given us the current picture of evolution. In this view, natural selection acts as the necessary force on a collection of variants produced by the contingency of mutation. As a result, any direction in evolution is only apparent direction, just as any purpose is only apparent purpose. For the neo-Darwinist then, the process is, at its core, directionless and purposeless.

How can we reconcile these various positions with theological perspectives? We will see that this stark view of nature has led some into the stance of scientific creationism (chapter 4) or the Intelligent Design theory (chapter 5). We will eventually come to our own position, that of theistic evolution, in which we will attempt to accept this scientific view within its own limits and couple it with our own theological proposals (chapters 6 and 7).

Darwinian Biology Versus Materialist Ontology

One the one hand, Darwinian evolution as a science has been used to justify the philosophical stance of naturalism, or what in chapter 1 we referred to as ontological materialism. Since natural processes can explain all of life, then there is no need to postulate anything but the material world itself. This is clearly stated by such contemporary writers as Richard Dawkins and Daniel Dennett.[33] It would not be too far-fetched to say that their philosophical position argues that the facts of Darwinian evolution prove that God does not exist. These are the "lineaments of a new religion," as Julian Huxley announced in 1959.

One great difficulty is sorting out the components of this mixture of science, metaphysics, and religion that is often presented to us in both academic and public arenas. The popularity of *The Blind Watchmaker* by Dawkins, for instance, presents the reader with the challenge of distilling out those parts of the brew that constitute the science rather than the philosophy. If one is after the clear taste of scientific research that is mixed within, then it will be necessary to have the proper tools for straining science out from the dregs of often undefended or unconscious materialist philosophical convictions.

Yet, in this book we want to argue that it is possible to be a believer in the biblical God and still hold that Darwinian evolution is an acceptable model for explaining the observed facts. To argue for compatibility between evolution and faith requires an analysis of the complex connection that already exists between evolution and unfaith. Richard Dawkins trumpets: "Darwin made it possible to be an intellectually fulfilled atheist."[34] Michael Ruse, in contrast, says, "No sound argument has been mounted showing that Darwinism implies atheism. The atheism is being smuggled in, and then given an evolutionary gloss."[35] We will rely on Ruse's judgment here.

Let us conclude our discussion of Charles Darwin with a quotation from the last chapter of *Origin of Species*. In the second and later editions, Darwin took note of the influence his theory was having, especially among religious people. He writes:

> I see no good reason why the views given in this volume should shock the religious feelings of any one. It is satisfactory, as showing how transient such impressions are, to remember that the greatest discovery ever made by man, namely, the law of the attraction of gravity, was also attacked by Leibnitz, "as subversive of natural, and inferentially of revealed, religion." A celebrated author and divine has written to me that "he has gradually learnt to see that it is just as noble a conception of the Deity to believe that He created a few original forms capable of self-development into other and needful forms, as to believe that He required a fresh act of creation to supply the voids caused by the action of His laws."[36]

Darwin could not have foreseen that the "transient" impression his book would make would last for nearly a century and a half after its first publication and would remain as a central issue of discourse today.

CHAPTER THREE

SOCIAL DARWINISM, SOCIOBIOLOGY, AND EVOLUTIONARY PSYCHOLOGY

Charles Darwin's work had a major influence on British society in particular and on Western society in general. However, his work was a product of that very society.

Darwin was a man of Victorian England, in which he was born, educated, and worked until his death. His only significant travel away from his homeland was the momentous voyage on the HMS *Beagle*. He was a member of the upper middle class. His father and grandfather were physicians. He married into wealth and lived a life that permitted him the time for pursuing his studies. But Darwin was also a scientist. He therefore interacted with and was influenced by the scientific culture and personalities of his day.

This heady mix of academic and societal factors must be taken into account when reading Darwin's work. At the same time, the milieu of England in the late nineteenth century was set to receive these writings in certain unique ways. The industrial revolution had affected England's class structure in a profound manner, changing the relationships among all levels of society and altering the cities with the influx of workers for the burgeoning factories. The far-flung British empire was at its height, with little premonition of the turmoil that its dissolution would bring a few decades in the future. So it was that a model of development that argued for the survival of those who are the fittest would fall on receptive ears, especially among those who were privileged to live in the upper strata of the society.

Darwin's second book, *The Descent of Man*, is rife with the attitudes that one would expect from a person of his social location. We do not say this in the post-modern sense of trying to rewrite the history of what happened. However, in discussing the social implications and applications of Darwinian evolution, we must understand the political and social context in which the theory took form.

Almost immediately upon the publication of *Origin of Species*, there arose discussions of how this theory would apply to human beings and to the societies we form. As we mentioned in the opening chapter, the Darwinism we encounter today is a mixture of biological science and social philosophy. If we ask what has gone into this mix, we can identify at least four major applications of the evolutionary model to society. In historical order they are: social Darwinism, the eugenics movement, sociobiology, and evolutionary psychology. We will discuss each of these in turn.

Herbert Spencer and Social Darwinism

Although the iconic figure of Charles Darwin looms continuously over the modern academy, the countenance and work of Herbert Spencer is little noticed. And yet, it was Spencer, not Darwin, who originally published the idea of biological evolution.

Spencer was born some eleven years after Charles Darwin, in Derby, England. He was more or less self-educated as a result of his readings in the natural sciences. Although early in his career he was employed as a schoolteacher and as a civil engineer for a railway, his main occupation was editor for the prestigious newspaper, *The Economist*. He worked there from 1848 until 1851 when a bequest from his uncle, the Reverend Thomas Spencer, allowed him to resign and spend the remainder of his life in pursuit of scholarly work.

Spencer had read the work of the geologist Lyell, as had Darwin, and was influenced by the developing notions of evolution and deep time. However, he disagreed with Lyell's criticism of the acquired inheritance model of Lamarck. Instead, Spencer would argue for Lamarckianism as the mechanism by which development took place. He published the first of a series of works designed to show, in a coordinated way, how everything from the organic forms in the biosphere to human societies obeyed the rules of evolution.

In 1851, he published *Social Statics* and, a year later, an essay entitled "The Development Hypothesis." It is interesting to see his language in this latter case, since it predates the publication of *Origin of Species* by seven years:

Those who cavalierly reject the Theory of Evolution as not being adequately supported by facts, seem to forget that their own theory is supported by no facts at all. Like the majority of men who are born to a given belief, they demand the most rigorous proof of any adverse belief, but assume that their own needs none. Here we find, scattered over the globe, vegetable and animal organisms numbering, of the one kind (according to Humboldt), some 320,000 species, and of the other, some 2,000,000 species (see Carpenter) and if to these we add the numbers of animal and vegetable species which have become extinct, we may safely estimate the number of species that have existed, and are existing, on the Earth, at not less than ten millions. Well, which is the most rational theory about these ten millions of species? Is it most likely that there have been ten millions of special creations? Or is it most likely that, by continual modifications due to change of circumstances, ten millions of varieties have been produced, as varieties are being produced still?[1]

Why is it, then, that Spencer is not regarded as the originator of this theory? Why do we not talk about "the neo-Spencerian synthesis"? For one reason, he was not the meticulous observer that Darwin was. In addition, he championed the idea of acquired characteristics as the mechanism of evolution, while both Darwin and Wallace proposed descent with modification through natural selection. As a result, Spencer's approach did not survive the test of academic inquiry.

To his credit, however, Spencer read *Origin of Species* and came to support the model of natural selection as presented by Darwin. In fact, the phrase "survival of the fittest" appears in the first volume of Spencer's *Principles of Biology*, published in 1864. Darwin then incorporated that phrase into later editions of *Origin of Species*.[2]

It was Spencer's contention that one could develop an overriding philosophy that subsumed all of the sciences, including sociology and psychology, under the aegis of the evolutionary model. As a result, he advocated a societal system that allowed for Darwinian principles. At the heart of his proposal was the idea that the individual has preeminence and that society evolves as the sum of the individuals within it.

Spencer would have defined himself as a liberal, in spite of the fact that our current view of his political and social agenda makes him seem right wing. After all, the result of his model would be the absence of governmental intervention to assist those less able to compete, as well as justification for the *laissez-faire* capitalism of John Stuart Mill that still characterizes our view of the conservative agenda today. However, in Spencer's own view, he was in favor of progressive policies. His liberal stance was in the sense of the Liberal Party or Whig Party in the early nineteenth century in England. Personal freedom was the watchword, and this fit nicely with Spencer's philosophical position. In fact, as the Liberal Party itself evolved at the end of the nineteenth century, Spencer became more critical of their increasingly interventionist proposals. Perhaps a better description of Spencer's political thought would be found in the current word "libertarian" rather than "liberal."

What was the result of the social Darwinism that Spencer proposed? As a philosophical position, it was embraced by thinkers such as John Stuart Mill. As a practical political and societal agenda it justified the efforts of the great capitalist Andrew Carnegie in the United States. It was Carnegie who sponsored a visit and lecture tour by Spencer.

The appeal was perfect for both the middle- and upper-class Victorian society of England as well as the burgeoning capitalist class of the United States. Certainly the positivist philosophy of that time celebrated progress for leading us toward improvement and the greater good. Therefore, if society, like species, were allowed the freedom to evolve, the greater good for that society would be achieved. And those who could not compete, be they individuals or groups, would not survive. The fit, and hence the good, would survive.

We remember Spencer for discerning the law of the jungle, survival of the fittest, and applying it to civil society. When it comes to the unfit, Spencer could say, "The whole effort of nature is to get rid of such, to clear the world of them and to make room for better. . . . It is best that they should die."[3]

Yet, this would not be the only form that a social ethic based upon evolution would take in the nineteenth century. Thomas Huxley was repulsed by Spencer's transfer of survival of the fittest to human morality. Huxley believed high minded humanistic values could carry us beyond our evolutionary origins. We can transcend our biological roots: "Ethical nature, while born of cosmic nature, is necessarily at enmity with its parent. . . . The conscience of man revolts against the moral indifference of nature."[4]

Both Spencer and Huxley expanded evolutionary biology into a social philosophy, evolutionary naturalism. Yet one saw an ethic for modeling society on nature, while the other saw human ideals transcending nature's past. Spencer's survival of the fittest yielded to nature blood "red in tooth and claw" (the words bequeathed us by Alfred Lord Tennyson's poem of 1850, "In Memoriam"). Huxley, in contrast to Spencer, envisioned a society governed by caring values that mark an evolutionary advancement from beyond where we have come.

Spencer would go on to propose his evolutionary model as an overarching structure for all disciplines. He envisioned the publication of a body of work that he called "The Synthetic Philosophy," in which he would bring all of the special sciences under one umbrella. He wrote a series of volumes with the word "principles" in the title, such as "First Principles," "Principles of Psychology," "Principles of Biology," and "Principles of Sociology," all of which would be included as a part of this synthesis. At his death in 1903, he left a trust to fund the completion and publication of a series entitled "Descriptive Sociology."

Spencer's revolutionary and controversial view of human biology and human society had a major influence on the thought of the late–nineteenth-century academy in Britain, Western Europe, and the United States. Coupled with the intellectual achievement of the Darwinian model, Spencer's bold proposals were a perfect fit for those intellectuals who saw science as a redeeming discipline that would free humanity from the ills brought about by the grip of religion. Here, at last, was an apparent "objective" way of thinking about and implementing social policy.

Francis Galton and the Eugenics Movement

If, as Spencer argued, societies evolve as the collection of individuals within them evolves, then it is logical for some to assume that influencing the evolutionary trajectory of those individuals would eventually lead to the improvement of the society. After all, agriculturists have been doing this for generations with both plants and animals. In fact, the first chapter of *Origin of Species* deals with the breeding of domestic animals. Why not apply the same thinking to humans to achieve the greater good as envisioned by Spencer?

Francis Galton was born in 1822 to Viola Darwin, the aunt of Charles Darwin.[5] Rather than wilting under the pressure of having so famous a cousin, Galton became preeminent in his own right, rising to be knighted as one of England's most accomplished scholars. He began his professional career as an explorer and meteorologist, leading an expedition to South Africa and joining in the famous search for the headwaters of the Nile River, led by Richard Burton and John Speke. Later, he became a statistician and a criminologist. It was Galton who argued for and popularized the use of fingerprints as an identification system, publishing a major work on this subject.[6] All told, he was a significant voice in the late-nineteenth and early–twentieth-century intellectual conversation of Great Britain.

However, he is mainly remembered today as a hereditarian and a eugenicist. Galton coined the word "eugenics" from the Greek word for "well-born." He championed the idea that derives from his cousin's model, namely, that variations in populations are subject to natural selection. Galton's goal was to improve the population. Those exhibiting the "best" characteristics—health, intelligence, industry, and so forth—should be encouraged to have more children, thus raising the possibilities for future generations. This idealistic notion is often termed *positive eugenics*, in contrast to the movements involving *negative eugenics* that arose in the United States and Germany, which we will discuss below.

Over the course of his life, which came to a close in 1911, Galton would argue vociferously for his views on the importance of eugenics as a principle for a society. In his autobiography he wrote: "I take Eugenics very seriously, feeling that its principles ought to become one of the dominant motives in a civilised nation, much as if they were one of its religious tenets."[7]

What did he mean by the notion of eugenics as a policy? In his published papers and books, including *Hereditary Genius* in which eugenics is first described,[8] he wrote eloquently in support of hereditarianism and its power to improve "the race." In his autobiography, he chose to summarize what eugenics means in one paragraph:

> This is precisely the aim of Eugenics. Its first object is to check the birth-rate of the Unfit, instead of allowing them to come into being, though doomed in large numbers to perish prematurely. The second object is the improvement of the race by furthering the productivity of the Fit by early marriages and healthful rearing of their children. Natural Selection rests upon excessive production and wholesale destruction; Eugenics on bringing no more individuals into the world than can be properly cared for, and those only of the best stock.[9]

What "race" is he improving? What are the standards by which he judges the "Unfit" from the "Fit"? As a product of his age and culture, Galton would naturally and unconsciously consider Western European civilization to be the pinnacle of evolutionary achievement. We do not mean this as a redaction from the view of the twenty-first century. It is sufficient to look into the publications of Galton to see what he meant by these terms and by race improvement.

In his major work on this subject, *Hereditary Genius*, Galton devotes a part of the appendix material to "the comparative worth of races." In this section, he takes as the standard for such comparison the "civilized" world of his own culture, that is, the white, Anglo-Saxon British Empire of the late nineteenth century. So, for instance, in comparing the cultural achievements of the "negro" race to this standard, he concludes that this is "a result which again points to the conclusion, that the average intellectual standard of the negro race is some two grades below our own."[10]

Clearly, Galton's eugenic standards are based on his own racial identity and culture. His plea for a eugenics policy in his own country is argued so that the civilizing influence of Britain on the world will not begin to overwhelm the abilities of the British middle and upper classes, to whom this was entrusted. He sees, as Rudyard Kipling called it, the "White Man's Burden" as something to be assumed as both a right and a responsibility. Here we have practical social policy coupled with the best science of the day, his cousin's model for natural selection and survival of the fittest.

A naive reaction to Galton's positive approach of encouraging the "ablest" to have more children would be to ignore it as something that would have no effect on the general population. This benign reaction ignores the racism inherent in the model. More important, it does not foresee the dangerous corollary that arises from acceptance of Galton's basic hypothesis. If racial improvement means increasing the number of the Fit in future generations, then this can also be achieved by eliminating those who are deemed Unfit from the breeding population. This approach is called *negative eugenics* and was the direction taken during the early twentieth century in the United States and in Germany.

The American eugenics movement had its home at the Cold Spring Harbor Laboratory on Long Island in New York. From 1910 to 1940, the Eugenics Records Office there collected materials and directed research and programs aimed at disseminating the practice of eugenics throughout the United States.[11]

The Eugenics Records Office was operated by Charles Davenport and Harry Laughlin. They had common interests as animal breeders and were much influenced by the rediscovery of the Mendelian laws of inheritance at the beginning of the century. Though the great geneticists of the time, including Thomas Hunt Morgan at Columbia, repudiated the ideas of eugenics, the proponents embraced the rules of heredity as support for their case. As a result, the social theories of Spencer and the racial improvement strategies of Galton took on a much more quantitative nature with pedigree charts and genetic trait analysis. Eugenics became a so-called science that was allegedly supported by the same objective data-gathering methods that applied to garden peas and fruit flies.

This appeal to quantitative inheritance measures characterized much of the eugenics movement in America. Davenport and Laughlin discussed the inheritance of traits such as "feeblemindedness" and "criminality" in the same language that Mendel had used for flower color of his peas and that Morgan was using for the eye color of his flies. Their tacit assumption was that each of these so-called traits could be treated as single, Mendelian genetic locus. The flaws in their research assumptions and methods were masked, we believe, by their own cultural biases and by the zeal with which they championed their cause.

Eugenics did find its supporters and popularizers. The cereal company founder J. H. Kellogg started the Race Betterment Foundation at his home in Battle Creek, Michigan. With his funding, conferences were held to explore the ideas of eugenic policies and their implementation. Throughout the country, at county fairs, Fitter Families Contests were held. On the surface, this sounds much like the program of Galton to encourage breeding of the ablest. However, there was a much darker side to the American eugenics scene.

Soon, in response to the program, sterilization laws and marriage laws began to appear in states. Those deemed "unfit" as mentally defective could be institutionalized and prevented from producing offspring by forced sterilization. A famous case involved the state of Virginia and the Buck family. The Supreme Court of the United States ultimately upheld the legality of the Virginia sterilization laws in this case, after presentation of evidence that a seven-month-old infant, the daughter and granddaughter of two women diagnosed as "feebleminded," was also judged to be feebleminded.[12] The majority opinion was written by the pillar of American jurisprudence, Justice Oliver Wendell Holmes, who said that "three generations of imbeciles is enough."[13]

Prohibitions against interracial marriage already existed in various states' laws. However, the eugenics movement gave them new impetus and justification. By the year 1915, some twenty-eight states had laws that invalidated or made criminal the marriage between a white person and an African American. Such laws remained on the books until 1967, when the U.S. Supreme Court declared unconstitutional the Racial Integrity Act, ironically, of the state of Virginia. At the time, such laws existed in sixteen states.

The relative success of the British and American eugenics movements drew the attention of German intellectuals during the decade following World War I. Adolf Hitler was attracted to Darwinism and Spencerism, combining "survival of the fittest" with his nationalism, anti-Bolshevism, and anti-Semitism. Hitler's thinking in "cosmic terms" became "combined with the principle of the struggle for life and of the survival of the fittest, resulting in a sort of eschatological Darwinism," writes Joachim Fest. Human society should look to the laws of nature and follow them, argued Hitler in his autobiography, *Mein Kampf;* and this means "only the urge for self-preservation can conquer."[14] Eugenics became one of the weapons by which Hitler's Aryan race would try to conquer. His political party, the National Socialist Party (the Nazis), promoted the idea of "inferior and superior races," with the ultimate goal of producing a "master race" that would lead Germany and the world into a bright, Aryan future.[15]

The Nazis tried to use the Darwinian model and the Mendelian laws of genetics to support their pseudoscientific approach to racial policies. As a result, they spoke and wrote of traits that were "unfit" and set policies for the eugenic control of future generations. Their targets for exclusion became the mentally retarded, mentally ill, criminals, and the physically infirm. But members of other races were also slated for deliberate extinction. Nazi ire was particularly directed toward people of Jewish heritage, whom they demonized as "hostile," "evil," and "unhealthy." The German eugenic philosophy was called "racial hygiene" (*Rassenhygiene*), and it sought to purify the Aryan race through purified breeding and through extermination of persons with unfit genes.[16]

With their rise to power and the establishment of the Third Reich, the Nazis were free to implement social policies that furthered their eugenic agenda. To begin with, the civil rights of Jews were limited by acts such as the Nuremberg Laws of 1935. Removal of Jews from public office and confiscation of their properties and businesses were legalized. By 1935, Jews were being expelled from the country or relocated into ghettos. Violence against Jewish people and businesses was mounting. Finally, in 1938, the process of elimination began. At first it was the euthanasia of the mentally and physically ill, along with criminals, antisocials, and others. But the policy soon extended to the Jews and other racial "types" deemed unfit, such as Gypsies, Slavs, and Africans. As other European countries came under the rule of the Nazis, their Jewish populations were also subjected to this treatment. Ultimately, with the Third Reich crumbled in ruins at the end of the war in Europe, the world saw the results of the "final solution to the Jewish question" as the infamous death camps were opened to reveal the unimaginable horrors of the Holocaust.

Edward O. Wilson and Sociobiology

The years immediately following World War II saw the birth of a new discipline—molecular biology—accompanied by the death throes of the eugenics movement that had culminated in the horrors of the Nazi regime. In fact, the scientific home of the American eugenics program, the Cold Spring Harbor Laboratory, became the campus for the new biology that attracted physicists such as Max Delbrück and physicians such as Salvador Luria. The "phage group," as they were called, would spend the academic year at the California Institute of Technology in Pasadena, California, and then drive in caravan cross-country to Long Island, New York, for the intense summer of work at Cold Spring Harbor.[17] Thus, the social Darwinism that gave rise to the eugenics proposals of Galton and others disappeared, leaving behind only the physical location that today houses one of the most famous biological research facilities in existence. However, the intellectual ferment of social Darwinism was not forgotten and lay buried in the subconscious of the academy until the arrival of the monumental work by Edward O. Wilson entitled *Sociobiology: The New Synthesis*.[18]

Wilson is now Professor Emeritus of Entomology at Harvard University. He published *Sociobiology* in 1975 based on his work with colonial insects such as ants. His analysis of insect behavior was coupled with the neo-Darwinian understanding of populations and genes to produce a thesis that argued for a strong genetic component to their behavior. From this background Wilson and his supporters would begin to make the case for a similar consideration for human behavior. Looking for genetic factors that structure social behavior in animals became the model for understanding social behavior in humans.

We believe that Wilson had no idea he was lighting the fuse on the firestorm of protest that his book would ignite. A reactive group of Boston-area scientists constituted themselves as "The Science for the People Sociobiology Study Group." Out of revulsions to past injustices and horrors buried in the academic psyche erupted the reaction: are social Darwinism and maybe even Nazism returning to haunt us once more?[19] Michael Ruse rose to Wilson's defense: "This criticism strikes me as being intemperate to the point of unfairness—even cruel. . . . The sociobiologists are not racists. . . . They are certainly not neo-Nazis."[20]

Whether justified or not, the critical reaction had an effect. Wilson found himself cast in the role of debating social policies with which he had no truck. He disavowed support for scientizing social discrimination. Yet Wilson's suggested genetic determinism evoked both disciples and detractors. Out of the environment that his work created would come such controversial works as *The Bell Curve*, purporting to show how racial and inherited differences in intelligence should provide criteria for structuring a social hierarchy.[21] Detractors such as Stephen Jay Gould and Richard Lewontin, colleagues in Wilson's own university, highlighted the social implications of these claims as reasons not only to disagree with Wilson's work, but also to suppress the development of the discipline of sociobiology itself. As a result, however strong or weak the claims of sociobiology might be, it is difficult to find an objective critique of the field of sociobiology as a science.

To Wilson's credit as a scientist and scholar, he did not attempt to justify his work in the face of outrageous claims made against it. Instead, he concentrated his efforts on the publication of what has become a well-received body of writings about human nature, evolution, and the modern synthesis.

In these beautifully crafted pieces, Wilson sets out his view that everything will be made clear when we see that human behavior is, at its very basis, a set of traits that are genetically based and subject to natural selection. This position is clarified and extensively discussed in *Consilience: The Unity of Knowledge*, one of his recent and most popular books.[22]

The key to unifying knowledge for Wilson is found in his doctrine of genetic reductionism and genetic determinism on the basis of which all human behaviors are reexplained. Central here is the doctrine of the selfish gene, a term given to the field of sociobiology by Oxford University professor Richard Dawkins. The concept of the selfish gene refers to the alleged principle that DNA sequences seek to replicate themselves; and it is this drive to replicate that leads to social structures that protect progeny and ensure that one's genetic code continues into future generations. Fitness is understood as reproductive fitness; and reproductive fitness is the product of the gene's effort to survive. It is the gene, not the organism or the person, to which survival of the fittest applies in the sociobiological worldview.

"Ruthless selfishness" characterizes gene activity, says Richard Dawkins.[23] What we know as human consciousness and human culture are the means the genes employ to ensure their continuance from one generation to the next. The DNA is in the driver's seat of every organism and of human culture as well. "The chicken is only an egg's way of making another egg," writes Wilson, so "the organism is only DNA's way of making more DNA."[24]

At the level of both animal society and human society, genetic selfishness expresses itself in groups as kin preference, protecting family members who share gene complexes and finding expendable competitors who are genetically distant. Because it is the gene's drive to persist to the next generation, we can explain group selection and kin selection in animals and, by analogy, what happens in human society. Wilson did not invent this idea, but he expanded on it. Kin selection is a Darwinian principle that explains both aggression and altruism by distinguishing persons who are genetically close from those who are distant. In 1971, R. D. Alexander said we could understand "calls for war to be waged in some relationship to degrees of genetic difference and [this] raises the question of the selective value and background of assisting one's closer relatives at the expense of nonrelatives or distant relatives. In any species engaging in the more violent kinds of intraspecific competition, ability to recognize and spare close relatives would be highly favored."[25] Patricia Williams comments on the ethical implications: "Under both group slection and kin selection, racism and genocide are natural. Only within groups is charity likely to flourish."[26] With this emerging doctrine of kin selection, sociobiologists believe they can explain human xenophobia against strangers and altruism toward relatives, because both are expressions of the selfish gene's desire to replicate.

How do sociobiologists arrive at these conclusions with these implications? What is their method of study? Wilson's method is to study social behavior in nonhuman animals—behavior such as aggression, sexual habits, reciprocal altruism, and such—and then by analogy apply this to human society. Because human beings share with nonhuman animals common descent in Darwinian terms, what we witness as human social organization is one more form of adaptation for the purpose of extending the future of the genes we carry. That the sociobiological argument rests not on empirical research with human beings but upon an analogy is worthy of note. Michael Ruse observes, "the sociobiologists argue that in some cases it is legitimate to argue from non-humans to humans. Hence, we have analogical support for the genetic basis of human behavior."[27] Now, Ruse believes "analogy per se is not a bad argument."[28] Yet we might ask: if sociobiology claims to be a science, then why does it not provide empirical study on the subject matter it deals with, namely, the connection between human genes and human behavior?

Despite our question regarding whether sociobiology can be considered scientific in its study of humanity, Wilson believes he can locate the unity of knowledge within science—consilience—by appealing to genetic explanations for a wide variety of phenomena, including human culture. Culture is reducible to a genetic analysis of evolutionary adaptation. Everything in culture serves reproductive fitness—that is, everything serves the gene's desire to survive to the next generation. Values and ethics and religion invisibly serve the selfish gene's agenda. "The genes hold culture on a leash," writes Wilson. "The leash is very long, but inevitably values will be constrained in accordance with their effects on the human gene pool."[29]

The leash holds loosely yet securely to all of human culture, including ethics, morality, and religion. Even though Wilson "favors a purely material origin of ethics," he does not advocate the brutal social ideology of Spencerism or Nazism.[30] Instead of an ethic of individual survival, Wilson says society ought to embrace altruism and cooperation. On what basis? Because "cooperative individuals generally survive longer and leave more offspring," he says.[31] Thus, he tethers his ethic of social cooperation to the leash of reproductive fitness. Despite the selfish gene and survival of the fittest, he contends we ought to support modern liberal values such as human rights in opposition to premodern tribalism and xenophobia. Is there a contradiction here? Does striving for universal human rights run counter to kin preference and the tribal values that serve the selfish gene? Can we override the dictates of genetic determinism? "Human nature can adapt to more encompassing forms of altruism and social justice. Genetic biases can be trespassed" in favor of universal social cooperation, says Wilson.[32]

This is inconsistent, complains Holmes Rolston III. How can Wilson tether all ethics to the genetic leash and then suddenly cut the leash?

> Just where is Wilson getting these *oughts* that cannot be derived from biology, unless from the insights of ethicists (or theologians) that transcend biology? This no longer sounds like a biologist biologicizing ethics and philosophy. It sounds like a biologist philosophizing without acknowledging his sources.[33]

It would seem that any biologist who is serious about rooting ethics in evolution would have to follow in the footsteps of Spencer and draw the conclusions of Hitler. To advocate such things as altruism, cooperation, or universal human rights would require appeal to ethical norms that are extrabiological, perhaps even theological. Intellectual honesty would require such acknowledgment, says Rolston.

Would E. O. Wilson want to acknowledge that his values derive from a theological vision that transcends the influence of the genes? By no means. This leads colleague and critic Stephen Jay Gould to categorize Wilson as one of the ultra-Darwinians—those reductionists who, in Gould's view, adhere to a strict and essentially fundamentalist interpretation of natural selection and adaptation.[34] In support of Gould's critique, we can see this in some of the statements found in *Consilience*. For instance, with respect to his view on the origins of ethics and religion in human societies, Wilson writes that these two behaviors derive not from a transcendent, theistic source, but rather from a genetically determined set of features for which there was selective advantage at some time in our ancestral past.

His use of the word "consilience" in his title is telling. The word means "a jumping together" and came into usage due to William Whewell, the nineteenth-century philosopher of science. Wilson uses it to mean that the results of different disciplines will be seen to come together in "the unity of knowledge." However, the leap, in this case, would be in one direction. What he means by this is that "empiricism" (his word for the objective, scientific viewpoint) must prevail over "transcendentalism" (his word for religion). The unity that he speaks of will come to be when religion rightly concedes that science has the answers. For instance, he writes:

> Which world view prevails, religious transcendentalism or scientific empiricism, will make a great difference in the way humanity claims the future. During the time the matter is under advisement, an accommodation can be reached if the following overriding facts are realized. On the one side, ethics and religion are still too complex for present-day science to explain in depth. On the other, they

are far more a product of autonomous evolution than hitherto conceded by most theologians.[35]

Wilson concludes this section with a revealing statement about his belief in the ultimate and universal validity of the empirical view: "Science for its part will test relentlessly every assumption about the human condition and in time uncover the bedrock of the moral and religious sentiments."[36] Wilson's belief in the final explanatory power of the neo-Darwinian model in every feature of human nature seems to justify Gould's characterization of him as a Darwinian fundamentalist.

Darwinian fundamentalist or no, Wilson's sociobiology has fascinated some theologians. Like offering a dish of milk to a feral cat, some are trying to coax sociobiology into the theological yard. Arthur Peacocke admonishes us to incorporate biological influence into a theological understanding of human nature. "Theologians would do well to recognize . . . the complexity of human nature and the fact that its basic foundational level is biological and genetic, however overlaid by nurture and culture."[37] Yet, sociobiology cannot be fully domesticated. "Where the Christian theist differs from the sociobiologist, as such, is in his affirmation of God as 'primary cause' or ground of being of the whole evolutionary process and, indeed, of God as the agent in, with, and under this process of creation through time."[38]

Evolutionary Psychology

In the sixth edition of *Origin of Species*, in the chapter entitled "Recapitulation and Conclusion," Darwin wrote:

> In the future I see open fields for far more important researches. Psychology will be securely based on the foundation already well laid by Mr. Herbert Spencer, that of the necessary acquirement of each mental power and capacity by gradation. Much light will be thrown on the origin of man and his history.[39]

To many, this prediction has come to fruition in the new and growing field of evolutionary psychology. Jerome Barkow, Leda Cosmides, and John Tooby are three of the leading scholars in this very active field. They have authored the principal text in the discipline, *The Adapted Mind*.[40] Cosmides and Tooby, at the University of California, Santa Barbara, have established the Center for Evolutionary Psychology for research in this field. On their web site they present a "primer" for the discipline, in which they define very carefully the nature of the field:

The goal of research in evolutionary psychology is to discover and understand the design of the human mind. Evolutionary psychology is an *approach* to psychology, in which knowledge and principles from evolutionary biology are put to use in research on the structure of the human mind. It is not an area of study, like vision, reasoning, or social behavior. It is a *way of thinking* about psychology that can be applied to any topic within it. In this view, the mind is a set of information-processing machines that were designed by natural selection to solve adaptive problems faced by our hunter-gatherer ancestors. This way of thinking about the brain, mind, and behavior is changing how scientists approach old topics, and opening up new ones.[41]

At the heart of evolutionary psychology is, of course, the neo-Darwinian model. Starting from this position, evolutionary psychologists utilize five basic tools—called, interestingly enough, the Five Principles, in perhaps an unconscious nod to the Fundamentals (see chapter 5)—in an attempt to understand the human mind. Those five principles, as described by Cosmides and Tooby, are:

Principle 1. The brain is a physical system. It functions as a computer. Its circuits are designed to generate behavior that is appropriate to your environmental circumstances.
Principle 2. Our neural circuits were designed by natural selection to solve problems that our ancestors faced during our species' evolutionary history.
Principle 3. Consciousness is just the tip of the iceberg; most of what goes on in your mind is hidden from you. As a result, your conscious experience can mislead you into thinking that our circuitry is simpler that it really is. Most problems that you experience as easy to solve are very difficult to solve—they require very complicated neural circuitry.
Principle 4. Different neural circuits are specialized for solving different adaptive problems.
Principle 5. Our modern skulls house a stone age mind.[42]

Of major importance in this viewpoint is the assertion that our brains evolved during a period of selective pressure characterized by a set of conditions known as the environment of evolutionary adaptedness or EEA. Ancient animals lived in a variety of environments, facing a variety of survival and especially reproductive challenges. Not all challenges were the same. The EEA for each organism is the set of reproductive problems faced by members of its species over evolutionary time. The evolutionary ancestors to modern humans faced their specific reproductive challenges and adapted. The adaptationist approach therefore seeks to identify human behaviors as the result of a natural selection process in a period during which those behaviors would have given our distant ancestors a survival advantage.

As an example, evolutionary psychology (along with sociobiology) seeks to identify the origins of the behavior we know as reciprocal altruism or cooperation. This is the idea that we establish social contracts in which a give-

and-take format is tacitly agreed upon. The researchers then argue that, if this is so, we must have also evolved the ability to detect those who would "cheat" on this contract and accept a benefit without the intention of a return. They proceed, then, to test for this innate ability to detect cheating. Such abilities, when identified, are correlated with the selective pressure present during the EEA, such that our ancestors who had this genetic trait would have a survival advantage.

The philosophical implications of observations about the survival advantage of altruism are significant because we have here an evolutionary-based scheme that at first seems to mitigate the cruel implications of survival of the fittest. If reciprocal altruism is natural, then perhaps acknowledging a natural origin for human morality is made more tolerable. Perhaps, or perhaps not. The difficulty, of course, is that genetically driven altruism is reciprocal, limited to one's close genetic kin group, and finally reducible to governance by the selfish gene. Altruism as a principle of evolutionary adaptation is not what Christians would call love because love in its most ethical sense aims at improving the welfare of someone who is other. Limiting love to genetic kin removes the element of seeking benefit for the other. So, if altruism is reducible to disguised selfishness, it does not pass the test an ethicist would exact. "One common reaction to the theory of reciprocal altruism is discomfort," writes Robert Wright. "Some people are troubled by the idea that their noblest impulses spring from their genes' wiliest ploys."[43]

Are the patterns of the adapted mind rising from the adapted brain reducible to the universal drive of the selfish gene? No, according to evolutionary psychologists. They wish to avoid any simple genetic reductionism. The adapted brain has evolved to levels of complexity that go well beyond gene expression. Reliance upon adaptation at this level distinguishes them from sociobiology, they believe. Yet, adaptation still means reproductive fitness; and the complex human brain still serves the goals of the selfish gene.

Evolutionary psychologists argue that they are less interested in differences, but more in common features of humans. In this way, they distinguish themselves from behavioral geneticists:

> In fact, evolutionary psychology and behavior genetics are animated by two radically different questions:
>
> 1. What is the universal, evolved architecture that we all share by virtue of being humans? (evolutionary psychology)
> 2. Given a large population of people in a *specific* environment, to what extent can *differences* between these people be accounted for by *differences* in their genes? (behavior genetics)[44]

Evolutionary psychologists also make a sharp distinction between their field and either social Darwinism or sociobiology. They point to their emphasis on commonalities rather than differences to separate themselves from the ideas of Spencer and Galton. And since sociobiology relies on studies of animal behavior rather than that of humans, one can argue that it is a subdiscipline of evolutionary psychology rather than a progenitor. In addition, evolutionary psychology emphasizes the physical brain adaptations themselves rather than adaptive behavior.

In contrast to this, however, some scholars look to sociobiology as the direct antecedent of evolutionary psychology. Richard Dawkins, for instance, in an interview with the online magazine *The Evolutionist*, refers to evolutionary psychology as no different from sociobiology:

> I think it's awfully easy to exaggerate the difference between evolutionary psychology and sociobiology. I've always assumed the reason for the new name was public relations. A whole lot of people have been brought up to think that sociobiology is a dirty word, so we'd better have a new word. The phrase "behavioral ecology" was invented for exactly the same reason: to distance the subject from sociobiology, which in ignorant circles has been taken up as a sort of red-rag word.[45]

Nevertheless, evolutionary psychology has, unlike sociobiology, become an accepted part of the academic landscape, at least in the United States.

Evolutionary psychology has garnered considerable criticism within the scientific community. Although individual reactions that disagree with the tenets of evolutionary psychology have been circulated, perhaps one of the most potent and accessible commentaries is the collection of essays edited and published by Hilary and Steven Rose, entitled *Alas, Poor Darwin*.[46] The book is the result of the eleventh Portrack Seminar, organized by the Roses in September 1998. The collection presents work by a number of leading opponents of evolutionary psychology, including biologists (Stephen Jay Gould, Gabriel Dover, Anne Fausto-Sterling, and Stephen Rose), sociologists (Ted Benton, Mark Erickson, Dorothy Nelkin, Tom Shakespeare, and Hilary Rose), ethologists (Patrick Bateson and Tim Ingold), philosophers (Mary Midgley and Barbara Herrnstein Smith), along with a psychologist (Annette Karmiloff-Smith) and the architect and postmodernist Charles Jencks who is the cofounder of this series of seminars.

Each essay in the collection takes a specific tack in arguing against the conclusions of evolutionary psychology. In the introduction to the book, the Roses lay out the case that they and the other contributors wish to make: "It is the argument of the authors of this book that the claims of [evolutionary psychology] in the fields of biology, psychology, anthropology, sociology, cultural studies, and philosophy are for the most part not merely mistaken, but culturally pernicious."[47]

Hilary Rose recounts the development of evolutionary psychology and its lineage. In her contribution, she tracks for us the rise of social implications and applications of the Darwinian model. Interestingly, the new theory was championed by both Herbert Spencer, whom we have discussed earlier, and Karl Marx. This apparent dichotomy is explained by Rose as an indication that the Victorian intellectual climate embraced the new science and immediately began to see ways in which it could be used for the unification of knowledge. In the same way, she argues, both sociobiology and evolutionary psychology represent attempts to house all of the social sciences under the rubric of the biological model, while condemning all previous formulations as based on outmoded, culturally based assumptions. She criticizes this program as the plan of "Darwinian fundamentalists" and concludes: "No wonder those who remain unconverted by the revealed truths of [evolutionary psychology] are made uneasy."[48]

In like manner, other authors challenge the genetics and evolutionary biology of Richard Dawkins and Daniel Dennett, or the cultural memes model espoused by both Dawkins and E. O. Wilson. Though evolutionary psychology is distinctly not racist, the place of women as seen through its lens is especially troubling to several of these critics. Should we bless patriarchy as adaptive? All in all, the text sets out to make a case that evolutionary psychology is bad science that could lead to even worse social policy. This fear is specifically referenced when Charles Jencks describes a talk by E. O. Wilson in which he commits the naturalistic fallacy by justifying the moral direction that comes from the research he reports.[49]

For our part, we can see how some of these criticisms arise from the literature, both original and popular, that the field has produced. Of greater interest for us, as scientist and theologian, is the paradox that arises from the argument for the primacy of evolution. On the one hand, an evolutionary psychologist would argue, we are the products of natural selection during the Pleistocene epoch for a set of fitness adaptations that became the modular brain we now employ. On the other hand, the proponents of the discipline argue that we are able to throw off the shackle of this genetic disposition to rebel and rise above and beyond the dictates of those fitness adaptations.[50] It would appear to us, then, that the proponents of evolutionary psychology have run into nearly the same conundrum with which theologians grapple: understanding the nature of human agency and choice in the face of divine omnipotence. In their case, it would seem, the conflict is not with the nature of God, but rather with that of the modern synthesis: evolution and genetic determinism.

Darwinian Social Philosophy

Whenever evolutionary biology is exploited for more than strictly its ability to describe biological processes, we need to be philosophically alert. We need to be alert especially when ethical or moral directions are said to be implied by what nature does. Sociobiologists accompanied by evolutionary psychologists in our own era appeal to nature's evolutionary history for both explanation of human nature and, directly or indirectly, for moral guidance.

Reproductive fitness has become the court of final appeal for moral understanding. "Natural selection *wants* us to behave in certain ways," writes Robert Wright.

> But, so long as we comply, it doesn't care whether we are made happy or sad in the process, whether we get physically mangled, even whether we die. The only thing natural selection ultimately "wants" to keep in good shape is the information in our genes, and it will countenance any suffering on our part that serves this purpose.[51]

With the doctrine of the selfish gene, nature now has a purpose—an allegedly scientifically discerned purpose—and everything that we human beings hold as precious means nothing as long as the selfish gene attains its own end: survival. Nature is nihilistic on every matter except genetic survival.

Is this ground sufficient for constructing a social ethic or a naturalistic worldview? We do not believe so. We find such proposals problematic for a number of reasons. First, strict biological scientists who wish to take advantage of evolutionary theory to pursue their research have invested considerable effort at expunging purpose from their methodological assumptions. With these new schemes of social Darwinism, purpose is surreptitiously slipped back into nature at the level of assumption. Just when we had thought we had cleaned out the closet, a new pile of dust appears.

Second, grounding ethics in nature alone commits the naturalistic fallacy. It is philosophically unsatisfying to base an *ought* on what is. Evolutionary biology tells us our past and present. How can it provide a vision of the good toward which we should work in the future?

Third, the fact that social theorists find ethical options—even contradictions—in evolution demonstrates the fruitlessness of appealing to nature for moral justification. Some find brutal selfishness; others find models of altruism. When we find both, we are forced to choose which model to follow. What is the criterion by which we make such a choice? Nature alone cannot answer.

As we saw, Herbert Spencer and Adolf Hitler go to evolution and appeal to survival of the fittest for their social ideal. "What was right for apes must be even more applicable to men," wrote Hitler in *Mein Kampf*.[52] Thomas Huxley and now Richard Dawkins, in contrast, go to evolution and appeal to high-minded humanistic values such as altruism that transcend our biological substrate. "Our genes may instruct us to be selfish," argues Dawkins, "but we are not necessarily compelled to obey them all our lives."[53] Nonselfish altruism becomes an option within an evolutionary ethic. It appears to us that naturalistic ethics cannot appeal to nature to decide which of these two options is right. Evolutionary ethics seems to be internally incoherent.

What is relevant to our study of the controversy over evolution is that when we confront Darwinian theory we confront far more than merely the science of biology. Trying to get to the science is like trying to get to one's E-mail for the day. Pop-ups and advertising and junk messages clutter the computer screen, just as social Darwinism and genetic reductionism and materialist philosophy clutter the basic Darwinian theory. For the theologian trying to assess the potential value of Darwinian theory for understanding human nature or divine creativity, the clutter makes reading the message more difficult. Yet, it is no less interesting, and no less worth the effort.

CHAPTER FOUR

SCIENTIFIC CREATIONISM

W e're at war. We're fighting for the American soul," said Duane Gish during a 2000 visit by a delegation from the Center for Theology and the Natural Sciences to the Institute for Creation Research in El Cajon near San Diego. What makes Darwinian evolutionary theory the enemy is that it is corrosive to the American soul. It teaches natural law without divine intervention, a materialist philosophy devoid of spirit or purpose. Worst of all, it teaches a social ethic of survival of the fittest that endorses *laissez-faire* capitalism, racism, and imperialism; it repudiates the divinely inspired vision of an ethic of love toward the weak, compassion for those who lose in the struggle, and care for those considered "unfit." On the surface, the war is being fought over a scientific explanation of human origins. Below the surface, the war is being fought over the essence of what it means to be a human being in a world created either by a loving God or by an uncaring natural selection.

This concern over theology and ethics should not obscure the fact that this is a scientific argument, intensely scientific. The question is this: Is Darwinian evolutionary theory good science or bad science? The creationists argue: Darwinism is bad science. The Darwinists argue that creationism is bad science. It is inaccurate to describe the controversy as just one more battle in the perpetual warfare between science and religion. This is a distortion. That a war is being fought is clear, but it is not a war with a religious army facing off against a scientific army. It is a war being fought over the question of what constitutes good science within a culture in which everyone respects and honors science.

What complicates the matter is that each side accuses the other of contaminating their science with ideology. Creationists accuse their opponents—whom they call "evolutionists" so as to connote believers in an ideology of evolution—of illegitimately going beyond what the science warrants to advocate a materialist philosophy that is deliberately atheistic. They accuse those whom they call "evolutionists" for conspiring to slip an atheistic philosophy into the American way of life under the smokescreen of unbiased scientific theory. Those defending evolutionary biology, in contrast, accuse the creationists of being fundamentalists, meaning they are locked into rigid dogmatic prejudices deriving from an out-of-date prescientific worldview, and, it follows, creationists are then incapable of admitting new knowledge produced by honest scientific inquiry. Each side sees the other as biased and stubborn.

As an ideological dispute, the battle looks at first like one being fought between Christian theism and materialist atheism. Yet, this would again be too simplistic. Among the evolutionary biologists who carry the science into the laboratory or the classroom, we find many devout Christian laypeople as well as persons of other faiths holding deep religious convictions. In such instances, these supporters of evolution see themselves as appreciating the science while not necessarily buying into a materialist ideology. The science does not dictate particular religious beliefs. Darwinism does not entail atheism. Some defenders of Darwinism are theists.

Are Creationism and Fundamentalism the Same Thing?

Are creationism and fundamentalism the same thing? No. That is the simple answer. What is fundamental to fundamentalism is appeal to the authority of a divinely inspired and inerrant biblical text. During the fundamentalist-modernist controversy of the 1920s, the authority of the Bible in matters of nature and history was at stake; and fundamentalists defended biblical authority in the face of what they perceived to be threats from liberal Christianity. Liberal Protestants in the late nineteenth century had imported higher criticism of the Bible from German and British scholarship; and this was intolerable to what would become the American fundamentalist reaction. Central to fundamentalism is biblical authority based upon inerrant inspiration. If this is the criterion by which we measure, then contemporary creationism is not fundamentalism, because creationism appeals not to the authority of the Bible but to scientific evidence to substantiate its claims.

So, no is the simple answer. However, this needs to be qualified. Some historical continuity exists between the fundamentalists of the early twentieth century and the creationists of the early twenty-first century. Today's creationists look back to that earlier era and claim fundamentalism's heroes such as William Jennings Bryan as their own. Creationists also hold the Bible in high esteem. Even though their focus is on what science reveals, they are confident that science, when properly pursued, will confirm what the Bible says. It is safe to say that biblical fundamentalism and scientific creationism are siblings, but not identical twins.

At the Institute for Creation Research, Henry Morris and John Morris and others customarily distinguish between *biblical creationism* and *scientific creationism*. The former appeals directly to what the Bible says; and it treats Scripture as authoritative. The latter appeals to science first, and this in turn supports what the Bible says. The ceding to science a certain level of authority to adjudicate scriptural claims and in principle to risk possible disconfirmation is what earns the label "scientific" in "scientific creationism."

Despite the high honor ceded to science here, creationists see themselves as carrying on the struggle begun by their fundamentalist forebears. In his *History of Modern Creationism*, Henry Morris devotes a lengthy subchapter to the 1925 John T. Scopes trial in Dayton, Tennessee. Even though Hollywood's movie version, *Inherit the Wind*, makes atheist attorney Clarence Darrow (named Henry Drummond in the movie), played by Spencer Tracy, the hero, not so for Henry Morris. Morris sees the humiliated and brow-beaten William Jennings Bryan (named Matthew Brady in the movie) as the hero because Bryan stood up for fundamental Christian commitments.

The historical William Jennings Bryan had been a liberal Democrat and Secretary of State under Woodrow Wilson and ran for the U.S. presidency three times; and in Dayton he was campaigning for biblical truth in American life. Even though he was in the courthouse as an attorney, Bryan took the stand at Darrow's request. On the stand, Bryan defended the infallibility of the Bible as the Word of God against scientific evolution; and he argued that scientific Darwinism led to social Darwinism and this in turn justified capitalist exploitation of labor and German militarism leading to the Great War, World War I. "With his oratorical brilliance, he had become probably the top spokesman for fundamentalism and creationism in the nation."[1]

Bryan, curiously enough, was not a strict biblical literalist; nor was he categorically opposed to evolutionary theory applied to biology. As a liberal social reformer dedicated to preventing war, Bryan's political passion became bolstering a healthy social morality. His reading of the history of Germany leading to the Great War convinced Bryan that Darwinian biology and social Darwinism had fostered the "law of the jungle" in that nation; and this led to the militarism and imperialism that nearly destroyed European civilization. This accounts for the passion with which he sought to prevent Darwinian evolution from attaining hegemony in the American public school curriculum, something the movie *Inherit the Wind* deletes when referring to Matthew Brady as a "bigot." Nothing could be more historically inaccurate.

Another historical fact is astounding. Historian Ronald Numbers observes that Bryan did not advocate a simplistic biblical literalism, nor was he totally opposed to evolutionary theory. Rather, Bryan held the *day-age* interpretation of the Genesis creation account. Bryan believed that each of the "days" mentioned in Genesis 1:1–2:4a could have referred to a long eon of time, thereby permitting the length of time recorded in geology and needed for evolutionary development. Further, Bryan could accept the idea of evolution of life-forms prior to the appearance of the human race. Common descent for humanity with other life-forms had not yet been proved scientifically to his satisfaction; but, in principle, he could accept it if and when it might be proved. Until such proof is in, Bryan felt we should keep the scientists on the defensive. In sum, he had no objection to "evolution before man but for the fact that a concession as to the truth of evolution up to man furnishes our opponents with an argument which they are quick to use, namely, if evolution accounts for all the species up to man, does it not raise a presumption in behalf of evolution to include man?"[2]

Our point in reviewing the Scopes Trial is that contemporary creationists associate themselves with the mission formulated by previous fundamentalists. Having said this, we need to proceed to note one more thing: Fundamentalism is not the equivalent of anti-evolutionism, despite its popular image. Still another historical fact well worth observing goes frequently unobserved, namely, the doctrine of creation did not appear on the original list of the Five Fundamentals. The movement we have come to know as "fundamentalism" takes its name from the Five Fundamentals adopted by the General Assembly of the Presbyterian Church in 1910, reaffirmed in 1916 and 1923. These were widely discussed in a series of twelve booklets called *The Fundamentals* published during this period. Fundamental to defining the Christian faith are belief in:

1. inerrancy of the Scriptures in their original documents;
2. deity of Jesus Christ, including virgin birth;
3. substitutionary atonement;
4. physical resurrection of Christ; and
5. miracle-working power of Jesus Christ.

The above five were approved. Items of theological importance nominated but not voted for inclusion were such things as Calvin's view on natural depravity, Luther's view on justification by faith alone, the premillennialist promise of a bodily return of Christ, and literal existence of heaven and hell. These four also-rans were held in high regard but simply were not approved for the list of fundamentals. Although these items are vital to orthodox Christianity, some well-respected theologians of the day were slightly nonconformist. J. Gresham Machen, for example, was a prominent Presbyterian fundamentalist who rejected premillennialism. Fearing a sectarian derailment and desiring to remain within the pale of classical orthodoxy, the assemblies dropped the bodily second coming from the central five.

Conspicuously absent from either the approved list or the secondary list is the doctrine of creation, let alone an anti-evolutionist interpretation of creation.

During this period, numerous orthodox theologians close to fundamentalism had incorporated Darwinian evolution into their respective theological belief systems. Stubborn resistance would not accurately describe the mood of the era. A. C. Dixon, the first editor of *The Fundamentals*, felt "a repugnance to the idea that an ape or an orang-outang was my ancestor"; nevertheless, he added that he was willing "to accept the humiliating fact, if proved."[3]

"Creation was not even listed as one of the 'five fundamentals' of the faith," sighs Henry Morris. "Several of the *Fundamentalist* booklets were actually written by men who were theistic evolutionists."[4] What we need to conclude here is that theological fundamentalism did not necessarily entail anti-evolutionism, because creation was not seen to be fundamental to the same degree that redemption and biblical inerrancy were. The startling fact of history is that some fundamentalists were able to reconcile their theology with evolutionary theory.

The first of the five fundamentals listed above affirms biblical authority and even inerrancy. One of the most articulate of the prefundamentalist Princeton theologians who formulated what would become accepted as the concept of inerrancy was B. B. Warfield. Here are Warfield's words as cited in one of the definitive books in creationist literature, *The Genesis Flood*, by John C. Whitcomb and Henry M. Morris. Warfield writes that the human words in the Bible were written "under such an influence of the Holy Ghost as to be also the words of God, the adequate expression of His mind and will. . . . This conception of co-authorship implies that the Spirit's superintendence extends to the choice of the words by the human authors (verbal inspiration) . . . thus securing among other things that entire truthfulness which is everywhere presupposed in and asserted for Scripture by the Biblical writers (inerrancy)."[5] As you will see in chapter 6, we place B. B. Warfield in the camp with other theistic evolutionists. This means that the first fundamental—biblical inspiration and inerrancy—does not in itself mandate a creationist position against evolution.

Even though contemporary creationists view fundamentalist Protestantism as their ancestor, some mutational changes are worth noting. As we have just seen, what was definitional for fundamentalism a century ago was passionate commitment to scriptural authority by virtue of the Bible's inspiration and inerrancy. This commitment was initially prompted by opposition to higher criticism applied to biblical hermeneutics in liberal Protestantism. The doctrine of biblical inerrancy was not formulated as a reaction against what was happening in the sciences. The enemies of fundamentalists are liberal Christians, not scientists. This should alert us to a pair of subtleties on the fundamentalist coin. On the one side, scriptural inerrancy itself does not require anti-evolutionism. On the flip side, contemporary creationists can freely celebrate science as a legitimate form of human knowing. Today's creationists are not encumbered by their fundamentalist heritage from making public appeal to scientific evidence rather than to the authority of the Bible. But, then, neither were those fundamentalists.

We are trying here to dispel two popular distortions. First, today's creationism cannot be reduced to yesterday's fundamentalism. Second, even yesterday's fundamentalism was not totally opposed to evolution. So, although most creationists are comfortable thinking of themselves as fundamentalists, the two belief systems are not identical. Not every fundamentalist is an anti-evolutionist, not every anti-evolutionist is a creationist, yet every creationist is an anti-evolutionist.

The Common Descent of Contemporary Creationism

Rather than fundamentalist forebearers in the broad sense, those whom Morris singles out as grandparents to contemporary creationism are conservative Christians who specifically argued against the validity of Darwinian evolutionary theory in behalf of a biblical account of world history. Morris singles out George McCready Price (1870–1962), a Seventh-day Adventist who provided scientific support for the biblical account of a worldwide flood in *The New Geology*. Price followed the teachings of his pre-Darwin Adventist architect, Ellen White, who claimed to have had a vision in which she was taken back to the founding of the world and saw how God created everything in six days and then rested on the seventh; this established the practice of the Seventh-day Sabbath rest.[6] Price's work purported to provide geological support for the Genesis account and to reconcile biblical faith with natural science. One of Price's students, Harold Clark, continued this line of scholarship with works such as *The New Diluvialism* (1946) and *Fossils, Flood, and Fire* (1968). Morris also lauds Presbyterian Harry Rimmer (1890–1952) for works such as *Modern Science and the Genesis Record* (1940) and *The Theory of Evolution and the Facts of Science* (1941).

Morris places Martin Luther in his theological family tree, contending that Luther was a six-day creationist. Few in the sixteenth century prior to the rise of modern science had an available alternative to the traditional literal view of Genesis, so one would simply expect Luther to be unquestioning on such a matter. Morris lifts up Luther's heirs in American Lutheranism to stand in as forerunners. He applauds Byron Nelson for writing *The Deluge Story in Stone*, published by Augsburg Publishing House in 1931; and he is especially appreciative of Concordia Theological Seminary faculty members such as Professor Theodore Graebner for his *Essays on Evolution* (1925) and *God and the Cosmos* (1943), as well as Alfred Rehwinkel who published *The Flood* in 1951. Four members of the Lutheran Church, Missouri Synod, joined Morris's Team of Ten in establishing the Creation Research Society in 1963: Walter E. Lammerts, John Klotz, John Grebe, and Wilbert Rusch.[7]

In addition to individuals, societies have begotten societies. The Creation Science Movement (CSM) began in London, England, in 1932, to protest the influence of Darwinism.[8] Contemporary creationism in America claims as ancestors the Religion and Science Association (1935–1937), which begot the Creation-Deluge Society (1938–1945). Morris cites an editorial from the Deluge Society's first bulletin supporting "the literal interpretation of the book of Genesis and other Scriptures relating thereto." Then he imparts confidence that the science will support the Bible's claims about Noah's flood: "If the Deluge did occur, it is believed that the scientific facts now available, or easily discoverable, will abundantly prove it."[9]

The American Scientific Affiliation (ASA) began during this same era, 1941, and its role in this story is a matter of dispute. Through the glasses of Henry Morris, it appears that ASA converted from young earth creationism to theistic evolution. ASA's members appeared to have committed themselves to opposing evolutionary theory; but over the years they gradually affirmed the indisputable veracity of scientific claims for an old earth and speciation, much to Morris's disappointment. The ASA "is no longer a *creationist* organization, with its leaders and most of its members having long since capitulated to theistic evolution."[10] In actuality, the ASA scientists never committed the organization to a specific position on the evolution question; so they could not convert from one to another. And those involved in the public controversy were hesitant to describe themselves as theistic evolutionists, preferring labels such as "progressive creationists." They affirmed geological evidence for an old earth and biological evidence for development from one species to another. Accordingly, God originally created many species, but in turn due to mutation and selection these led to development of a number of new species.[11] Today's heirs to progressive creationism are the Old Earth Creationists, willing to live with a 13.7-billion-year history of the universe and a 4.5-billion-year history of our planet.[12] Because some progressivists hold to episodic divine interventions, many are now moving in the direction of Intelligent Design, which we will discuss in the next chapter.

Aware of this checkered ancestry, the Creation Research Society (CRS) gave birth to itself in 1963 with a statement of faith that could not be reversed, a strategy to avoid the reversal apparently taken by ASA members who converted to what looks like theistic evolution. The Creation Research Society required of its members commitment to the following: (1) inerrancy of Scripture and the simple historicity of the Genesis record of creation; (2) special creation of the various "kinds" of organisms in the Genesis week of creation; (3) the global extent and effects of the Genesis flood; and (4) the historicity of the Fall of Adam and Eve, the need for a Savior, and salvation only through accepting Christ as Lord and Savior.[13] Today's heirs of this family line are the Young Earth Creationists.

CRS begat the Institute for Creation Research (ICR) in 1972; and from its center near San Diego, California, it now beams waves of influence all over the world. With Henry Morris as founder and his son, John Morris, directing expeditions to find Noah's Ark on Mount Ararat, along with indefatigable campus debater Duane Gish, ICR broadcasts the above-mentioned commitments as part of a philosophical and political campaign to oppose the hegemony of Darwinian evolution in the public school system. Through literature, debate, and courtroom testimony, ICR champions the cause of a worldview that includes a creator God against competing worldviews in which God is absent.

Although creationism began as a struggle for the American soul, this form of creationism—Young Earth Creationism—has spread to more than thirty nations who now host broadcasting centers of their own.[14] ICR supports a museum on creationism near San Diego, California, and Ken Ham's Answers in Genesis worldwide ministry supports a new theme park in northern Kentucky just across the river from Cincinnati. Creationism as an "ism" is battling against evolutionism for the human soul. Ham told the *Los Angeles Times*, "It's heating up. They need to know: We're coming."[15]

Gospel and Creation

Commitment to the doctrine of creation is not an end in itself. For the creationists, it supports the gospel message. What is the gospel? Henry Morris turns his eyes toward Jesus Christ: "The Gospel focuses especially on the person and work of the Lord Jesus Christ, the incarnate Creator (John 1:1-3, 14), who died in our place for the sin of the world (John 1:29)," he writes. "An understanding of faith in His bodily resurrection requires an acknowledgment that only He has conquered death, and, therefore, that He is Lord of all, able and sure to restore the whole creation someday to its primeval perfection." Note here the identification of the creator with the savior. Note also the identification of redemption with the creation prior to the Fall. "Thus, the Gospel is based on the good news that Christ Himself is the true Creator of all things and the good news that He, therefore, is King of Kings and Lord of Lords, sovereign of the universe, coming again someday to purge all evil and consummate all His purposes in creation."[16] Morris embraces a high Christology; and he objects that so few theologians appeal to the doctrine of creation to support Christology. One task of creationism is to rectify this oversight in contemporary theology.

Ken Ham identifies the Christian gospel with the entire story of creation, Fall, and redemption. We were created originally by God to live in paradise, the Garden of Eden. In Eden was peace. Even animals were vegetarians, living without killing. When the human race fell into sin, death was introduced into the world. The incarnate Jesus Christ suffered the same death we do; yet his resurrection instantiated the will of God for resurrection and redemption from sin, suffering, and death. "Every time we celebrate the Lord's Supper, we remember Christ's death and the awfulness of sin. Each Lord's Day we rejoice in Christ's resurrection, and thus the conquering of sin and death. But evolution destroys the very basis of this message of love. The evolutionary process is supposed to be one of death and struggle, cruelty, brutality, and ruthlessness. It is a ghastly fight for survival, elimination of the weak and deformed. This is what underlies evolution."[17]

Creationists find that the apathetic and cold-blooded interpretation of nature proffered by the Darwinian worldview contradicts what Christians know about the love and grace of God. The theodicy problem receives indirect attention in their repudiation of evolutionary history. Darwin's waste due to predation and extinction is as revolting to creationists as it was to Darwin.

> Evolution is inconsistent with God's nature of love. The supposed fact of evolution is best evidenced by the fossils, which eloquently speak of a harsh world, filled with storm and upheaval, disease and famine, struggle for existence and violent death. The accepted mechanism for inducing evolution is overpopulation and a natural selection through extermination of the weak and unfit. A loving God would surely have been more considerate of His creatures than this.[18]

Curiously, both Darwin, the atheist/agnostic, and Morris, the theist, agree on this point: The God of the Bible simply could not employ a process such as Darwin describes "with all its randomness, wastefulness, and cruelty."[19]

The original state of creation when it left the divine hand was "very good," say the creationists. The historical Garden of Eden enjoyed harmony in nature with no violence, suffering, or death. These things we know as evil came later as a result of the fall into sin. What scientists think of as evolution, creationists think of as devolution—that is, subsequent to the lapse into sin, the natural world has become subject to a cursed existence. The only existence contemporary science can study is nature under the curse; the prelapse Eden is unavailable to scientific examination.

The problem of evil is a problem all sensitive Christian theologians must face with honesty. When contemporary neo-orthodox and liberal Protestants assert that predation, suffering, and death are simply parts of nature, even necessary parts of nature, and therefore not to be subject to moral valuing, they tacitly remove the creation from the realm of the creator. The Christian claim is that the creator of all things is loving and gracious; and the overwhelming scope of "waste" should cause unease and tension with this Christian claim. The method for handling this unease or tension followed by the creationists is denial; they deny that evolution ever happened. The method for neo-orthodox and liberal theologians is also a form of denial; they deny that predation, suffering, and death can be assigned moral value.

We need here to ask the kind of question a systematic theologian would ask: Is this a coherent view? Does the commitment to scientific creationism imply or cohere with a high Christology? In our judgment the answer is methodologically no and theologically yes. In terms of methodology, the employment of scientific argumentation to support a young earth without speciation simply could not apply to what is said here about the redemptive work of Jesus Christ. Knowledge of redemption must come from special revelation, from Scripture. In terms of theology, to view the natural world we live in as scientists do is to see the world as fallen, as replete with violence, suffering, and death. Creationists can speak of this world as fallen because they posit a prefallen state of paradise, and they look forward to a redeemed state of paradise. In between, the natural world is the one scientists study through experience and reason. Paradise remains invisible to science, imaginable only to eyes of faith.

What Do Young Earth Creationists Actually Believe?

Since the rise of modern geology and speculations about deep time, conscientious Christian thinkers have sought ways to reconcile Genesis 1–3 with science. How can the sequence of events in a six-day creation fit with deep time? One trial balloon has been the *day-age theory*, according to which each of the six days in Genesis 1:1–2:4*a* represents not twenty-four hours, but rather long stretches of time, perhaps millions of years. Another trial balloon has been the *gap theory*, according to which a time gap opens up between Genesis 1:1 and 1:2. Gap theorists suggest that a pre-Adamic creation arose and was destroyed prior to God's sweeping over the face of the waters and calling for light. The remnants of this first creation are found in the ancient fossil record. The gap theory accounts for deep time as well as a subsequent special creation in six days leading to Adam and Eve. *Old Earth Creationism* has been aided by the day-age and gap theories when interpreting Genesis in light of modern science.

The contemporary controversy between evolutionary theory and scientific creationism does not center around the day-age theory or the gap theory. Rather, it centers around speciation through natural selection and related matters. What we have come to know as *Young Earth Creationism* is committed to a model depicting the origin of life that includes a half dozen basic principles.[20] Dare we call them the Six Fundamentals of Creationism?

First, sudden creation of the cosmos from nothing by divine action. The term "creationism" can refer quite generally to the monotheistic doctrine that the universe we live in is the product of a divine creative act and not an eternal metaphysical principle or a product of strictly physical principles. Like orthodox Christians in Roman Catholic, Protestant, and Eastern Orthodox circles virtually everywhere, Young Earth Creationists affirm fundamental doctrinal beliefs such as creation out of nothing, *creatio ex nihilo*—that is, God brings the entire cosmos into existence from nothing preceding it. Time and space and matter and energy and the laws of nature are all products of God's creative Word, and the created order is a product of God's design and purpose. Even though contingency and accident and unpredictability occur within the course of creation's history, the very existence of creation issues from divine love and direction. In itself, the doctrine of *creatio ex nihilo* does not distinguish creationists from other Christians, nor does it favor either evolution or anti-evolution.

Scientific creationists are emphatic that they share a commitment with the entire Western monotheistic tradition. "There are essentially only three modern creationist religions," write Henry Morris and Gary Parker, "orthodox Judaism, orthodox Islam, and orthodox Christianity. These are all founded upon belief in one self-existent eternal Creator, who called the universe itself into existence in the beginning, as well as all its basic laws and systems."[21] What we need to remain clear on is this: Most Jews, Muslims, and Christians affirm divine creation out of nothing but do not necessarily give it the twist we find in scientific creationism.

What distinguishes scientific creationism from garden variety contemporary Christian theology is the assertion that the "creation was 'mature' from its birth."[22] This is a no-growth theory of creation. No substantive changes. No Big Bang with subsequent development. What is produced by God's creative Word is a world complete with an apparent, not a real, past. Because we have an apparent rather than a real past, the creation could have come into being yesterday or billions of years ago; the time scale is not essential. Even so, creationists tend to think the divine creative act occurred within the last ten thousand years.

Anyone who disagrees with the creationist model gets called a nasty name— an "evolutionist." Swept up into the evolutionist dust bin for discarding, then, are Asian metaphysical religious traditions such as Buddhism and Hinduism along with Western Humanism and, of course, liberal Christianity. It would be a shock of dumbfoundment for a Buddhist monk or a Hindu sanyasin to wake up one morning to be told that he or she has been an evolutionist all along. It is also curious that liberal Christianity is said here to deny *creatio ex nihilo* because this element in the doctrine of creation is retained by liberals even when incorporating evolution. As we see it, nineteenth-century Darwinian biology simply has nothing to do with the great Eastern religious traditions that preceded modern science by two millennia; nor does acceptance of evolutionary biology mandate rejection of *creatio ex nihilo* by liberal Christians.

More is at stake than merely turning our attention to the very beginning of all things, to the origin of the cosmos. The question of ultimate origin does not interest evolutionary biologists. Only the origin of life does. Life presupposes the existence of matter, and *creatio ex nihilo* deals with the origin of matter per se. This is why no conflict need break out between creation and evolution. Nevertheless, the creationists carry the conflict onto the battlefield of the origin of life. They reject the idea that life could arise spontaneously from nonliving chemical reactions. Even the chemicals we find in DNA, say the creationists, have no inherent tendency to evolve into living cells. This means that *"life also is the result of creation."*[23] What we see here is the application of the concept of creation of the natural order to what happens *within* the natural order, what traditional theologians have called "providence" and recent theologians have called "continuing creation." For the creationists, God creates life within the cosmos the same way God had previously created the cosmos as a whole.

As an aside observation, this tenet illustrates partial continuity with creationism in another form, namely, the Vatican commitment to the special creation of each individual soul. German theologians distinguish these two by spelling them differently: *Kreatianismus* refers to the belief that each human soul is immediately created by God for each person, a doctrine that stands in opposition to traducianism and the idea of preexistent souls. *Kreationismus* refers to the beliefs we here associate with scientific creationism.[24] In English, our word "creationism" does double duty, hence the ambiguity. Yet, it may be an advantageous ambiguity at this point because both usages indicate what is tantamount to *creatio ex nihilo* within the already-created order.

Second, insufficiency of mutation and natural selection to explain development of all living kinds from a single point of origin. Microevolution is affirmed, while macroevolution is denied. Creationists object to natural selection on two levels. First, on the broad level, they object because it is a godless naturalistic explanation. It appears to be a deliberate attempt to explain natural processes without reference to God; hence, it is atheism under the guise of science. Second, at the level of research, creationists contend that proof is lacking that one species evolves into another. Curiously, once these two commitments have been made, creationists proceed to affirm both natural selection and evolution. How?

Creationists affirm both natural selection and evolution, but they confine them to microevolution, to what happens within a species or a so-called kind. What they reject is macroevolution, the transformation of one species or kind into another.[25]

It may appear that the creationist model rejects the principle of natural selection categorically. But a closer look will show that creationists are convinced that natural selection is operative in the natural world and that it affects the relative populations of variants within a species—that is, it applies to what happens within microevolution. What is repudiated is that natural selection explains macroevolution because no such thing as macroevolution exists.

One of the hot topics in the debate is the interpretation of industrial melanism in the peppered moth, *Biston betularia*. Peppered moths have two varieties, light and dark. The dark-colored form is known as the carbonaria or melanic form. It is estimated that prior to the industrial revolution, the light-colored variant amounted to 95 percent and the dark only 5 percent. If you take a photo of these moths on a tree you can see how the wing coloring of the light peppered moth matches the speckled gray lichen on the tree, lichen that covers the dark-colored bark, while the dark variant stands out. Birds can spot those dark moths on a light background; so many moths do not live to reproductive age. During the late nineteenth and early twentieth centuries, pollution from industrialization gradually killed off the lichen, leaving the dark-colored tree bark exposed. Now the light-colored moths could be more easily seen by birds, and the darker moths enjoyed the camouflage. The relative population reversed, so that by the middle of the twentieth century the dark moths outnumbered the light ones. Natural selection over time clearly affected the distribution of genetic traits within *Biston betularia*.

Is this evidence of macroevolution? No, say the creationists. What it demonstrates is that natural selection affects genetic variance within a given species. It affects microevolution. It simply has nothing to say to Darwin's theory that natural selection explains the origin of species.[26]

Creationists insist that macroevolution simply is not a scientific concept, because it has never been demonstrated. It has not been demonstrated in the laboratory, nor has anyone ever witnessed it in nature. What appears to count as evidence for macroevolution at best describes transformations that occur within the inheritance range of an already-existing species.

Third, changes occur only within fixed limits of originally created kinds of plants and animals. This extends what was just said. The word "kind" is important in this preformitarian position. It comes from the Bible, where in the first creation account, Genesis 1:1–2:4a, God creates creatures and asks them to multiply according to their own "kinds" (Hebrew: *min*). Creationist interpreters find ten "kinds" in Genesis: (1) grass; (2) herbs; (3) fruit trees; (4) sea monsters; (5) other marine animals; (6) birds; (7) beasts of the earth; (8) cattle; (9) crawling animals; and, finally, (10) the human race. Creationists believe that God intends for each kind to remain within its "own particular structure. . . . One 'kind' could not transform itself into another 'kind.'. . . Many different varieties can emerge within the basic framework of each kind, but at the same time such variations can never extend beyond that framework."[27]

Just what does the word "kind" refer to in today's nomenclature? At this point the creationists do two things. First, they grant that the biblical word "kind" is less than fully clear, that what belongs within and without this category is not biblically specified. Second, they tacitly yet rigorously equate it with "species." Each species is a kind. Each species puts up its own "no trespassing" sign. No overlap of species is permitted by God. Although creationists readily acknowledge that evolution takes place within a species—microevolution—what they deny is transformation of one species into another—macroevolution. "During the creation week God created all of these basic animal and plant kinds, and since then no new kinds have come into being. . . . Each kind was created with sufficient genetic potential, or gene pool, to give rise to all of the varieties within that kind that have existed in the past and those that are yet in existence today."[28]

The denial of macroevolution is what distinguishes creationists from the wider scientific community. "Evolutionists ultimately believe . . . that frogs turn into princes. . . . Creationists don't believe that frogs turn into princes at all, of course, but rather that frogs and people were separately created from the same kinds of molecular building blocks."[29]

One of the chief arguments raised by creationists against macroevolution is the alleged absence of transitional forms, what we popularly call the "missing links." If one species gradually gave way to a subsequent species and then died out, one would expect its fossil remains to chronicle the transition. Yet, claim the creationists, no such fossil record of transitional species has been found. "Evolutionists should expect to see transitional forms in the fossil record. . . . The fact is, however, that the same kinds of gaps exist in the fossil record as in the living world. All of the great phyla (the basic structural plans) of the animal kingdom seem to have existed unchanged since the earliest of the supposed geological ages. . . . There are no transitional forms."[30]

There are, however, varieties within species, and lots of them. Acknowledging variation over time is necessary to the creationist argument in order to prevent Noah's ark from being overloaded. Two representatives of each kind must fit into this one vessel; so the smaller the number of kinds, the more likely that all could fit. What we know as *flood geology* within scientific creationism places approximately one million animals on Noah's ark—the ark was a giant barge of 1,396,000 cubic feet, with the carrying capacity of 522 standard stock railroad cars—for 371 days during a worldwide deluge. From these one million representatives all the countless varieties have subsequently developed. Every kind was represented on the ark; what we see today are varieties within these Noahic kinds. "These 'kinds' have never evolved or merged into each other by crossing over the divinely established lines of demarcation, but they have been diversified into so many varieties and sub-varieties . . . that even the greatest taxonomists have been staggered at the task of enumerating and classifying them."[31]

Fourth, no common descent; apes and humans have separate ancestry. Even though we commonly use phrases such as "I'll be a monkey's uncle," contemporary evolutionary theory does not actually contend that monkeys were our uncles. Rather than say that we human beings have descended from apes, the theory posits that both apes and humans descended from a common ancestor. "Common descent" refers to the position that all life shares a single evolutionary ancestry.

Given what has been said above, then it should come as no surprise that creationists are not happy with the idea of common descent inclusive of human beings. "Today there is only a single species in the Hominidae, the family of man—*Homo sapiens*, or modern man. In the creationist view, man has always been separate and distinct from all other creatures, a unique created being."[32] Theologically, the human being is a special creature, a distinct "kind." Scientifically, no missing links can be found to establish the claim for common descent. "What about the evidence in the fossil record for transitional forms leading up to the modern apes—gorillas, chimpanzees, orangutans, gibbons— and those leading up to man's putative ape-like ancestor, the australopithecines? They are nowhere to be found."[33]

Fifth, earth's geology is explained by catastrophism, including a worldwide flood. Flood geology is a subdiscipline within creationism that provides an alternative explanation for the fossil record, an alternative to uniformitarianism. Uniformitarianism holds that fossils were formed at a uniform rate over deep time. The uniformitarian model, coming from Lyellian geology, correlates rock strata containing fossils with the biological history of the development of new species. Creationist catastrophism, in contrast, ascribes to Noah's flood in Genesis 6–8, dated three to five thousand years before Abraham, the reason we find so many fossils in sedimentary rock. This flood, which creationists say covered the entire globe, killed off human beings and animals and plants of all sorts in a one-year natural catastrophe. Sediment piled up on the corpses, preventing immediate decay and preserving their structures. The fossil record supports catastrophism, say creationists, because preserved remains of all life-forms can be found together in the same geological strata. Rather than finding simple life-forms in the lower strata with more complex allegedly newer species in the upper strata, lumped together we find fossils for all plants, animals, and human beings, both extinct and contemporary.

Footprints of both dinosaurs and human beings were apparently uncovered in the limestone bed of the Paluxy River near Glen Rose, Texas, indicating that dinosaurs had not become extinct prior to the arrival of *Homo Sapiens*. Human footprints appeared to be crossing the path of footprints made by a T-Rex. If dinosaurs and humans were contemporary, then we find fossil support for belief in a young earth. The creationist method is to examine the fossil record and provide an explanation compatible with the biblical flood account. "It is not the facts of geology, but only certain interpretations of those facts, that are at variance with Scripture."[34]

The creationists are not the only ones impatient with Darwin's uniformitarian or gradualist approach to speciation. Among the catastrophists we can place Stephen Jay Gould. The notion of punctuated equilibrium he developed with Niles Eldridge suggests that natural catastrophes accompanied jumps or leaps in the establishment of new species. The natural mechanism remains allopatric speciation—that is, geographic isolation followed by reproductive isolation. Natural catastrophes simply speed up this process on some occasions. Some creationists interpret Gould's punctuated equilibrium as support for their cause. Gould, on the other hand, locates his version of catastrophism within the broader Darwinian model.[35]

The creationists reject the Darwinian model, using catastrophism as evidence, especially Noah's flood. Historian Ronald Numbers is puzzled: Why does flood geology give such energy to the creationist argument? His surmise is that with flood geology, creationists are now able to put forth a positive research program, a theory that provides an alternate explanation for the evidence all scientists share. It connects the Bible to the rocks and fossils. And it does not require tricky nonliteral interpretations of the Bible, such as interpreting days as ages, in order to squeeze out deep time. Biblical literalists can now enter the fray with a proposed scientific explanation of their own.[36]

Sixth, a young earth, less than ten thousand years old. The above argument against uniformitarian deep time suggests that the earth need not be as old as the scientific community presumes. Young Earth Creationists do not feel compelled to defend a young earth; but they do so anyway. The question of evolution can be distinguished from the question of the geological age of the earth. Whereas "the concept of evolution does suggest an *old* earth," writes Henry Morris, "Creationism is free to consider *all* evidences regarding the earth's age, whether old or young."[37] Darwinists are stuck with an old earth, while the creationists have the option of young or old.

Why do creationists think the universe and our earth are young? First, they believe the second law of thermodynamics disproves Big Bang cosmology. If the universe began with an explosion, then we would expect the universe to be chaotic and then devolve due to entropy. Evolution as an upward movement could not occur. In sum, creationists can do without Big Bang cosmology, thereby permitting the creation of a universe basically as we observe it now. Second, they refute the notion that the earth is an open system, absorbing the sun's energy, and rising through chaos to higher levels of self-organizing order. Again, the second law is appealed to rendering impossible the conditions necessary for evolution to occur. Third, their confidence in catastrophism and belief in a single worldwide flood provides an alternative explanation for what appear to be ancient geological formations. Such arguments permit, though not require, a young earth. Finally, they wish to equate the second law itself with the Adamic story. They contend that the existence of entropy (disorder) and its inevitable increase as dictated by the second law is a result of sin. Thus, their inclination is to equate thermodynamic chaos with natural evil as a result of the Fall.

In addition to shying away from Big Bang cosmology and the law of entropy applied to the universe, scientific creationists also repudiate claims for deep time on earth based upon radiometric dating. Carbon-14 dating methods apply only to samples a few thousand years old and cannot be extrapolated accurately to distant points in the past. Appeals by radiochronologists to such things as uranium-lead or thorium-lead or potassium-argon ratios in today's mineral-bearing rocks cannot help, because no empirical knowledge of the original ratios exists. Radiochronologists must rely upon a large set of unprovable assumptions, so their methods cannot be trusted. "Not only is there no way to verify the validity of these assumptions, but inherent in these assumptions are factors that assure that the ages so derived, whether accurate or not, will always range in the millions to billions of years."[38] In short, arguments for deep time based upon radiometric dating are circular and hence fallacious. The earth is young.

Why do the universe and our planet appear old, then? Why would Henry Morris say that the "universe had an 'appearance of age' right from the start"?[39] It appears old because of so many complex physical and biological functions. When God created the world instantly by calling it from nothing, God created it with all functions running pretty much as we observe them now. If we assume that these observable functions were not created but rather developed slowly over time, then projection of an old cosmos and an old earth becomes corollaries to an unnecessary assumption. So, even if our physical world "appears" old, it is not. "The Creation Model quite reasonably implies that these initial conditions were produced in the system by the processes of creation and were of whatever nature and magnitude they needed to be for that system thenceforth to function optimally in the completed world as created."[40]

It is significant to note one item about the preformitarian model adopted by scientific creationists. They do not see themselves as disciples of Archbishop James Usher, who is known for calculating on the basis of the Bible that the earth was created on October 23, 4004 B.C. at 9:00 in the morning. The Usher view is perpetuated in works such as the *Scofield Reference Bible* and *Halley's Bible Handbook,* read widely in fundamentalist circles, but not authoritative in creationist circles. Biblical literalism does not require creationists to support a young earth; rather, affirming a young earth is optional.

Opposing Social Darwinism

The dust kicked up by creationist objections to evolution involves much more than merely defending Genesis or providing an alternative scientific explanation for geological and biological data. Values are at stake. Our very souls are at stake. The love of God for us is at stake. Our love one for another is at stake. The fabric of Western culture and all that it stands for is at stake. If evolution would come to us in its limited form as a scientific theory about biological origins, it could be calmly debated and readily absorbed into Christian theology. But that's not how it comes packaged. It comes packaged as naturalistic philosophy, as a set of social values, as an arrogantly revolutionary way of life. Evolution comes touted as something modern, as a new way of life that will replace our outdated religious traditions. And the way of life proffered by a social ethic based upon evolution is antithetical to what Christians believe and teach.

Fundamental to the Christian gospel is the belief that God loves the human race and all the creatures of nature. In fact, Christian theology teaches God created this world as an expression of eternal love. When we turn from creation to redemption, we see that God became incarnate and suffered on the cross. What this indicates is that divine love has a self-sacrificial dimension to it. When Jesus admonishes us to love one another as God has loved us, this self-sacrificial dimension becomes our ethical mandate. Christian ethics through the ages has cultivated a sensitivity for those who suffer from disease, misfortune, social marginalization, and injustice. To give food to the hungry and drink to the thirsty is to serve God as God serves us. No Christian, creationist or mainline, can surrender these commitments.

Yet, say the creationists, these values are the very ones derided by evolution in the various forms we know as social Darwinism (see chapter 3 for a detailed discussion of this movement). Any ethic constructed on a naturalist base of "survival of the fittest" cannot be reconciled with the Christian ministry to the weak or Christian love for the unfit. Darwin's own era in the late nineteenth century witnessed the damage done to the social fabric by the robber barons such as John D. Rockefeller and Andrew Carnegie, the capitalists who made themselves rich on involuntary sacrifices of the poor. These capitalists deliberately "applied the survival-of-the-fittest philosophy in their business dealings. . . . The laissez-faire capitalism of the American industrialists was only one of the deadly fruits of evolutionary theory."[41] A *laissez-faire* capitalism—in which the rich are judged as fit and the poor as unfit—that justifies neglect of the needs of the poor cannot be reconciled with Christian values. Creationists fear that the teaching of social Darwinism in the public schools will corrupt the souls of our young people and lead to a heartless and cruel society.

Militarism and imperialism parallel capitalism in appealing to social Darwinism for scientific and, hence, ethical justification. Philosophers such as Friedrich Nietzsche who took Darwinism on board celebrated victories of the strong over the weak and looked forward to a future stage in human development, in Nietzsche's case to the *Übermensch* (superman). Responsibility for the two World Wars started by Germany are placed at Darwin's feet. As we saw earlier, U.S. Secretary of State William Jennings Bryan attributed the military expansionism of Germany leading to World War I as the product of belief in Teutonic superiority fostered by a philosophy of the survival of the fittest. In the decades leading up to World War II, Darwinism in the form of eugenics was incorporated into Nazi philosophy by Adolf Hitler, depicting the Aryan race as Nietzsche's *Übermensch*. In Germany,

> racism, the growing belief that the white race (some even narrowed this to the Teutonic race) had demonstrated its superiority in the struggle for existence and was thus destined to control or eliminate the other races. Neither imperialism nor racism originated with Darwinism, of course, as both have been present in one form or another throughout history. . . . However, Darwinism finally provided racist imperialism with an apparent scientific justification.[42]

Contemporary creationists are racial egalitarians. Creationists emphasize the unity of the human race. They lift up the concept of species here, recognizing that all human beings regardless of race are able to interbreed with one another. The human race is a single species, scientifically defined. What appears to us as racial difference is trivial, say creationists, noting how there is more genetic variation *within* any group than there is *between* one group and another. This means apparent racial divisions are not scientifically justifiable divisions; and this helps combat attempts at moral or social divisions.

In an earlier era, when evolutionary theory was widely used to justify racial superiority, racist ideologies presumed that the inferior races were closer to the animals than the more evolved and hence superior races. Such racial differences were supported by depicting racial groups as different branches on the evolutionary tree. Creationists square off against the now-outdated evolutionary doctrine of separate branches for human development. "One of the biggest justifications for racial discrimination in modern times is the belief that, because people groups have allegedly evolved separately, they are at different stages of evolution, and some people groups are less evolved," write Ken Ham, Carl Wiel, and Don Batten. Then they apologize for racism practiced among Christian believers. "This sort of thinking inspired Hitler in his quest to eliminate Jews and Gypsies and to establish the 'master race.' Sadly, some Christians have been infected with racist thinking, through the effects on our culture of evolutionary indoctrination that people of a different color are inferior because they are supposedly closer to the animals."[43]

It is of decisive theological importance to emphasize that the human race is a single species, according to creationists. The Bible does not use our term "race," they point out; rather, Scripture describes "all human beings as being of 'one blood' (Acts 17:26)."[44] Essential to Christian anthropology is the oneness of the human race with Adam and with Christ, the second Adam. In Adam, we all die. In Christ, we are all made alive. Jesus Christ is the image of God (*imago dei*) in incarnate form, an image in which we all share. Racial divisions simply cannot be considered fundamental, from a theological point of view; and the creationists argue this point with considerable passion.

Now, we might ask: Is it necessarily the case that evolutionary biologists must be racists and creationists egalitarians? No. To draw the picture this way would be a distortion. Evolutionist commitments to such things as common descent combined with opposition to the doctrine of progress, on which the split between superior and inferior depends, could be conscripted as support for racial equality. Evolutionists and creationists could find themselves in ethical agreement here. "Virtually all evolutionists would now agree that the various people groups did not have separate origins; that is, in the evolutionary belief system, the different people groups did not each evolve from a different group of animals. So they would agree with biblical creationists that all people groups have come from the same original population."[45] Note the method here: The proper interpretation of evolution as science supports a previous commitment made to what the Bible says about racial equality.

At times the list of moral calamities in society blamed on evolutionist thinking can get quite long. In addition to capitalism, Nazism, and racism already mentioned, evolutionary thinking is accused of cursing the modern world with communism, Freudian psychoanalysis, abortionism, the sexual revolution, homosexuality, the drug culture, and New Age spirituality. All these "deadly social philosophies" are allegedly the "corrupt fruits of evolutionism."[46]

Criticizing the Science of Creation Science

We now turn to the question, should creation scientists be permitted to call themselves "scientists"? Should they be excluded from membership in the club of real scientists? If creationists use science to support what they believe to be biblical truths, does this automatically define them as religious and, if religious, then unscientific?

What we believe to be relevant in asking this question is the self-understanding of creationists. One fact demands honest attention, namely, scientific creationists see themselves as engaging in science. Thus, we would like to give an affirmative answer to the opening question: Yes, scientific creationists should be treated as scientists. We answer yes because this is what creationists want. A second question that could be posed would be this: Does the quality of their scientific research equal that of what we know as university level science? Our answer is: probably not. What we want to avoid is defining creationists as religious when they want to be defined as scientific. Now, what is going on here?

Does scientific creationism have any connection to biblical creationism? Yes, at the point of departure, at the point of basic assumption and hypothesis projection. Here again we find a subtlety. Creationists do not necessarily feel obligated to produce new scientific data; rather, they debate how the existing scientific data ought to be interpreted. "We do not presume to question any of the data of geological *science*," write Whitcomb and Morris. Then they define scientific method in terms of experiment and reproducible knowledge regarding how nature works in the present. Science, they say, is limited to present knowledge. It cannot provide empirical knowledge of things past or future. Any extrapolation to the past or to the future is nonscientific. When one speculates about prehistoric origins, one must build in assumptions that are extrascientific. These assumptions, then, are a matter of faith. They are a matter of faith whether one is a biblical Christian or a materialist scientist. Once the faith assumption has been articulated as a hypothesis, say Whitcomb and Morris, then it is time to assess existing data to see if it corroborates it.

> Extrapolation of present processes into the prehistoric past or into the eschatological future is not really science. Such extrapolation necessarily involves assumptions and presuppositions and is therefore basically a philosophy, or even

a faith. . . . We believe that the Bible, as the verbally inspired and completely inerrant Word of God, gives us the true framework . . . one of special creation of all things, complete and perfect in the beginning, followed by the introduction of a universal principle of decay and death into the world after man's sin, culminating in a worldwide cataclysmic destruction of "the world that then was" by the Genesis Flood. We take this revealed framework of history as our basic datum, and then try to see how all the pertinent data can be understood in this context.[47]

The creationist method, understood as interpretation of data from an assumed stance of faith, is said here to be comparable to what established scientists do. Standard evolutionary theory and scientific creationism should be viewed as competing models of equal intellectual stature, they contend.

In the debate setting, Henry Morris relies on scientific, not theological, arguments. "We are always careful to stick strictly to scientific arguments, especially using the fossil record to show that macroevolution has not occurred in the past, the characteristics of mutation and natural selection to show that it is not occurring in the present, and the laws of thermodynamics to show that it could not occur at all. Also the principles of probability are used to show that complex functioning systems could never arise by chance."[48] Morris complains that his scientific opponents fail to stick to the science; rather, they criticize creationists for having "religious motivations" or attack "our personal character or credentials. . . . But one thing they will not do is give any real scientific evidence for macro-evolution."[49] Unmistakable here are two things: first, their opposition is to macroevolution from one species to another and, second, the self-understanding of creationists that they are mounting a distinctively scientific argument.

Brown University cell biologist Kenneth Miller does not think this constitutes an adequate scientific argument. He is critical of creationism on both scientific and theological grounds. His scientific critique is that Henry Morris and his ICR colleagues fail to handle the fossil evidence with accuracy or integrity. Miller finds the geological evidence for an old earth so overwhelming that to deny it on behalf of a young earth theory is absurd. The arguments in behalf of flood geology are massively contradicted by what is found in the layers of rock under investigation. For example, flood geologists argue that during the flood, nonswimming animals drowned first so that their fossils lie at the lowest levels of sediment, while swimming animals died later and their fossil remains lie in the upper regions. Miller points out that plants are geological latecomers to the history of the planet, hence their fossils can be found in the upper strata. Miller asks, how could these plants swim up near the surface during the alleged flood? Furthermore, radiometric dating has confirmed the evolutionary hypothesis that our planet is very old, 4.5 billion years, in fact.

> The consistency of the data drawn from each of these samples is nothing short of stunning. When it comes to the geological age of our planet, true controversy is a thing of the past, and not because of evolutionary dogma. Rather, it is the concordant music of the data itself that overwhelms claims to the contrary. . . . The actual pattern of life over geologic time doesn't even come close to matching what would have happened in a single worldwide flood.[50]

Are there transitional forms, the missing links creationists deny? Yes, indeed. Miller refers us to two important fossil finds, one on each side of the fish-to-amphibian transition. He finds decisive the detailed skeleton of *Acanthostega gunnari*, a remarkably fish-like tetrapod.[51]

Scientifically, Young Earth Creationism cannot account adequately for the data. But scientist Miller offers a theological objection as well. He notes how Henry Morris and his ICR confreres recognize the indisputable evidence of an earth 4.5 billion years old; yet they argue that the earth only has the "appearance" of being ancient because the divine creator ordained this misleading appearance. Our creator God is said to have deliberately fashioned a bogus astronomical and geological history measurable by our scientific instruments. Nature's evidence for an old earth, then, becomes a trick that God is playing on human perception. Miller asks rhetorically, what kind of a view of God is at work here? "What saddens me," he writes, "is the view of the Creator that their intellectual contortions force them to hold. In order to defend God against the challenge they see from evolution, they have had to make Him into a schemer, a trickster, even a charlatan. . . . In other words, their God has negated science by rigging the universe with fiction and deception. To embrace that God, we must reject science and worship deception itself."[52]

In disgust, Miller denies the appellation of "science" to "scientific creationism" as well as repudiates the theology that underlies it. It is ironic, Miller says, that creationists "invoke the name of science itself, as in 'scientific creationism,' even as they reject science. This lack of honesty is most revealing. . . . Such so-called creation science, thoroughly analyzed, corrupts both science and religion, and it deserves a place in the intellectual wastebasket."[53]

Calvin College physicist and astronomer Howard J. van Till offers a parallel evaluation. He criticizes scientific creationism for its selective mustering of evidence and for promulgating the idea that God is deluding us by making a young universe appear to be old. This is poor science and poor theology, he contends.

> I am fully convinced that "scientific creationism" is a travesty of natural science and a sad parody of biblical theology. . . . It appears that persons motivated by a sincere desire to praise God as their Creator have become trapped in an unbiblical approach to the realization of that desire. I heartily commend the desire

but wish to suggest a more biblically faithful manner for expressing the highest praise of our Creator-Redeemer.[54]

A Conflict Between Science and Faith?

Ian Barbour classifies the controversy between evolutionary biology and scientific creationism as one of conflict. Barbour interprets this as a conflict between science and religion, not a conflict within science. He locates scientific creationism within "biblical literalism" and then denounces it as "a threat to both religious and scientific freedom. . . . When absolutist positions lead to intolerance and attempts to impose particular religious views on others in a pluralistic society, we must object in the name of religious freedom."[55]

Ted Peters has disagreed with Barbour's assessment. That a conflict is upon us is obvious; but it is less than fully accurate to describe this as a conflict between science and religion. This is because the creationists see themselves as debating within the scope of science, not as pressing a religious case against science. Contemporary creationists understand themselves as appealing to science, not to biblical authority, to make their case.[56] Henry Morris states it flatly: "Scientific creationism is *not* based on Genesis or any other religious teaching. . . . Indeed, the scientific case for creation is based on our knowledge of DNA, mutations, fossils, thermodynamics, geology, and other sciences."[57] How much clearer could he be? Before we can draw an accurate picture of what is going on, we must allow the self-understanding of the creationists to enter the picture and be accounted for.

Just what is the line being drawn that identifies the conflict? Actually, two such lines divide. First is the line between evolutionary theory and creationist theory to account for the scientific facts. Creationists believe that before the bar of science their model is at least as adequate if not superior to that of established Darwinism. Duane Gish exemplifies this self-understanding of the conflict and its potential resolution:

> If, without the philosophic presuppositions of either the materialist or the theist, creation and evolution are used as models to predict the nature of the historical evidence, it can be seen that the creation model is just as credible as the evolution model (and, I believe, much more credible). And I reiterate: the one model is no more religious or any less scientific than the other.[58]

Note that Gish does not appeal to the literal interpretation of Scripture, as Barbour would presume; rather, he appeals to criteria of evaluation he believes all scientific theories share in common. In sum, the conflict is between theories or models, not between religion and science.

Yet, reflected in Gish's challenge is concern over extrascientific ideology, namely, concern over materialist philosophy. Creationists are energized over what they perceive to be the threat to faith mounted by materialism and atheism supported by Darwinism. This marks the second line that divides. "This is a spiritual battle," writes Henry Morris; "and the battle plans and tactics can only really be understood in spiritual terms."[59] So, Barbour is correct; there is conflict here. Yet the enemy of creationism is not science per se. It is materialist ideology.

Materialist ideology is the enemy as creationists perceive it. But creationists have their own sworn public enemies, an army of opponents who by all objective measures is out to get them. One military commander is science fiction writer Isaac Asimov. His chief weapon is to deny to creationism its claim to be scientific. Asimov believes he can defeat the movement by establishing a defensive perimeter around the laboratory, by keeping creationists in outside religious territory. He contends that the word "scientific" in "scientific creationism" is "nothing but a disgraceful imposture." Then he describes creationists as strict biblical literalists devoid of science. Creationism "cannot endure the intellectual marketplace, since it will not allow its basis to be questioned. The literal words of the Bible are asserted as true to begin with; how, then, can there be any questions, any arguments, any controversy? This is, of course, unscientific gibberish."[60]

Stephen Jay Gould agrees. Repudiation seems obvious: Dogmatic commitments such as inerrancy of Scripture are simply incompatible with scientific method. Science pursues empirical evidence wherever it leads. Dogmatic commitments threaten honesty in research because they appear to determine the conclusion of research in advance. On this basis Gould denies to the creationists the right to join the club with real scientists. After criticizing them for misusing the theory-fact relationship, Gould adds that the term "scientific creationism" is "meaningless and self-contradictory, a superb example of what Orwell called 'newspeak.'"[61] Because scientific creationism is not genuine science, Gould would prefer that the word "science" be removed from their name.

Yet, as we have seen, the creationists distinguish between biblical and scientific creationism. The latter does not depend methodologically on the former. Henry Morris even concludes one of his books by saying proudly, "There is not a single quotation from the Bible in this entire book!"[62] His self-understanding is that when creationism is scientific it does not rely upon biblical authority. Those who demand to interpret the conflict as a conflict between science and religion are forced to label creationists "religious" when they do not want to be.

To be sure, creationists by no means abandon Scripture. While defending biblical inerrancy and making the "case for creationism," Wayne Frair and Gary Patterson put it this way: "We believe that a Christian does not need to abandon a biblical perspective in order to carry out effective science. Accurate exegesis and reliable interpretation of the Bible along with valid scientific conclusions are the goal of all scientists who are Christians."[63]

Our point here is not to advocate that establishment scientists adopt creation science as their own; nor are we offering an evaluation of the science of creation science. Our point is that the self-understanding of creationists is that they are pursuing a scientific argument. More, creationists have a high regard for science in general. It is this point that renders it inaccurate to dub the controversy over evolution as a simple example of alleged warfare between science and religion.

What Does It Mean to Be Scientific?

Even so, at issue is whether or not creationists have the right to consider themselves scientists. "This has been a movement led, not by churchmen, but by scientists—scientists with Ph.D. degrees from recognized universities, holding responsible scientific positions and using cogent scientific data and argumentation," exclaims Henry Morris.[64]

In tacit alliance with Asimov and Gould, theological critics such as Langdon Gilkey try to take away from creationists their door key to the scientific clubhouse. Gilkey says that creationists confuse categories. Science deals with finite causes in the temporal world. Religion, in contrast, deals with the infinite ground of reality, with God who is transcendent. Gilkey accuses the creationists of confining all knowledge to a single level of truth—to the level of factual knowledge regarding finite cause and effect. They see God as one finite cause among other finite causes. This, to Gilkey's mind, is a mistake because it confuses theological language about our transcendent God with scientific language about the facts of the present world.[65]

Henry Morris grieves this situation; but he responds with increased resolve:

> There is much resistance to this message, of course. The scientific community insists that creation is a purely religious concept, not scientific. The liberal and evangelical religious communities often insist that it is not even an important religious concept. Our message thus must often deal with both objections, demonstrating that creation is both critically important and truly scientific, meriting full commitment of both mind and heart.[66]

The question regarding the scientific status of creationism came to a head in 1981 in the Little Rock courtroom of Judge William Overton, trying the constitutionality of Arkansas Law 590 in *McLean v. Arkansas Board of Education*. This law would require that public school teachers who talk in class about human origins must discuss creation as well as evolution. The scientific status of evolution was not in question. The legislation did, however, describe creationism as scientific.

> "Creation-science" means the scientific evidences for creation and inferences from those scientific evidences. Creation-science includes the scientific evi-

dences and related inferences that indicate: (1) Sudden creation of the Universe, energy and life from nothing, (2) The insufficiency of mutation and natural selection in bringing about development of all living kinds from a single organism, (3) Changes only within fixed limits of originally created kinds of plants and animals, (4) Separate ancestry for man and apes, (5) Explanation of the Earth's geology by catastrophism, including the occurrence of a world-wide flood, and (6) A relatively recent inception of the Earth and living kinds.[67]

The American Civil Liberties Union (ACLU) contracted with the New York law firm of Skadden, Arps, Slate, Meagher, and Flom to fight Arkansas Law 590. The ACLU brought a number of expert witnesses in both science and religion to testify against the scientific character of creationism: Michael Ruse, Francisco J. Ayala, Stephen Jay Gould, Langdon Gilkey, plus others. Quite decisive in the testimony was the observation that scientific creationists had not published articles in recognized scientific journals over the previous two decades, indicating that they were not engaged in recognized progressive research programs. The court also found it relevant, and therefore damning, that the creationists personally believed in a literal rendering of the Genesis account of creation. That they sought scientific support for their biblical beliefs did not spare them losing credibility because they held such biblical beliefs.

Creationists were depicted in Little Rock as we saw Barbour depicting them earlier, namely, as absolutist and a threat to academic freedom. In his rendering of the Arkansas 590 story, Michael Ruse reports his excitement at having been chosen by the ACLU to travel to Little Rock to fight for academic freedom against the creationists. He reports he "wanted to prove not merely that Creation-science is not science, but that it is a dishonest and thoroughly corrupt enterprise, violating every standard of intellectual integrity." He referred to "the Creation-scientists as 'sleazy.'"[68] This charge of sleaziness is based upon the alleged habit of creationist authors to quote evolutionist authors out of context, leading to distortions of what evolutionary biology actually teaches. Sleaziness is not scientific, obviously.

University of Chicago theologian Langdon Gilkey testified against the creationists as well, locking them out of the scientific establishment and consigning them against their will to religious house arrest. Before expelling them from the laboratory, Gilkey shows he understands their claim to be scientific; he recognizes that their credentials such as doctorates in the natural sciences make them "'scientists' by any normal, useful, or descriptive definition of that word."[69] What denies them admittance to laboratory status is that they fail to produce a progressive research program—that is, they fail to lead us toward predicting confirmation of hypotheses and new knowledge. "As for the theories of creation science, they cannot claim to be science, but not because their proponents are religious or religiously inspired. On the contrary, it is because their theories or models fail to accord with the canons of science, because they cannot be tested in experience, and because they cannot usefully predict."[70]

Yet Gilkey adds nuance missed by most commentators. Gilkey recognizes that evolutionary theory cannot claim to be pure science either; it too has philosophical overtones and undertones that make it a form of religious perspective on reality. Creationists are not the only ones whose religious perspective influences their scientific agenda.

> Perhaps the trickiest intellectual problem of the trial—far more subtle than just proving creation science wrong or even unscientific—would be to distinguish the scientific from the religious elements of *both* creationism and evolutionary science. . . . In any case, it became at once clear to me as I studied the documents that creation science had misunderstood and confused its own religious speech or conceptuality with scientific speech or conceptuality, and that that represented one of the major problems of the case.[71]

Can Ian Barbour rightfully describe this situation as a conflict? Yes. However, what we are looking at is by no means a conflict between science and religion. It is a conflict between science and science, and it is a conflict between religion and religion.

CHAPTER FIVE

INTELLIGENT DESIGN

I t is our common observation that living organisms are incredibly complex and appear to act with or toward a purpose. Yet, what is it we are observing? Is purpose really there? Are natural phenomena designed so as to fulfill a purpose? As we have seen in the previous chapters, evolutionary theory is a cauldron boiling over with questions and debates about designs in nature and the purpose of evolutionary development.

That complexity exists in nature is not a question for debate. It is the origin of this complexity and the mechanism by which it arises that has engendered the most intense debate. Until recently, arguments about purpose or direction or design were carried on outside the specific arena of the biological sciences, *qua* science. Those evolutionary biologists who chose to take a position were doing so within the philosophical or social setting, even when they did not realize or admit to this. Enter now the Intelligent Design theorists, who argue vehemently that the complexity present is purposeful and did not arise as one of many chance possibilities. This proposal for Intelligent Design is being made using the methods and framework of science itself.

In this chapter we will review the history of the so-called design argument and discuss the work of the most prominent of the contemporary Intelligent Design advocates, Phillip Johnson, Michael Behe, and William Dembski.

The Philosophical Setting of Modern Biology

In many ways, the neo-Darwinian synthesis that is the central paradigm of modern biology is a product of nineteenth-century thought. In spite of the appeal to the random or chance nature of mutations, an event that can be explained only by quantum theory, the central assumptions of the discipline remain mechanistic and deterministic. The mechanistic mind-set has pervaded the most ambitious project to date of so-called Big Science, namely, the Human Genome Project (HGP) pursued by molecular biologists. Begun during the final decade of the last century and still continuing, HGP has sought to sequence the nucleotides and identify the genes in human DNA. Surrounding the research is an aura of significance, the widespread belief that DNA is the alleged "blueprint" of each individual person. In schizoid fashion, DNA is elevated to the rank of determining the very essence of who we are and then dropped immediately into the materialist vat where everything is a mere collection of chemicals. When in the popular mind molecular biology is combined with sociobiology the result is belief in genetic determinism, what some label the "gene myth."[1] At the laboratory bench, molecular biologists tend to dismiss genetic determinism; yet the gene myth has firmly established itself in our biologically informed culture.

The mechanistic and deterministic mind-set deliberately expunges purpose. Modern biology has inherited this mind-set from the seventeenth-century philosopher David Hume. As a staunch empiricist, Hume argued against the use of any kind of teleological explanations in science. He believed and persuasively wrote that to attribute purpose to any system that could be subjected to the scientific method would be adding an unnecessary layer to the problem. As an advocate of reductive methodology and epistemology, Hume said such layers should be avoided whenever possible.

The heritage of Hume's thought in modern science is that the method employed is essentially blind to purpose of any kind. Francisco J. Ayala has discussed this and noted that even though teleological explanations work best in some cases, still a common scientific reaction is to deny that such exist.[2] Cells divide by mitosis, and in the process, each daughter cell receives the identical number of chromosomes that the parent cell had. This is carried out in an elegant way by the spindle apparatus, with its web of fibers traversing the dividing cell. However, it is not proper to speak of this result as the "purpose" of the spindle apparatus. In fact, biologists will say that this is a teleonomic explanation, one that appears to have purpose, but really only has function. According to Ayala, we cannot say evolution as a whole follows a grand design, even though we can see functional coordinations toward local or limited purposes within the life of organisms.

What was Hume rejecting in his argument against teleology within nature? As we shall see the philosophical link between purpose and theological reflection creates a slippery slope down which Hume believed, perhaps rightly, science could not afford to slide. We suspect that much of modern science continues unconsciously to flee this possibility.

Thomas Aquinas and the Aristotelian System

Spain in the twelfth century was a society that we can certainly envy today for its intellectual fruitfulness and multireligious harmony. Living together in intellectual and religious harmony were the three major monotheistic religious traditions that cannot seem to find such peace today. Christianity, Judaism, and Islam were, for a brief moment in history, able to flourish side by side. In the midst of this *pax Abrahama* came a rediscovery of critical import for our discussion.

The writings of Aristotle had been all but lost in the Western world, save for the library in Constantinople. However, these manuscripts had been translated into Arabic and commented on by Islamic scholars, notably, Ibn Sina (Avicenna) and Ibn Rushd (Averroes).[3] They took the ideas of the Greek school and filtered them through the cloth of their own theological reflections. It was through the recovered Greek text and the commentaries of the Muslim scholars that the works of Aristotle returned to the West and became the intellectual framework of the high Middle Ages.

Thomas Aquinas entered the relatively new Order of Preachers (the Dominicans) against the wishes of his prominent southern Italian family. The order, after its beginnings as mendicant preachers in the campaign against the Albigensians, had settled into a place within the central academic structure of Western Europe. It was here that young Thomas came under the tutelage of Albert von Bollstädt, called Albert the Great. Albert was a scientist and a biologist in the tradition of Aristotle. He was also one of the new breed of Aristotelian philosophers. It was from him that Thomas, the "dumb ox" as Albert liked to call him, became a practitioner of this new philosophical system.

Thomas's great accomplishment would be the synthesis of Christian theology with the Aristotelian philosophical system. He wrote voluminously on many topics, producing both philosophical as well as theological commentaries. One of his most renowned texts is the *Summa Theologica*, a work so influential that it was standard reading for centuries and now is found in the collection of the *Great Books of the Western World*.

Aristotle's system is an attempt at describing the observable world. He wrote treatises on the sciences of physics, zoology, and human biology. However, for Aristotle, all of these fell into the category of natural philosophy. As those of us who have Ph.D.s in the sciences should have been told at our final oral examinations, our degrees are really doctorates in natural philosophy in this sense. When Aristotle sought to explain the nature of knowledge or of reality itself, he needed to go "beyond the physics" or into metaphysics.

In his metaphysics, Aristotle formulated a system for understanding and describing objects in the real world. He stated that everything has four "causes," a word that has a very different meaning in our lexicon than in his. For him, the causes were the key to understanding a thing. The cause was that which brings a thing into being. He argued that each thing has four causes: the material, the formal, the efficient, and the final cause.

Aristotle used analogy in an attempt to explain these aspects of a thing. So, for instance, consider a wooden chair. The material cause in the analogy of the chair would be the wood out of which the chair is made. The formal cause of the chair would be the shape of the chair. The efficient cause can be thought of as the agent—in the case of the chair, the carpenter who builds it. The final cause is the purpose for which the chair is built, that is, as something upon which to sit. The final cause in Greek is the *telos*, from which we get our word "teleology."

Thomas's synthesis of Christian theology with this new system of philosophy was cutting-edge intellectual work in his day. He utilized Aristotle's concept of cause as coming into being, as well as this description of things themselves. His *Summa Theologica* was written as a definitive seminary text for priests in training.[4]

In the *Summa*, Thomas opens with a defense of the existence of God. Using the Aristotelian system, he argues that there are six ways we can know something about God. Notice here the word "ways." Thomas does not call these "proofs" for God's existence, as many later commentators have mistakenly termed them. Rather, he points to Aristotelian-inspired notions of the "unmoved Mover" or the "uncaused Cause" as arguments in favor of the existence of an eternal Supreme Being.

In his second argument or way, Thomas introduces the idea of a primary cause. Employing the Aristotelian concept that something cannot preexist itself and therefore cannot cause itself, he develops what is called the argument from efficient cause: "The Second way is from the nature of the efficient cause. Among sensible things in our world we find an order of efficient causes. There is no case of a thing being the cause of itself, nor is such a thing possible, for then it would exist prior to itself, which is impossible. Therefore it is necessary to admit a first efficient cause, which we call 'God.' "[5]

The first efficient cause is also called the primary cause. Using this argument, we can define secondary causes as everything else observed to bring things about or make things happen. We will come back to the appeal to primary and secondary causes as defined in this way. For now, let us state that secondary causes are the objects of science.

It is the fifth of Thomas's arguments, the fifth way, that has been miscast as the so-called proof from design. In the *Summa*, Thomas says:

> The fifth way is taken from the governance of the world. We see that things which lack intelligence, such as natural bodies, act for an end, and this is evident from their acting always, or nearly always, in the same way, so as to obtain the best result. Hence it is plain that not fortuitously, but designedly, do they achieve their end. Now whatever lacks intelligence cannot move towards an end, unless it be directed by some being endowed with knowledge and intelligence; as the arrow is shot to its mark by the archer. Therefore some intelligent being exists by whom all natural things are directed to their end; and this being we call God.[6]

Notice that this employs Aristotle's final cause in the sense that purpose is apparent in the natural world, even for things to which we do not impute intelligence. Here, Thomas uses analogy, with an archer, arrow, and target, rather than a chair, carpenter, and a place to sit. In reading this excerpt, keep in mind that this was written to make a specific theological point—God can, in some sense, be appreciated by observing nature.

The Thomistic/Aristotelian synthesis was to dominate the Western academy for nearly three hundred years, to such an extent that it became a caricature of the novelty with which Aquinas worked. The scholastics of the French university system, with their slavish adherence to the text rather than the spirit, drove René Descartes away from the university and into his time of meditation. Out of this reflection came the kernels of thought that blossomed into the Enlightenment. This, coupled with the great Copernican cosmological revolution, paved the way for science to transition into the modern enterprise with which we are familiar. In this transition, however, the philosophical setting changed, such that the links between science and theology so apparent to Aristotle and Thomas would be severed. Thus, a rejection of teleological explanations by Hume, while opening the way for methodological naturalism as the path of choice for the advancement of science, might also be seen as the final break with the *Summa* as the text of record.

So, from what are scientists fleeing? Justifiably, they flee any attempt to return to explanatory systems that are not testable by methodological naturalism. If this means avoiding discussions of purpose, even when purpose appears to be present, then that is the way they will have it.

The Natural Theology of the Reverend William Paley

During the seventeenth and eighteenth centuries, the natural philosophers of the Enlightenment assumed, for the most part, that design was evident in Nature and that such design was the result of the actions of the Creator. In fact, Isaac Newton considered that his equations of motion only showed more precisely the mechanics by which all of creation functioned. The bias against teleological explanations entered the philosophical setting of science with Hume, as we have mentioned above. In this intellectual climate it is easy to see how the presence of design in the natural world would be used as a basis for theological argumentation.

The Reverend William Paley was an Anglican priest who lived from 1743 to 1805. His career as a theologian was quite illustrious, with a variety of prestigious appointments, both academic and religious. His most influential work for our consideration was *Natural Theology: Or, Evidences for the Existence and Attributes of the Deity, Collected from the Appearances of Nature*. First published in 1802 and then as a second and revised edition in 1803, this book was one of the most used textbooks of the nineteenth century. We have already discussed above its influence on Charles Darwin and his development of the theory of evolution.

In his *Natural Theology*, Paley introduces the analogy of the watch and watchmaker:

> In crossing a heath, suppose I pitched my foot against a *stone* and were asked how the stone came to be there, I might possibly answer that for anything I knew to the contrary it had lain there forever; nor would it, perhaps, be very easy to show the absurdity of this answer. But suppose I had found a *watch* upon the ground, and it should be inquired how the watch happened to be in that place, I should hardly think of the answer which I had before given, that for anything I knew the watch might have always been there. Yet why should not this answer serve for the watch as well as for the stone? Why is it not as admissible in the second case as in the first? For this reason, and for no other, namely, that when we come to inspect the watch, we perceive—what we could not discover in the stone—that its several parts are framed and put together for a purpose . . . the inference we think is inevitable, that the watch must have had a maker—that there must have existed, at some time and at some place or other, an artificer or artificers who formed it for the purpose which we find it actually to answer, who comprehended its construction and designed its use.[7]

Paley's watchmaker, in this case, is both the architect and craftsman—the one who both designed and built the watch. In like manner, then, he continues, that such features of the biosphere as the human eye must also be objects of purposeful design. And, he concludes, the designer is none other than God.

We see in this argument echoes of Thomas Aquinas and his fifth way. However, unlike Thomas, Paley uses the design of the natural world as full proof for the existence of God. In addition, Paley's designer is not simply involved in the "governance of the world," as Thomas asserted, but is the craftsman of the structures. So, unlike the arrow whose direction is determined by the archer, Paley would have the designer also construct the bow and arrow itself. This is not a trivial point, since it extends the argument into the details of the biosphere that science is exploring. In the philosophical system of Aristotle, we are dealing with secondary causes rather than primary cause.

Of course, Richard Dawkins meant to confront exactly this kind of theological position in his book *The Blind Watchmaker*. Certainly, he argues, there appears to be design in the natural world, especially in the case of such elaborate structures as the vertebrate eye. However, just as Darwin had stated, Dawkins holds that such design evolved by gradual steps over time. And, within the framework of the modern synthesis, there is no direction to this process since the steps involve the random or chance operation of mutational events, coupled with the contingency of natural selection for reproductive fitness. Thus, it seemed that Paley's theological proof had been put to rest by the progress of biological investigation.

Intelligent Design Versus Scientific Creationism

The new toddler in the schoolyard of evolutionary controversy is Intelligent Design, also nicknamed ID. The family ancestry, as we have just tried to show, goes back to scholastic arguments for God's existence and the design proofs of William Paley. Today's ID proponents ascribe speciation in macroevolution to saltations by a divine designer.

Many commentators on the contemporary controversy insist on identifying Intelligent Design advocates with creationism. To force this perspective, some have coined the phrase, "Intelligent Design Creationism."[8] Neither creationists nor ID scholars will accept this simple identification. Whereas creationism rejects evolution, Intelligent Design affirms it. This is a decisive difference. What both share is a fervent opposition to the materialist and mechanistic philosophy that accompanies Darwinism in the public square.

We have therefore chosen to treat Intelligent Design separately from creationism. In fact, most (if not all) ID proponents separate themselves, at least in writing, from the scientific creationists. Some testimonies from the work of our three Intelligent Design theorists will suffice to justify our decision:

Phillip Johnson in *Darwin on Trial:*

> I am not a defender of creation-science, and in fact I am not concerned in this book with addressing any conflicts between the Biblical accounts and the scientific evidence.[9]

Michael Behe in *Darwin's Black Box:*

> As commonly understood, creationism involves belief in an earth formed only about ten thousand years ago, an interpretation of the Bible that is still very popular. For the record, I have no reason to doubt that the universe is the billions of years old that physicists say it is. Further, I find the idea of common descent (that all organisms share a common ancestor) fairly convincing, and have no particular reason to doubt it.[10]

William Dembski in *The Design Inference* and *No Free Lunch:*

> First off, intelligent design is not a form of anti-evolutionism. Intelligent design does not claim that living things came together suddenly in their present form through the efforts of a supernatural creator. Intelligent design is not and never will be a doctrine of creation.[11]

It may be argued by critics of ID that these published statements hide the true agenda of Intelligent Design, that is, they secretly support the agenda of the scientific creationist. However, we have chosen to take these statements at face value and discuss and critique the Intelligent Design movement as an independent body of thought.

Locating the Intelligent Design Theorists Within the Spectrum

As before, we wish to provide a graphic representation of how we interpret the positions of the three representatives of the Intelligent Design position, using our spectra of divine action and causal explanation.

Although all three are quite close, in our estimation, we can spread them in the subspectra as shown in the accompanying two figures.

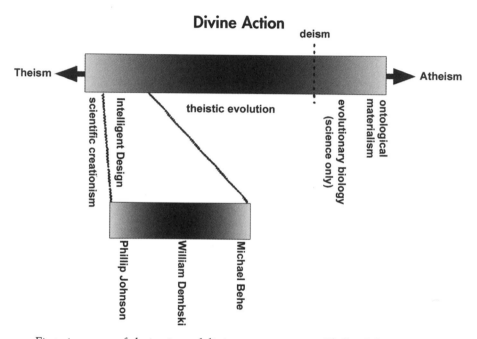

First, in terms of their view of divine action, we see Phillip Johnson as most affirming of an interventionist God in contrast to Darwinian evolution. William Dembski and Michael Behe rely increasingly on evolution as change over time, both requiring episodic or punctuated transcendental influence on evolutionary advance. We emphasize that this does not put them that far apart; it merely reflects our reading of their statements.

With respect to causal explanation within evolutionary advance, Phillip Johnson seems to be more focused on primary cause (the purpose and design within nature is due to divine intervention), while Dembski and Behe allow a bit more room for secondary causes (the behavior of the laws of the natural world). Intelligent Design advocates debate which causes are effective in evolutionary advance. This distinguishes ID sharply from scientific creationism, which removes all divine causation from evolution by denying evolution.

Causal Explanation

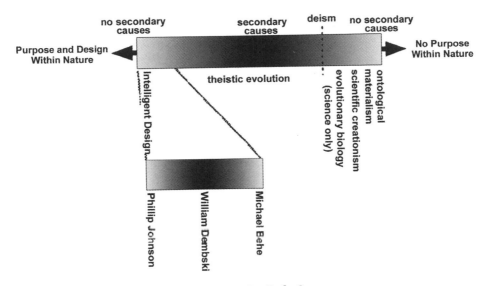

Phillip Johnson: The Lawyer's Brief

"They don't want to find evidence for what they think of as an 'interfering' God, meaning a God who does not leave everything to law and chance," argues prosecutor Phillip Johnson. He continues with his indictment of Darwinian evolutionists. "Hence they will refuse to see evidence of design that is staring them in the face until they are reassured that the designer is something whose existence they are willing to recognize."[12]

Phillip Johnson is Professor Emeritus of Law at the University of California, Berkeley. He has had a distinguished career in the judicial system, being a clerk for chief justices of both the California and United States Supreme Courts. His legal specialty is criminal law and, more recently, evolution and naturalism as a philosophical system.

In 1991, Johnson published *Darwin on Trial*, an examination of both the science and court proceedings surrounding the teaching of evolution in U.S. schools. Johnson is not trained as either a scientist or a theologian; nor has he ever practiced either discipline. His analysis of evolution is, therefore, based upon his own reading of the lay literature to which he has access and the interpretation of the scientific literature by popularizers. As a result, his book does not represent, in any sense, a professional (that is to say, scientific) critique of Darwinian evolution. Nor does it break new ground theologically. Nonetheless, its publication was successful, and he has had an active career on the lecture circuit as a result.

His arguments against the scientific claims of evolution focus on the gaps in the fossil record, the lack of what he considers credible evidence supporting speciation, and difficulties of classification raised by the newer molecular analyses of existing species. For example, he challenges what he calls the "fact" of evolution by calling into question any support for macroevolution as a central tenet of Darwinism. In response to the microevolutionary examples cited by Darwinists, Johnson retorts: "But what sort of proof is this? If our philosophy demands that small changes add up to big ones, then the scientific evidence is irrelevant. . . . What the Darwinists need to supply is not an arbitrary philosophical principle, but a scientific theory of how macroevolution can occur."[13]

In brief, Johnson argues first that evolutionary theory is a form of naturalistic philosophy that is closed off to evidence for divine intervention into the course of natural events. Second, the purported scientific evidence to support evolutionary theory is weak. Third, if naturalistic philosophy were not present to protect the weak scientific arguments, then evolutionary theory could legitimately open itself up to incorporate divine action in nature.

For Johnson, then, the task is not to substantiate the case for Intelligent Design or to provide other alternate explanations for Darwinian evolution. Rather, he is after examining the "evidence" in a legalistic sense and passing a judgment against Darwinism based on that examination. In spite of the fact that we have included his work within the Intelligent Design category, he does not actively propose this as an alternative to the Darwinian process. In fact, one could argue from a reading of *Darwin on Trial* that, in spite of his aversion to creationism cited above, he is more sympathetic to the scientific-creationist stance on the divine action spectrum than he would admit.

Michael Behe: The Biochemist's Dilemma

Michael Behe is a professor of biochemistry at Lehigh University. He has an active research program that specializes in the evolution of proteins. However, his career has taken a dramatic turn with the publication of *Darwin's Black Box: The Biochemical Challenge to Evolution*. Note that Behe is himself a committed evolutionist.

Behe begins his argument from the standpoint of a biochemist. Darwin, he says, did not know about the internal working of cells, the details of which have been elaborated during the twentieth century. Therefore, looking at evolution from the aspect of whole organisms is different from examining the complexities of intracellular pathways.

His central thesis is that there exist structures that are irreducibly complex. By "irreducible complexity" he means that the structure will not function if one part of it is removed: "By *irreducibly complex* I mean a single system composed of several well-matched, interacting parts that contribute to the basic function, wherein the removal of any one of the parts causes the system to effectively cease functioning."[14]

Thus, he says, such structures could not have arisen by standard Darwinian gradual processes. Notice the emphasis on "gradual processes" in this argument. We will come back to this point below.

Behe uses a mousetrap analogy as his model for an irreducibly complex structure. How could evolution produce such a structure by gradual, single-step changes? What would the selection pressure be for the function of the spring in the absence of the catch? He asks these same rhetorical questions about five biochemical systems and cellular structures: the cellular cilium and bacterial flagellum, the blood clotting cascade, the intracellular trafficking system, the immune system, and pathways of intermediary metabolism. In each case, he describes the system in detail and makes the argument that it could not have arisen by standard gradualist mechanisms in the Darwinian model, again using his argument that such systems are irreducibly complex. He then concludes that there must have been an Intelligent Designer who arranged each of these systems with a specific purpose in mind.

Does Behe present us with a full-fledged theology of evolution? No. He affirms Intelligent Design within evolutionary history, but he stops short of providing attributes to the designer. "We can hold the conviction of design much more strongly than a conviction about the identity of the designer."[15]

William Dembski: The Mathematician's Formulation

"Intelligent design is just what the doctor ordered for both science and theology," says William Dembski.[16] Dembski has exceptional academic credentials. He has earned doctorates in mathematics and philosophy from the University of Chicago and holds a Master of Divinity from the Princeton Theological Seminary. He is currently a faculty member at Baylor University and is a senior fellow of the Discovery Institute. The institute's Center for Renewal of Science and Culture (CRSC) is dedicated to challenging the antireligious bias in science and science education. Dembski's earlier book, *Design Inference*, opened a novel approach to the Intelligent Design discussion.[17] He followed this with a more detailed exposition in *No Free Lunch*.

Complexity is the issue for Dembski as well as Behe, although from a mathematical and philosophical point of view. In his recent book, *No Free Lunch*, Dembski sets out a method for determining if a structure is specifically complex. He uses the term "specified complexity." When specified complexity is present, we have evidence for Intelligent Design.

This is not simply a restatement of Behe's irreducible complexity. Dembski produces an algorithm that, he argues, allows one to calculate whether or not specified complexity exists in a particular case. This is called the explanatory filter. The detection of specified complexity requires that the filter answer three questions: Is the event or object contingent, is it complex, and is it specified?[18]

Contingency means that the event, such as the properties of water leading to the formation of ice crystals, can be explained by the operation of physical necessity coupled with the nondirectedness or random nature of the process. Complexity, at least for Dembski, means that the event or object cannot be explained as arising by chance, where chance here refers to the action of all natural process, both known and unknown. In this regard, Dembski introduces a universal probability bound of 1 in 10^{150} as the limit below which it is improbable that chance was the source of the event or object. This number is a product of the estimated total number of elementary particles in the universe (10^{80}) times the age of the universe in seconds (10^{25}) times the number of events that can occur per second (10^{45}, or the Planck time).[19] Finally, an event or object is said to be specified if the pattern detected is detachable from the event or object itself. This condition is one that Dembski spends a good deal of time discussing in *No Free Lunch* and one that has engendered much criticism. Dembski states this criterion as follows: "Detachability can be understood as asking the following question: Given an event whose design is in question and a pattern describing it, would we be able to explicitly identify or exhibit that pattern if we had no knowledge which event occurred?"[20]

This is a critical part to the argument, since a no answer to this question allows the explanatory filter to relegate the event or object to the category of chance. As we shall develop, this has become one of the central critiques of Dembski's Intelligent Design proposals.

What Dembski believes he has accomplished here is a refutation of the adequacy of appealing strictly to law and chance to explain complex life-forms in evolutionary history. According to the criterion of specified complexity, nature at identifiable points shows evidence of Intelligent Design. This is a scientific conclusion, a scientific conclusion that evades the unwarranted restrictions of naturalistic philosophy. Does it imply a doctrine of God? No, not necessarily. "Intelligent design can be formulated as a scientific theory having empirical consequences and devoid of religious commitments."[21]

A Critique of Johnson and Behe

The criticism of the modern Intelligent Design proposals we have discussed falls into two general categories: errors in scientific interpretation and philosophical objections. We will discuss Johnson, Behe, and Dembski with respect to each of these.

Johnson, in *Darwin on Trial*, bases his criticism of the Darwinian model on what he calls an examination of the science upon which it is based. As he states: "My purpose is to examine the scientific evidence on its own terms, being careful to distinguish the evidence itself from any religious or philosophical bias that might distort our interpretation of that evidence."[22]

Herein lies the source of much of the criticism directed at Johnson's conclusion. In this statement, he intends the word "evidence" to have the same kind of meaning that is given in a legal setting. That is, he looks at the science as a set of logical statements that he can, as an "academic lawyer," reason out in terms of their value. The problem arises when it becomes apparent that Johnson does not fully understand the character of scientific evidence, in terms of the methodology and the data. For instance, he discusses the concept of mutational change producing the variations upon which natural selection acts over time. Johnson concludes that mutations are "nearly always harmful."[23] This is not the case, since most mutational changes are silent or conservative, meaning that they alter the structure of the encoded protein not at all or only slightly. True, individual silent mutations will not have an effect on evolution, although there is a very influential idea called the neutral mutation theory that contradicts this.[24] However, the idea of gradualism is that an accumulation of such changes, both neutral and otherwise, can ultimately lead to significant variations in the population. Johnson seems to forget that such accumulations take place on a geological time scale.

He also uses the word "random" in a variety of ways in his discussion of mutational changes. One of his scientific errors is to assume that random change means that virtually any kind of change is possible. He states by analogy: "A random change in the program governing my word processor could easily transform this chapter into unintelligible gibberish, but it would not translate the chapter into a foreign language, or produce a coherent chapter about something else."[25]

However, if Johnson examined all of the variants that his program produced, he could conceivably find one that was in perfect Spanish. This process is called selection, and it is this feature of evolution that Johnson ignores in his analysis of mutations. We will come below to a discussion of probability as, for instance, of finding the Spanish version arising by simple mutations of the word processor program when we examine the work of William Dembski.

A second kind of objection to Johnson's arguments is his confusion of science as a method or a particular way of viewing the natural world and the *scientism* practiced by certain Darwinians. By "scientism" we mean the metaphysical use of scientific information to create a philosophical worldview that relies upon materialism or naturalism. Johnson is on target when he criticizes certain scientists who speak or write about the ideological meaning of Darwinian evolution, when they draw philosophical inferences that have nothing to do with the science *qua* science.[26] However, Johnson does not explain why this philosophical and admittedly intellectually misguided error should be grounds for rejecting the entire body of evidence presented by the scientific method. Is Johnson throwing the baby out with the bath water?

For instance, Johnson rejects the compelling genomic analysis that shows the genealogical relationships of living systems at the level of protein structure. As support for this rejection, he mentions the apparent "conflicts" between the sequence analysis data and the fossil record. As an example, he cites comparisons of the protein cytochrome as found in bacteria with the version found in higher organisms (a number of different plants and animals). He notes correctly that the sequence divergence ranges more than 60 percent between the bacterial cell and the higher organisms. He then concludes that this does not represent genealogical linkage, since no "intermediates" have been located. Johnson states that this invalidates the molecular data as any support for the Darwinian model. This is the same argument that he and others use against the fossil record.

His line of reasoning does not recognize the extraordinary correlation between the molecular data and the model itself, especially given the evolutionary distance between prokaryotes and higher eukaryotes. Terry Gray, a professor of chemistry at Calvin College, has criticized this position with respect to the specific case of a nonactive gene for vitamin C synthesis in primates. It has been discovered that, with respect to the mammals, all have the gene for making vitamin C except guinea pigs and primates. However, analysis of the genome of these two organisms shows the presence of an inactive "pseudo-gene" for vitamin C synthesis. Gray says: "Now we could argue that in God's inscrutable purpose he placed that vitamin C synthesis look-alike gene in the guinea pig or human DNA or we could admit the more obvious conclusion, that humans and primates and other mammals share a common ancestor."[27]

Another rhetorical device that Johnson uses to his advantage is to assume that any disagreement between scientists on issues surrounding evolution is tantamount to saying that the entire model is to be discarded. Thus, he quotes extensively from Stephen J. Gould and his proposal for punctuated equilibrium as a way to deal with the sudden (in geological time scale) appearance of new forms in the fossil record. Whereas, Gould does not wish to throw out the Darwinian model in any of his writings, Johnson assumes that the disagreement is with the fundamental structure of the model—natural selection.

Finally, Johnson attempts to characterize natural selection and the survival of those most fit as a tautology: "The theory predicts that the fittest organisms will produce the most offspring, and it defines the fittest organisms as the ones which produce the most offspring."[28]

Michael Ruse has refuted this argument, we think effectively.[29] Ruse has three points that invalidate Johnson's objection. First, natural selection depends upon the fact that more offspring are produced than can survive. This is an observation that predates Darwin. Second, there are traits that differ between those

110

members of the population that survive and those that do not. These trait differences can, in fact, be shown to be related to survivability. Finally, he notes that successful traits can also be shown by experiment to yield like results in like situations. These three criteria mean that Johnson's simplistic tautology is actually an observational fact of some merit to the Darwinian model.

We come next to the work of Michael Behe. Although he has correctly noted the amazing structure of the intracellular systems that serve as his exemplars of irreducible complexity, he has, in our opinion and that of others, made the error known as the God of the gaps. This fallacious theological position argues that anything that cannot apparently be explained by known physical laws must be ascribed to the intervention of God. In Behe's case, of course, it is an Intelligent Designer who assumes the role of filling in the gaps.

The problem with this position is that by placing God (or the Designer) within the gaps of our knowledge we run the risk that when science advances such that a natural explanation is found, the place for God disappears. Kenneth Miller, referred to earlier in the chapter on creationism, has made just this critique of Behe. In his book, *Finding Darwin's God*, Miller discusses each of the Behe exemplars of irreducible complexity and presents references that support a naturalistic explanation rather than an appeal to Intelligent Design. After reviewing a number of literature examples that counter Behe's statements, Miller concludes:

> Michael Behe's purported biochemical challenge to evolution rests on the assertion that Darwinian mechanisms are simply not adequate to explain the existence of complex biochemical machines. Not only is he wrong, he's wrong in a most spectacular way. The biochemical machines whose origins he finds so mysterious actually provide us with powerful and compelling examples of evolution in action. When we go to the trouble to open that black box, we find out once again that Darwin got it right.[30]

Behe has responded to these criticisms and has engaged Miller in an active debate, both in person and on the Web. However, it still remains that the logical result of filling gaps with Darwinian explanations for the evolution of Behe's examples is a theological pitfall of the argument. As we shall develop in detail later, this confuses primary cause (divine action) and secondary causes (the lawlike behavior of the universe).

Critique of Dembski

The work of William Dembski is more challenging to critique since his argument relies not simply on an analysis of the scientific claims of the Darwinian model. Unlike either Johnson or Behe, Dembski presents a model of his own—specified complexity. He does not reject the fossil record or the molecular evidence, as Johnson does. Like Behe, he argues that design is apparent in the structures found in the living world. Unlike Behe, however, Dembski offers what he calls a testable hypothesis. If specified complexity exists in nature, there are ways it can be detected.

Dembski's arguments are mathematical and philosophical, rather than strictly biological. He approaches the question from a radically different direction than do either of the other two writers we have considered. He has been criticized vociferously in print and on the Web. He has responded at length to these critiques, both in print (*No Free Lunch*) and on the Web.[31] These exchanges of views are ongoing and involve everything from the details of Dembski's mathematical arguments to the philosophical and theological positions maintained by each writer or commentator.

We do not intend to review the entire structure of this discussion here. Instead, we wish to focus on the position taken by Dembski with reference to our spectrum of divine action and causal explanation. In this case, how do we see the work of Dembski in relationship to the other scholars we have discussed? What do we interpret as the limitations of his position?

Although Dembski argues for the status of Intelligent Design as a research program with testable hypotheses, he also deals with the question of who or what the intelligence is that is responsible for the design. There are two ways he treats this question. One is to argue for two kinds of causal explanations: intelligent causes and natural causes. The second is to argue that Intelligent Design, as a scientific research program, is not concerned with the nature of the designer.

In the first case, Dembski contrasts natural and intelligent causes throughout *No Free Lunch*. In the introductory material of this book, he is quite specific about what natural causes are: "Natural causes, as the scientific community understands them, are causes that operate according to deterministic and nondeterministic laws and that can be characterized in terms of chance, necessity, or their combination."[32]

This definition is in concert with what we mean throughout this work by secondary causes—that is, efficient causes other than Thomas's first efficient cause. However, what does Dembski mean by "intelligent causes"? He assumes that such causes are defined in contradiction to natural causes. Thus, any causes that have telic properties would be intelligent causes. Are these then also to be included as secondary causes, in the Thomistic definition? If so, then Dembski's argument is with the philosophical underpinning of science, which does not, in the standard Darwinian model, include any teleological explanations. Francisco J. Ayala has also raised this criticism.[33]

On the other hand, if Dembski means by "intelligent causes" (note his use of the plural) the direct intervention of God, then are we to assume that all of these causes are subsumed in Thomas's first efficient cause? If this is the case, then the discussion becomes theological and not scientific at all.

112

In fact, it is the theological aspects of Dembski's work that interests us in this analysis. One model for divine action in nature is the "front-loading" concept, wherein the lawlike behavior of the universe is placed there from the beginning by God. Dembski correctly calls this a deist position. However, he sees no other alternative to this than to invoke an interventionist position that is inconsistent with the methodology of science in which natural processes have natural explanations (secondary causes). He accuses theistic evolutionists such as his critic van Till of using process theology to "keep this from degenerating into deism."[34]

However, is this the only philosophical or theological position to take? Consider the writings of Robert John Russell or William Stoeger. Their assessments of how divine action can take place without compromising the methods or observations of science come from their understanding of the quantum view of the world.[35] Their ongoing research program into *noninterventionist objective divine action* is to consider that the quantum nature of the world, including such properties as quantum indeterminacy and quantum nonlocality, allow a place for divine action without violation of the observed lawlike behavior of the universe. Though they have not resolved all of the philosophical and theological issues that this raises, they have provided another way of considering divine action as a primary efficient cause and yet as a continuing force in ongoing creation (*creatio continua*).

It would appear then that Dembski's retreat into an interventionist deity and rejection of naturalistic causes as "incomplete" may be premature.

Howard J. van Till is a sympathetic critic of Intelligent Design. He suggests that a weakness in the ID demand for episodic intervention is that it implies God withheld something valuable at the onset of creation. So, in complementary contrast, van Till recommends taking a fully gifted creation perspective. Van Till affirms that the created world was "fully gifted" all along and that "the search for gifts withheld is replaced with the celebration of each new creaturely capability discovered by the sciences as further evidence of God's creativity and generosity."[36]

A Critique of the Critics

Almost uniformly the critics of Intelligent Design have included the work of ID theorists in the same category as that of the scientific creationists. We have tried to show, using our spectra of divine action and causal explanation, that this is not the case. Though it may be closer to the truth for Phillip Johnson, in spite of his protestations, it is certainly not true for either Michael Behe or William Dembski.

Perhaps we should ask why this has been done? In chapter 4 we discussed the stance taken by the scientific creationists and contrasted it with that of biblical creationists. We covered the historical antecedents and links of both programs. We concluded that these two programs are distinctly different. We observed how scientific creationism accepts the legitimacy of the scientific method while rejecting the interpretation that leads to Darwinian evolution. For the critics of Intelligent Design theory, confining ID within the domain of scientific creationism makes it easier to dismiss ID, since the methodology of science ceases to be at stake.

However, Intelligent Design theorists, especially William Dembski, are challenging something more fundamental—the philosophical assumptions of science itself. Notice that Duane Gish and Henry Morris do not challenge the assumptions of the scientific method. Dembski, on the other hand, argues that the method is based on an assumption that does not allow for the existence of purpose as an explanatory device. Perhaps this poses a much more difficult challenge to confront on its own merits. It may be, therefore, that critics want to equate ID with scientific creationism in order to reject it out of hand rather than debate ID claims on common scientific ground.

If the scientific research program proposed by Dembski in *No Free Lunch* were allowed to proceed, would it not rise or fall based on its explanatory merits? What is there to fear in this? In the history of science, many alternate proposals have been raised and, with the test of experiment, have either succeeded (quantum theory) or failed (phlogiston). Perhaps some trust in the open process of scientific criticism might be called for here as we search for the most adequate explanation for what we observe in nature.

CHAPTER SIX

THEISTIC EVOLUTION: A SURVEY

The position we are here calling *theistic evolution* is actually a collection of positions that share in common some degree of reconciliation of Christian faith with evolutionary biology. We would like to place a subspectrum for theistic evolution within the larger divine action spectrum we introduced in chapter 1. At one end of the subspectrum we find some Christian theologians who reluctantly consent to the truth of evolutionary theory on the grounds that it is scientifically credible. They find themselves almost stuck, so to speak. Because theology is committed to truth, these theologians find themselves obligated to accept evolution whether they like it or not. At the other end of the subspectrum, we find Christian theologians who enthusiastically embrace a developmental and even evolutionary worldview; and these thinkers celebrate the creative and providential directing of God within natural processes.

Those are the two extremes within theistic evolution. Most scholars at work today in the field we know as Science and Religion stand between these two; they reconcile the teleologically blind contingencies of natural selection with divine purpose by offering a free-will defense of God as creator—that is, most theologians in the middle of the spectrum adopt the view that God freely constricts divine power so as to open up room in creation for the contingent history of natural selection and for the eventual appearance of free will among the resulting creatures. According to this view, God provides the regularities of natural law combined with chance openings in natural history as the way to give birth to an evolving creation. This divine setting of initial cosmic conditions, within which evolution can occur, requires only deism. When free-will defenders assert a more active theist position, they usually rely upon a version of secondary causation to explain divine action after the evolutionary process gets underway.

In nearly all cases, residents of the theistic evolution camp are conscientious and committed Christians, seeking integration of scientific truth with the view of reality reasoned out from their experience with divine revelation. Revered here is truth; and when the theory of evolution appears to have truth on its side, then people of faith take it seriously. In some cases, the story of evolution provides an inspiring vision to theologians who celebrate God's creation as a long epic history leading to the present chapter, the arrival of the human race.

We the authors have been wrestling with a matter of vocabulary, between using the terms *theistic evolution* or *evolutionary theism* to describe this collection of positions. The latter term uses the word "evolutionary" to modify "theism." An analog would be *process theism*, according to which God as well as the universe are organically in process with each other. So, the term "evolutionary theism" could imply that God evolves. However, the scholars we plan to report on in this chapter do not posit an evolving God as their central concern. Rather, they wish to make God somehow responsible for what happens in biological evolution. So, it is "evolution" that we wish to modify with "theistic" to affirm divine creativity or divine providence in evolutionary history. Should one wish to use the term *atheistic evolution* to describe a strict naturalism, then *theistic evolution* would designate the counterposition. Thus, we have elected to employ the term *theistic evolution*.

For this chapter, we prefer *theistic evolution* over other related terms that have appeared from time to time in the discussion. Some evangelicals have experimented with *progressive creationism*, a position that accepts evolution understood as change over time but adds that God intervenes at strategic thresholds to guide the process. Rather than a single event of creation at the beginning of the universe, progressive creationists view creation taking place in a series of stages over millions of years. *Evolutionary creationism* holds that God directly guides the process we otherwise know as evolution; and *providential evolutionism* seems to propose basically the same thing. In this chapter, we issue club membership invitations to quite a variety of scientists and theologians whom we call "theistic evolutionists." Ordinarily, people in this group are not likely to show up at the same party. What they have in common is a commitment to theism, rather than deism or panentheism or other "isms." They believe not only that God is the world's creator, but also that God continues to be active within the world, even the natural world. Yet, these theists wrestle with incorporating into their theological vision the self-organizing or autopoietic status of natural selection. They assume: If it is true in science, it must be true in theology as well.

On the minimalist or *truth only* end of the subspectrum within the divine action spectrum, we will look briefly at the late–nineteenth-century Princeton theologian Benjamin B. Warfield, a classical theist many would put in the fundamentalist camp. On the other end of the subspectrum, the *evolutionary world-*

view and spirituality end, we will look at Teilhard de Chardin. Close to Teilhard we will place theist Philip Hefner and naturalist Ursula Goodenough, who build an entire worldview based upon the Epic of Evolution. In the middle, where most contemporary, classical theists are located, we find divine *free-will defenders* such as Arthur Peacocke, Kenneth Miller, and Denis Edwards. Robert John Russell's noninterventionist theory of divine action in quantum events will be given special attention. Also, here in the middle of the subspectrum we will give special attention to scholars such as John Haught who invoke the Theology of the Cross in attending to the theodicy problem. In the following chapter, it will be our plan to make a constructive case for theistic evolution. We will present this case only after showing the adequacies and inadequacies we find in the array of closely related positions.

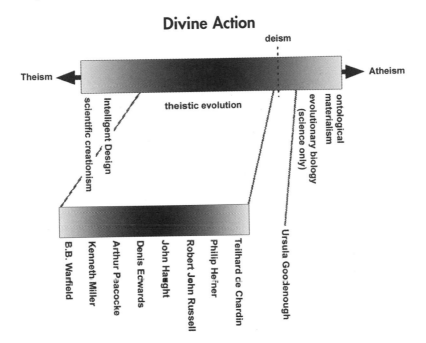

Five Questions for Theistic Evolutionists

What credentials must one show to be initiated into the club of theistic evolutionists? Obviously, a minimum of two: belief in an active God and acceptance of natural selection. Yet, there is more. Let us list a number of questions that members of this school of thought need to address, even if their answers may differ somewhat from one another and most likely differ from atheistic evolutionism, creationism, and Intelligent Design.

1. *Deep time*. Can theology take on board the possibility that it has taken life 3.8 billion years to develop on a 4.5-billion-year-old planet earth? And, if certain theories prove to be correct, could it admit that life may have begun still earlier on an extraterrestrial world and was transplanted to earth? Or, must theology repudiate geological time on behalf of a recent dating of our young earth?

2. *Natural selection*. Can theology accept that contingency, randomness, and chance characterize the process of speciation, that evolution from one species to another is not predesigned nor guided by a scientifically discernible inner telos or purpose? Can theology accept that nature is self-organizing, that natural selection is one form of self-organization, and that no straight line of progressive development is discernible?

3. *Common descent*. Can theological anthropology incorporate the evidence that biological continuity between human life and all other forms of life exists, and that the DNA found in roses and rats is the same kind of DNA found in our heart and brain cells? Can theologians properly appreciate the evolutionary contention that the contemporary human race shares a biological ancestry with primates?

4. *Divine action*. For theistic evolution to distinguish itself from atheism or deism, it must posit that God acts within time. But how? Three options avail themselves to theologians: *interventionist divine action*, according to which God becomes one efficient cause among others, perhaps even violating nature's laws such as we see in miracles; *noninterventionist divine action*, according to which God acts in nature without abrogating any natural laws, sometimes described as secondary causation; and *uniformitarian divine action*, according to which God initially selects the laws operative throughout cosmic and evolutionary history and withdraws from subsequent intervention in individual events. Interventionism typifies classical theism, while uniformitarianism tips toward deism. In what follows, we will see how a noninterventionist form of divine action is being proposed by some theists.

5. *Theodicy*. Can theological affirmations of divine love and omnipotence be reconciled with what Charles Darwin called "waste," namely, the eons and eons of deep time in which animals of prey suffered at the hands of predators, in which sentient beings suffered from disease and disaster, in which 98 percent of all species have perished? Not all theologians affirming divine action in evolution address this question; yet we believe that it should appear on the agenda of theistic evolutionary thought.

What will we find as we ask those proffering the theistic evolution position to produce their credentials? On the one hand, we will find that they honor evolution as a science, but, on the other hand, we will see how difficult it is to reconcile theology with all five items.

What makes it possible for theology to incorporate evolution is usually an appeal to *secondary causation*. This appeal admits an autonomous world of nature replete with law and chance that can be thoroughly studied by scientific means. God, as primary cause, is not subject to scientific analysis because science is methodologically limited to perceiving secondary causes. This permits the theologian to assert both the autonomy of natural selection as well as divine action, each on a separate plane of reality. Any given natural event would simultaneously result from a divine primary cause followed by a natural secondary cause. The two levels complement each other.

Even with appeals to secondary causation, reconciliation is still difficult because of biologists' overt repudiation of discernible design or purpose or *telos* or progress in nature. Theologians feel constrained to posit that a creation coming from the hand of a loving God must possess, if not benefit from, a divinely imparted purpose and meaning. The latter is required for a theist who believes God acts in the natural world. The result of these two conflicting tendencies leads evolutionary theists to affirm most, but not quite all, of what we find as acceptable in evolutionary theory as scientists understand it.

The question of *telos* within evolution is subtle. Even apart from theological motives, many want to keep teleology in some form. One secularized form of teleology is turning complexity into a goal toward which evolution allegedly develops. The evolutionary tree is actually a bush with branches growing sideways as well as upward; and the further we go toward the end of each branch, we find increasing complexity. "Evolutionary history does indeed show a *directionality*, a trend toward greater complexity and consciousness," writes Ian Barbour.[1] Some theologians, such as Teilhard de Chardin, will pick up on this and divinize complexification.

Biologist Francisco J. Ayala, following Darwin, expunges any grand or overall direction or purpose in natural history. Yet, he cannot do without teleology completely. He invokes it when looking at the design of the eye, for example, and admits that the parts function according to the purpose of the eye, namely, to see. "Teleological explanations are necessary in order to give a full account of the attributes of living organisms."[2] Key to Ayala's point here is that such design is the result of self-organization within natural selection alone; it is not the product of an external intelligent design or an internal entelechy guiding all of evolution. This is the gauntlet laid down by evolutionary biology for the theologian to take up.

To make the gauntlet more daunting, Ayala denies that even complexity counts as an overall direction. Finally, he says, maybe all complex forms of life will go extinct and only the microbial prokaryotic cells will survive. Nothing in evolutionary theory would prohibit such an outcome. The challenge for theologians is this: no *telos* is inherent within evolution.

Theistic evolutionists define themselves by taking up the challenge of incorporating natural selection into their doctrines of creation and providence.

Although the theistic evolutionists we plan to look at in this chapter are individual scientists and theologians, the wider institutional context favors this perspective. Contemporary Christians and Jews favor evolution, not so much because it appears to have indispensable value for theological reflection; rather, evolution appears to be a ticket to get on the train of modernity. For liberal church bodies, it marks a departure from earlier fundamentalism. The former United Presbyterian Church, for example, took a stand against the "imposition of a fundamentalist viewpoint." It identified with scholars in the "mainstream of Protestantism, Roman Catholicism, and Judaism. Such scholars find that the scientific theory of evolution does not conflict with their interpretation of the origins of life found in Biblical literature."[3]

Tacitly siding with theistic evolutionism, mainstream denominations generally tend to oppose efforts on the part of creationists to get their voice heard within the science curricula of the public schools. A General Convention of the Episcopal Church in America affirmed its "support of the sciences and educators and of the Church and theologians in their search for truth in this Creation that God has given and entrusted to us." Then it proceeded to take a political stand against creationism. It authorized a lobbying effort "to encourage actively their state legislators not to be persuaded by arguments and pressures of the 'Creationists' into legislating any form of 'balanced treatment' laws or any law requiring the teaching of 'creation-science.' "[4]

Under the political smoke and cinders that mainstream Christianity feeds by putting anti-creationist logs on the fire of controversy, we suspect lie glowing coals of concern for the truth. What conscientious church leaders presume, even if they are not articulate about it, is that scientifically credible theories about our evolutionary origins are simply true. If true, they cannot in good conscience be denied. Whether they like it or not, church leaders find themselves lined up against their fellow Christian travelers on the side of secular science and defending the public institutions that fund and promote it. Division among the Christian faithful is preferable to compromise on commitment to truth. Such is the unhappy context for contemporary theistic evolution.

Because It's True!
B. B. Warfield

At the far end of the divine action subspectrum we place those theistic evolutionists who welcome Darwinian evolution into the household of faith like a mother welcomes home her family for the holidays. Evolution is given the honored chair at the theological dinner table. On the near end of the subspectrum we place those theistic evolutionists who only reluctantly and guardedly look into evolutionary biology like a homeowner standing at the mailbox opening the monthly electric bill. It simply cannot be avoided. Just as the monthly bill makes a claim on us, so also does truth make a claim on the Christian conscience. If evolutionary biology contains any truth whatsoever, then heed must be paid.

The Christian faith is utterly dependent upon the truth of its fundamental convictions. As such, this faith reveres truth in all its forms, even scientific truth. Ambrose of Milan is remembered for saying, "All truth, no matter by whom it is uttered, comes from the Holy Spirit" (*Omnis veritas, a quoquo dicitur, e Spiritu Sancto est*). With this kind of confidence, Pope John Paul II could write, "If scientific endeavor, philosophical inquiry and theological reflection are to bring genuine benefit to the human family, they must always be grounded in truth."[5]

No verifiable truth can upset Christian faith, because that faith is directed toward the truth itself. The question at hand is this: Can claims made by evolutionary biologists be judged to be true? If true, then Christian theology is obligated to seek reconciliation between evolution and faith. Short of demonstrating apodictic truth for evolutionary theory, Christian theology is obligated to consider reconciliation merely on the basis of hypothetical claims made by evolutionary theory on the prospect that such claims may eventually be confirmed as true.

This characterizes the cautious yet open approach of Princeton theologian Benjamin Breckinridge Warfield (1851–1921). "We may be sure that the old faith will be able not merely to live with, but to assimilate to itself all facts [of evolution]," wrote Warfield in the 1895 essay "The Present-Day Conception of Evolution." "The only living question with regard to the doctrine of evolution is whether it is true. . . . We may hold it to be probably true, and yet agree that it is still upon its trial and has not yet been shown to be true."[6] Probable truth awaiting further scientific confirmation was sufficient reason to take evolutionary biology seriously as a theological matter.

B. B. Warfield the theologian grew up with his father, William Warfield, a shorthorn cattle breeder. William, the father, had written a book, *The Theory and Practice of Cattle Breeding*, and his son, B. B., served for a period as editor of *Farmer's Home Journal* in Lexington, Kentucky. Like Darwin himself, these two had firsthand experience with evolution through animal breeding. Both read with delight Darwin's work on this subject.

At Princeton, a picture of engagement between theology and evolution had been previously drawn by James McCosh, who had been widely recognized for adaptation if not accommodation. McCosh embraced a variant of evolutionary transformationism, even though he rejected an orthodox Darwinism that appeared materialistic or atheistic. In addition to McCosh, the theological Titan Charles Hodge had weighed in on the evolution controversy, publishing a book titled *What Is Darwinism?* Hodge had criticized Darwin's rejection of the supernatural in favor of the natural and objected to Darwin's rejection of design and final causation. Darwinism was the equivalent of atheism, thought Hodge. McCosh and Hodge had painted the landscape when Warfield entered the picture.[7]

What is of dramatic significance in Warfield's positive appropriation of evolutionary transformationism is the compatibility between biblical inerrancy and biological evolution. Biblical inerrancy does not forbid evolution. How can this be? The version of inerrancy Warfield sponsored made room for human perspective, for human finitude in the writing and interpreting of Holy Scripture. Warfield labels his view *concursus*, a hermeneutical version of secondary causation, according to which a concord or cooperation exists between the divine Word and the human hand that transcribes the divine Word. "The biblical basis of *concursus* is found in the constant scriptural representation of the divine and human coauthorship of the biblical commandments and enunciations of truth, as well as in the constant scriptural ascription of Bible passages to both the divine and the human authors, and in the constant scriptural recognition of Scripture as both divine and human in quality and character. . . . The Scriptures are the joint product of divine and human activities. . . . The whole Bible is recognized as human. . . . The whole Bible is recognized as divine."[8] The human component in the Bible's coauthorship provides hermeneutical wiggle room. The concepts in the Bible are not purely the concepts in God's mind; they are viewed through the human lenses and perspectives of the persons involved in the writing. The Scriptures, having been written prior to the appearance of the theory of evolution, could not be expected to contain the concept of evolution. Hence, Warfield concludes that the ancient Bible could be compatible with contemporary theories of evolution even though evolution itself is not a subject the Bible takes up.

What is at stake here is not simply a matter of a war between Bible and laboratory. What is at stake is the explanatory adequacy of evolutionary theory itself. That evolutionary theory has successfully explained some facts, Warfield grants. He finds the scientific community in the position of testing the hypothesis, to see just how much the theory will eventually prove to explain. He cautions the scientific community against *hubris*, the premature pride at claiming more than the theory can deliver. "The doctrine of evolution has served us, we will say, in our endeavors to unravel some exceptionally hard problem[s]. In the enthusiasm of this experience we declare it able to unravel all similar problems. This is the natural history of all panaceas. It is scarcely stringent logic, however, to infer from the fact that a theory can account for some facts, that it therefore can account for all facts. Yet this is a logic from which advocates of evolution have not kept their skirts free."[9]

This leads Warfield to provide both an acceptable theological incorporation of evolution by appeal to secondary causation as well as a word of caution about the dangers of evolutionary philosophy. On the one hand, evolution taken to be a scientific theory regarding natural processes could be reconcilable with the

Christian understanding of creation and providence by appealing to the concept of secondary causation. Just as the Bible has coauthorship, so also does the natural world work both according to its own natural laws and simultaneously according to God's providential guidance. If science restricts itself to studying secondary causation within nature, no conflict with theology should arise. On the other hand, evolutionary theory taken to be a materialistic philosophy that denies divine participation in order to support either atheism or pantheism could not be reconciled with Christian belief in a living and acting God. Science is compatible with faith, but materialist philosophy is not. The science of evolution does not entail its materialist interpretation. Atheism would be an unnecessary superimposition upon evolutionary biology and an enemy to theology.

Responding to the late–nineteenth-century works of Thomas Huxley, Joseph LeConte, and E. D. Cope, Warfield sees their all-inclusive ontologies as inappropriately anti-theistic. By appealing strictly to natural causes and positively eliminating divine participation in natural selection, these views constitute an unnecessary philosophical addition to what the science requires. Such evolutionary philosophy

> leaves no place for the Christian's God, who is not the God afar off of the deist, and not the simple world-ground of the pantheist, but the living God of the Bible—at once above the world and in the world, the author of the world and its strong governor who is not far from any one of us but yet is a being outside and above us, who is to the world and to man at least an external power making for righteousness.[10]

Warfield eschews atheistic evolutionary philosophy, but he welcomes evolution's biological corroboration of the biblical commitment to human unity. Theological and ethical concerns make the unity of the human race indispensable to the Christian view of reality. Theologically, the human race is united in sin and united in redemption. We are one with the first Adam at our origin, and we will be one with Christ, the second Adam, in our destiny. What evolutionary biology provides is complementary evidence of common descent (common descent within the human race is important here, not common descent with apes). Referring to the "unity of the human race," Warfield says

> the whole structure of the Bible's teaching, including all that we know as its doctrine of salvation, rests on it and implicates it. . . . The prevalence of the evolutionary hypotheses has removed all motive for denying a common origin to the human race, and rendered it natural to look upon the differences which exist among the various types of man as differentiations of a common stock. . . . [I enjoy] our natural satisfaction over this agreement between Scripture and modern science with respect to the unity of humanity.[11]

The question of human unity also has ethical implications. Warfield sought to combat racial pride and racial prejudice. Previously promulgated nineteenth-century theories of separate origins for separate races had served to justify racial division and racial discrimination. The Christian commitment to human unity repudiates such biological justifications for racial pride; and Warfield saw in evolution support for this Christian commitment. The concept of the "unity of the human race" is the basis of the entire scheme "of restoration devised by the divine love for the salvation of a lost race," and it is "the basis of a demand that we recognize the dignity of humanity in all its representatives, of however lowly estate or family, since all bear alike the image of God."[12]

How does Warfield address our credential questions? With regard to deep time, Warfield holds that the age of the earth has no theological significance. Dating geological time and evolutionary development is strictly a scientific problem to be worked out by scientists. Time becomes important only at the advent of the human race, only with Adam and Eve. This means that Warfield would not feel compelled to join young earth creationists in repudiating deep time. With regard to natural selection, Warfield repudiates a strictly materialist interpretation as atheistic; he would prefer to impart divine providence as a guide to evolutionary development. With regard to common descent, all members of the human race share the same biological history, but he does not affirm or celebrate having a monkey for an uncle. With regard to divine action, Warfield would be an interventionist on miracles; yet, his notion of *concursus* and secondary causation places him in camp with the noninterventionists.

The picture we paint here of Warfield is that he belongs on one extreme of our spectrum of theistic evolutionists. The late–nineteenth-century context with its ferment over evolution compelled theologians to face the truth question: If evolutionary theory is true, then it will have consequences for theology. Rather than actively pursuing evolution as a theological partner, Warfield reluctantly responded and adapted to the intellectual forces surrounding him. His Calvinist Protestantism was guided by commitments from within, and it was energized by confidence in a Bible that was inspired and inerrant. Though his treatment of the evolutionary hypothesis was honest and sympathetic, it was peripheral to his central theological agenda.

Having said this, however, one wonders if Warfield did not experience moments of intellectual temptation to reconstruct doctrines such as creation and anthropology around the evolutionary vision. When explicating John Calvin's doctrine of creation, Warfield points out that the Reformer limited creation to what God does *ex nihilo*, out of nothing. The term "creation" then refers to the origin of the world when God brought it from nonbeing into being, and it refers to the special creation of each human soul *ex nihilo* (a doctrine also known as "creationism"). When God creates, God is the primary cause, the first cause. By consigning and hence limiting creation to *ex nihilo* and to primary causation, Warfield speculates, we could then speak of transformations in the history of nature as the result of secondary causes. We could, in short, assign the history of nature to evolution. Warfield retrojects his theory into Calvin's systematic theology. "Calvin doubtless had no theory whatever of evolution, but he teaches a doctrine of evolution. . . . Calvin's ontology of second causes was, briefly stated, a very pure and complete doctrine of *concursus* . . . a very pure evolutionary scheme."[13]

At Princeton, a century after Warfield, we find J. Wentzel van Huyssteen teaching in the first chair in America devoted to "Theology and Science." In wrestling with the challenges to theology posed by postmodern nonfoundationalism, van Huyssteen proffers what he calls an "evolutionary epistemology" for theologians. "Our theological reflection is radically shaped not only by its social, historical, and cultural context, but also fundamentally shaped by the biological roots of human rationality. . . . All our knowledge, including our scientific and religious knowledge, is grounded in biological evolution. And if human knowledge results from evolution, then the study of evolution will be of extreme importance for an understanding of the phenomenon of knowledge and, therefore, for epistemology."[14] Rather than a mere grudging acceptance of evolution on the grounds that it may be true, van Huyssteen fully incorporates evolution into theological method. Now the study of evolution becomes the self-study of theological rationality.

Evolving Toward Point Omega
Teilhard de Chardin

Some Roman Catholics in the late nineteenth and early twentieth centuries grasped for solid ground amid the turbulence by permitting a *moderate evolution* that involved transformation of life-forms; but they strongly rejected any philosophical or social Darwinism in the form of materialism, atheism, or an ethic of survival of the fittest. This evolutionary transformationism could include all life-forms up to humanity, but whether Adam's and Eve's bodies were the result of common descent with apes was debated. What was not debated was the origin of Adam's and Eve's souls: They were immediately created by God and involved no evolution at all. Critics of accommodationism rejected any common descent between animals and humans, claiming such a view would violate the notion of our being created in the divine image.

The debate over evolution was caught up in a much larger debate regarding modernism, which for Roman Catholics included academic freedom for the sciences, academic freedom for European theologians known as *Catholic Modernists*, German biblical criticism, and the threat of Americanizing the church in the new world. By 1907 Pope Leo X had banned modernism in all of the above forms, and by 1910 priests were required to take an anti-modernist oath to become ordained. Despite this whelming tide of anti-modernism, some Catholic theologians still sought breathing room for including evolution in their thought. They maintained that "theistic evolution did not fall under the ban on modernism and that a modified form of Darwinism was therefore acceptable. . . . It was fashionable among Roman Catholic apologists to claim that true religion had nothing to fear from true science."[15]

During the 1890s, Notre Dame University priest and chemistry professor John Zahm, author of *Evolution and Dogma*, openly sought a positive incorporation of the science of evolution while repudiating Darwin's *The Descent of Man* for being a source for social discrimination. Evolution has an overall direction, he maintained, from the simple toward the more complex. Zahm tendered a thesis that God, having created matter directly, gave the material-created order the power of subsequently evolving into various forms. In interpreting the creation account in the book of Genesis, Zahm argued that God did not create the plants and animals directly; rather, God caused them to be produced from previously existing material. In addition to the Bible, Zahm appealed to Augustine and Thomas Aquinas for support for common descent between humans and other animals. Theistic evolution explains the origin of our human bodies, Zahm contended, even though Catholics must still affirm that God creates each soul immediately. "As matters now stand, evolution is not contrary to Catholic faith; and anyone is at liberty to hold the theory, if he is satisfied with the evidence adduced in its support."[16]

Such openness toward something modern was not applauded in Rome. Zahm's critics at the Vatican lumped together his advocacy of theistic evolutionism with biblical higher criticism and the misguided attempt to adapt the church to modern American culture; so in 1898, his book, *Evolution and Dogma*, was placed on the Index of Prohibited Books and banned.

Thus, the mood at the beginning of the twentieth century within Roman Catholic circles was one of suspicion toward modern science in general and fear of disruptions to dogma and church authority represented by nontheistic Darwinism and theistic evolution alike. Quietly and unobtrusively, Teilhard de Chardin's remarkable career began in this context.

Perhaps the most thoroughgoing synthesis of evolutionary history with Christian theology and spirituality can be found in the epic vision of the French Jesuit paleontologist, Pierre Teilhard de Chardin (1881–1955). Teilhard's self-appointed vocation as a theologian was to recast the essential Christian message in its awesome grandeur by expressing it in a conceptual matrix consonant with evolutionary science. His mysticism penetrated and pervaded his science; he saw his own empirical research as itself the adoration of God. He published 150 refereed scientific articles and is remembered as part of the archaeological team that discovered the 400,000-year-old skull of *Pekinensis* (*Sinanthropus*), known as "Peking Man," at Choukoutien in China in 1929. A prolific writer whose complex thought is most comprehensively summarized in his book first completed in

1938, *The Phenomenon of Man*, he appeared to violate the standards of orthodoxy as the Vatican appraised it. His theological writings were banned during his lifetime and only published following his death on Easter Sunday, April 10, 1955.

Teilhard marks the worldview edge of the theistic evolution subspectrum within the divine action spectrum. Here evolution has become a comprehensive epistemology, metaphysics, and spirituality. Divine purpose is thoroughly embedded within the logos that propels evolutionary advance; and there *is* an advance. Progress is built into nature. Evolution, for Teilhard, defines the reality within which we understand ourselves, our world, and the divine. "Is evolution a theory, a system or a hypothesis?" he asks. "It is much more: it is a general condition to which all theories, all hypotheses, all systems must bow and which they must satisfy henceforward if they are to be thinkable and true. Evolution is a light illuminating all facts, a curve that all lines must follow."[17] Evolution sits in the driver's seat of nature. Evolution becomes the maternal subject that nurtures its own pregnant potentials until giving birth to conscious sentience, to us, who in turn reflect evolution back onto itself. "Man discovers that *he is nothing else than evolution become conscious of itself.*"[18]

Our knowledge of evolution becomes virtually an end in itself as well as the decisive factor for the future of human evolution. Our knowledge of evolution is the instrument by which evolution will now further its own progress. Teilhard's high reverence for science transforms an apotheosized knowing into a creative natural force; knowing transforms being. "Intellectual discovery and synthesis are no longer merely speculation but creation. . . . *Knowledge for its own sake.* But also, and perhaps still more, *knowledge for power. . . . Increased power for increased action.* But, finally and above all, *increased action for increased being.*"[19]

The concept of evolution with which Teilhard works is much broader than merely the development of new species by natural selection. It includes our entire cosmic history, past and future. Evolution is the epic that begins with energy and matter and passes through primitive to advanced life-forms until thought and, finally, shared consciousness transcend the original physical beginning. The pulsations giving rise to primitive geochemistry and geotechtonics are the same pulsations giving rise to geobiology. Geogenesis promotes biogenesis; and biogenesis promotes psychogenesis. With psychogenesis we arrive at the doorstep of thought. Psychogenesis actualizes an ancient preanimate potential, the potential for a "within" as well as a "without"—that is, a sense of interiority in addition to external objective relations to other objects. Rocks or roses or rats have a within or a center that radiates energy outward.

Cosmogenesis—that is, the entire evolutionary process—is following a twofold path toward complexification and convergence. Complexification is the all-pervading tendency toward more elaborate organization; and it characterizes the passage from subatomic units to atoms, from atoms to inorganic and, later, organic molecules right on up to living organisms and human beings. Convergence countervails while complementing complexification; it is

Teilhard's anticipated future unity of an increased number of complex organizational centers.

The next step beyond psychogenesis is a giant one in the history of complexification, namely, *noogenesis*. This marks the arrival of mind. With mind we human beings can experience interiority consciously. Even more, we can engage in reflection, which is consciousness of consciousness. Reflection is the awareness of awareness. With the aid of mind, evolved creatures can now look into a mental mirror and see themselves; and this reflective consciousness marks a giant pace forward in cosmic history.

Hominisation is evolution's key step toward the *noosphere*, the sphere of mind that will eventually envelope planet earth. Teilhard defines "hominisation" as the leap from instinct to thought; yet it is a leap that maintains continuity with its physical precedent. It is the "progressive phyletic spiritiualisation in human civilization of all the forces contained in the animal world. . . . With hominisation, in spite of the insignificance of the anatomical leap, we have the beginning of a new age. The earth gets a new skin. Better still, it finds its soul."[20]

Teilhard's heart sings with the entire universe a prayerful song. His prayer involves soul, body, and cosmos. Spirituality is not the pursuit of disembodied spirit. Rather, spirituality is a welling up of the physical within us and surrounding us toward a shared cosmic unity. With the aid of knowing evolution, we find ourselves today capable of experiencing and discovering "God in the whole length, breadth and depth of the world in movement. To be able to say literally to God that one loves him, not only with all one's body, all one's heart and all one's soul, but with every fibre of the unifying universe—that is a prayer that can only be made in space-time."[21]

Evolution is an ascent toward consciousness, says the priest-scientist. Therefore, he adds, it should culminate in some sort of supreme consciousness. This future supreme consciousness should transcend and unite the individual consciousness we currently experience within ourselves and encounter in interpersonal relationships. This culmination of consciousness will be convergent and hyperpersonal and final. This leads the scientist-theologian to label it *Point Omega*, after the final letter in the Greek alphabet, omega. As a radiating center of consciousness, Point Omega does not obliterate but incorporates all other sub-centers of interior thought and awareness. "By its structure Omega, in its ultimate principle, can only be a *distinct Centre radiating at the core of a system of centres;* a grouping in which personalization of the All and personalisations of the elements reach their maximum, simultaneously and without merging, under the influence of a supremely autonomous focus of union."[22]

Is Point Omega divine? Yes, because "God is the Centre of centres."[23] The French Jesuit majestically enunciates an evolutionary theism with an emerging panentheistic divinity. "I mean the rise on our inward horizon of a cosmic *spiritual* centre, a supreme pole of consciousness, upon which all the separate consciousness of the world may converge and within which they may love one another;

the *rise of a God*."[24] Teilhard is enthralled in anticipation of the eschatological unity of the entire cosmic history of spirit and matter in the divine life. "Within a now tranquil ocean, each drop of which, nevertheless, will be conscious of remaining itself, the astonishing adventure of the world will have ended. The dream of every mystic, the eternal pantheist ideal, will have found its full and legitimate satisfaction. *Erit in omnibus omnia Deus* [God all in all]."[25]

How does Teilhard handle our credential questions? First, he clearly celebrates deep time; the long process of evolution only increases the scope and hence the magnificence of the nature's cosmic history. Second, for Teilhard, natural selection has a clear direction, so clear that progress can be measured. The direction is toward ever greater complexity, and life is virtually unstoppable in its pursuit of complexification. More complex centers of radial energy converge and cooperate and unite. Teilhard can forecast an eschatological stasis of intense individuation and unity, a convergent noospheric unity of all that has historically been physical. Third, Teilhard celebrates common descent, the continuity of human beings with earlier life-forms and even inanimate matter. Physiologically, the jump from primates to humanity is a small one, while the leap in mental activity is a giant one. Teilhard is impressed by both the continuity and the transcendence brought by hominisation. Fourth, divine action is uniformitarian in an ongoing pantheistic sense—that is, the divine purpose guiding evolution is internal to nature as it is internal to the divine life.

Fifth, with regard to the question of theodicy, it must be said that Teilhard trivializes evil. Evil is but a temporary dip in the otherwise upward curve of evolutionary progress. Evil takes the form of barriers to complexification such as disorder, decomposition, solitude, and the struggles of growing. "There are no summits without abysses," he writes.[26] In the final stages of the noosphere on earth, evil will be reduced to a minimum. Evil can be so reduced because, for Teilhard, evil is a defect in consciousness that can be healed by more consciousness. Like ancient Gnosticism, evil is the result of ignorance, and ignorance can be healed with knowledge. With the rise of God at Point Omega, shared consciousness and shared knowing will provide the unity that evil had previously sundered.

In the era immediately following the conclusion to World War II and the dropping of the first atomic bombs on Hiroshima and Nagasaki, Teilhard offered commentary and interpretation. Rather than attend to the human carnage and suffering wrought by fireballs of mass destruction, Teilhard celebrated the science that discovered how to engineer atomic energy for human designs. The urgency of ending the war warranted a concentration of scientific resources that led to a rapid leap in new knowledge. "Thus the greatest of Man's scientific triumphs happens also to be the one in which the largest number of brains were enabled to join together in a single organism, at the same time more complex and more centred, for the purpose of research."[27] The triumph of scientific research provides Teilhard with the optimism that we will in the future be able to eliminate war. "Thanks to the atom bomb it is war, not mankind, that is destined to be eliminated. . . . The atomic age is not the age of destruction but of union in research."[28]

Deism or Theism?
The Free-will Defense of Divine Self-limitation

With Warfield at one end of our subspectrum and Teilhard on the other, now we can turn to various options in the middle. What we find in the middle is a wide array of theistic evolutionists who, despite interesting differences, share one item in common: they offer what we are calling here the *free-will defense* of God. They take steps to remove God from the plane of evolutionary advance so as to permit autopoiesis and self-organization on the part of the natural world. We refer to "free will" here because this form of theistic evolution is reminiscent of classical arguments among theists who wanted to protect human free will from being overridden by divine determination. Actually, the word "free" applies twice here. First, God freely decides to limit divine power so as to permit creaturely self-determination; and, second, we human beings thereby experience free will in self-determination. This classic concern for God's freedom and human freedom returns in theistic evolution in order to make room for natural selection as the mechanism for speciation. However, once God's action is removed from the created order, the result is not coherent theism but tacit deism.

Our objection to the free-will defense is that it misconstrues the way divine power works. God's power does not restrict human freedom but makes it possible. The God of Exodus and Easter exerts power in order to liberate. Karl Barth emphasizes that when God exerts divine power it is an expression of grace; and, as grace, God's power makes our freedom possible. The divine Spirit and the divine Word do not compete with, but rather complement, our own free activity. "If God works by His Word and Spirit there is no reason whatever why the activity of the creature should be destroyed or suppressed by His omnipotent operation. On the contrary, it is necessarily the case that the omnipotent operation of God not merely leaves the activity of the creature free, but continually makes it free."[29] Rather than flee divine determination, we believe faith should seek it and be glad for it. What remains to be worked out is how this understanding drawn from debates over freedom might be applied constructively to contingency, chance, and creativity in evolution.

To establish *theistic* evolution in distinction from mere *deistic* evolution, we must believe that God acts in or through or under evolutionary creativity. The doctrine of secondary causation usually takes care of this. Free-will defenders, however, tacitly and perhaps unintentionally reject secondary causation, presuming rather that divine power and creaturely freedom belong on the same plane. This is our critique of the free-will defenders. However, we note that they themselves typically affirm secondary causation. Our critique is that they occasionally contradict themselves unnecessarily.

One of the easiest ways to marry divine power with evolutionary creativity is to place God's action back at the beginning, to draw a picture of God as the architect who designed the evolutionary process but then left the process to carry on in his absence. This is what the deists did. If we retrieve the deism of the eighteenth century so familiar to America's founding political leaders and to Freemasonry, we picture God as the great architect of the universe. According to this image, God designs the physical world, constructs it, even sets in it motion. Then, like human architects, God's work is done. God can leave the scene. What God has constructed stands on its own. In the world of Newtonian mechanics, where the physical material and the laws of nature constitute a closed causal nexus, this is readily understandable. Parallel to the architect is the picture of God as the clockmaker. Like a clockmaker, God designs and manufactures the world, establishes the mechanistic principles with precision, winds it up, and then leaves the world to function on its own.

A difficulty here is that images of God as the architect or clockmaker require a corresponding mechanistic understanding of nature. The mechanistic picture of nature was easy to come by in the days of Newtonian physics. Since the birth of evolutionary biology at the end of the nineteenth century plus the birth of quantum theory in the new physics at the beginning of the twentieth century, Newton's closed causal nexus has gone the way of the used car. It may sit in the garage available for short runs to the grocery store; but we now drive the new model with accessories such as physical indeterminacy and nature's self-organization. The child has matured and ventured out on its own. New pictures of God to correspond to the new picture of the physical world are in short supply.

Marrying Materialism with Theism
Kenneth Miller

"The Western God stands back from His creation," writes Brown University cell biologist Kenneth R. Miller, "not to absent Himself, not to abandon His creatures, but to allow His people true freedom."[30] Miller is a scientific materialist and an evolutionary theist. "There is neither logical nor theological basis for excluding God's use of natural processes to originate species, ourselves included," he writes; "There is therefore no reason for believers to draw a line in the sand between God and Darwin."[31] Miller readily takes on board deep time, natural selection, and common descent. But what does he mean by divine action in nature? Just what does he mean by affirming natural processes in combination with a God who acts?

131

As a materialist, material explanations are all he needs. Miller rules out the influence of the divine from any particular natural phenomenon by applying deterministic reductionism in his scientific method. He excludes any possibility of the spiritual playing the role of an immediate cause in a natural event. Everything in nature can be reduced to material determinants. All levels of nature connect according to defined rules, which the scientist is capable of understanding. With this strong denial of divine intervention, one would think he must take either an atheist or deist position.

Yet Miller believes in God, and the deistic form of belief is inadequate for him, so he says. He contends that deism is no longer viable since the rise of quantum theory in physics in the early 1900s, since the work of Max Planck, Albert Einstein, Werner Heisenberg, and Erwin Schrödinger. The new physics holds that underlying the machine-like behavior of nature upon which Newtonian mechanics was based are the probabilistic activities of electrons and photons and other particles. These fundamental subatomic particles behave individually in unpredictable ways. Electrons and photons do not behave like machines; they do not fit the model of the mechanism. In large groups, and at large size scales, patterns emerge, to be sure. These patterns can be measured and predictability of the Newtonian type begins to return. However, at the quantum level, that is, the atomic level, the indeterminacy of the natural world remains.

Now the application of the mechanistic model to fundamental physical reality is, Miller thinks, gone forever.

> A deist lawgiver might have been great and wise, but if he was thought of in the context of the Newtonian clockwork, our lives would become about as interesting as billiard balls, each move governed only by the forces and collisions of particles already set in motion. Lucky for us, that depressing prospect would never prevail—because at the very beginning of the twentieth century the clockwork upon which it depended would be broken forever.[32]

How does this retrieval of quantum physics aid in understanding evolutionary biology? Miller's answer is that unpredictable quantum activity is responsible for unpredictable genetic mutations. Our physical bodies are much larger than atoms, something obvious yet in this context quite profound. Our size and complexity make us immune on a daily basis to the unpredictable behavior of the subatomic particles in our cells. Our daily life operates at the level of Newton's laws. Yet, underlying this, things change; and they change in ways that cannot be foreseen. Quantum physics makes it possible to understand how this can be.

Miller points us to changes in one of the four chemical bases that make up our chromosomal DNA. At any point in replication, one of these nucleotides can change; and no intermediate chemical process can be detected. This is a quantum effect.

As a result, events with quantum unpredictability, including cosmic ray movements, radioactive disintegration, and even molecular copying errors, exert direct influences on the sequences of bases in DNA. . . . Mutations, which provide the raw material of genetic variation, are just as unpredictable as a single photon passing through a diffraction slit. . . . In other words, evolutionary history can turn on a very, very small dime—the quantum state of a single subatomic particle.[33]

What we experience in our lives and in evolutionary history is the physical amplification of invisible indeterminate quantum events.

Note what Miller has done and not done here. He has appealed to quantum indeterminacy in order to open up the Newtonian closed causal nexus so that chance and creativity can occur. He has not said that God works through quantum events. He has not proposed divine intervention at the subatomic level.

What, then, is God's role in natural events? For Miller, God is the architect of subatomic indeterminacy. Indeterminacy is "a key feature of the mind of God."[34] Further, chance events mean that "the physical world has an existence independent of God's will."[35] Note that the world is "independent" of God's will. Yet, for Miller, God did not completely abandon the creation after he designed it. God remains active. Miller needs to assert some sort of divine action if he is to hold a theistic rather than a deistic position. Miller wants to pray to God; so God must be more than merely a supreme principle of nature. "I am interested in a traditional view of God," he writes, "the one described by the great Western monotheistic religions" of Judaism, Christianity, and Islam.[36] This God is responsible for a number of things: First, God is the personal creator of everything in the universe; second, God intentionally created us human beings, endowing us with free will and providing the opportunity to love God; and third, God has revealed himself to us through the prophets, Jesus and Muhammad. In addition, we must make a distinction between the material and the spiritual—that is, God is a nonmaterial spiritual being. The spiritual reality surpasses the material. Miller's commitments are characteristic of classical theism.

Can Miller get what he wants and still be coherent? Miller wants both exhaustive material explanations that include chance mutations plus meaningful divine action in the physical world, and he wants both without conflict. To accomplish this, he distinguishes what can be understood and what cannot be understood. Science can understand material causation; theology cannot understand divine causation. This is curious, if not humorous. "God's means are beyond our ability to fathom, and just because events seem to have ordinary causes, or seem to be the result of chance, does not mean that they are not part of that divine plan. . . . God, if He exists, surpasses our ordinary understanding of chance and causality."[37] As long as we cannot understand divine action, we can affirm it without having it conflict with material causation.

Do miracles occur? Well, yes, according to the testimony of almost every theist. What can science say about miracles? Nothing, says Miller. "By definition, the miraculous is beyond explanation, beyond our understanding, beyond science."[38] Miller just leaves the subject of miracles here; he does not employ miracles to explain saltations or punctuated evolutionary leaps.

Although Miller claims classical theism as his ancestor, it is less than clear just how the biblical God connects with what actually happens in the overall evolutionary process. He seems to shy away from interventionism. His distinction and even separation of matter and spirit, locking God into the nonmaterial realm of spirit, renders God unable to function as one natural cause among others. Does this mean, then, that Miller advocates noninterventionist divine action? Even this is less than clear, because Miller does not point to anything that could count as a divine act within the natural world. God is the creator who is responsible for the world's existence, to be sure; yet Miller seems to leave no point of contact—*keine Anknüpfungspunk,* to use Barthian language—between God and the natural world. Does this place Miller in the uniformitarian camp by default? Does this mean that, despite eschewing deism, Miller tacitly retreats into the deistic camp?

This brings us to God's will in light of evil, suffering, and death. How does Miller handle the theodicy problem? How does he evaluate the brutality and cruelty of the predator's treatment of prey and the struggle for survival? Miller seems to have an investment in defending nature's moral reputation. He lashes out against theological criticism. He mounts two defenses. First, he offers an argument from relativism, from perspective. "Cruelty is relative," he says.[39] When he drops a lobster into a pot of boiling water, it's cruel from the point of view of the lobster but not for those sitting down to dinner. Therefore, nature is not exhaustively cruel, because some creatures benefit from the results of the struggle to survive.

Second, he offers a *tu quoque* or "you too" argument. If nature is cruel, then so is God.

> Ironically, anyone who believes that evolution introduced the idea of systematic cruelty to human nature is likely overlooking many acts of biblical cruelty, especially God's killing of the Egyptian firstborns, Herod's murder of the innocents, or the complete and intentional destruction of the cities of Sodom and Gomorrah. Evolution cannot be a cruel concept if all it does is reflect the realities of nature, including birth, struggle, life, and death.[40]

Miller's second argument seems to be operating with a two-step logic. By saying that the biblical God is just as cruel as evolution, he thinks this somehow exonerates evolution. Then he moves without an intervening premise to the conclusion that if we are dealing with the "realities of nature," they simply cannot be judged as cruel or brutal. It appears that Miller is caught in an intuitive reaction here, leading him to throw reason and logic to the wind.

Miller goes on to paint a picture of evolution as "nice." He picks up on the work of sociobiologists E. O. Wilson and Richard Dawkins to point out that kin preference leads to "nice" behavior on the part of animals who are genetically close to one another. Why are

> there . . . so many examples of animals being *nice* to each other? . . . Darwinian evolution can produce cooperation and care just as surely as conflict and competition. The care and self-sacrifice seen in animal families are not exceptions to evolution—rather, they are the straightforward results of natural selection acting to favor instinctive altruism.[41]

With nature so "nice," one wonders where the very idea of predation, survival of the fittest, and selection even came from. As we saw in earlier chapters, the altruistic argument fails to paint nature as nice because kin altruism is pressed into the service of the selfish gene and the larger march of the competition to survive in which suffering and death become universal.

Miller concludes with a creedal crescendo, a testimony of a scientist who is a believer: "Only those who embrace the scientific reality of evolution are adequately prepared to give God the credit and the power He truly deserves. By recognizing the continuing force of evolution, a religious person acknowledges that God is every bit as creative in the present as He was in the past. That—and not a rejection of any of the core ideas of evolution—is why I am a believer."[42]

Evolution as Continuing Creation
Arthur Peacocke

Perhaps the most thorough and articulate among theistic evolutionists whom we identify as free-will defenders is Arthur Peacocke. Like Teilhard, Peacocke interprets evolutionary history as an epic novel with human consciousness arriving in the present chapter. In the wake of the Big Bang, the interplay of microevents and lawlike necessities has caused matter on our planet to become more and more complex. Increased complexity has given birth to self-reproducing systems capable of receiving information from their environment and reacting and even transforming that environment. With the rise of human beings, complexity in the form of consciousness has developed; and with consciousness comes increased independence of, and freedom over against, the environment. Not only the environment. Conscious freedom makes possible human independence from God, our creator. Such freedom and independence are the inevitable consequences of the evolutionary advance to human consciousness. In fact, believes Peacocke, this is what God intended all along. Freedom is a divine achievement just as it is an evolutionary achievement. "God intended that out of matter persons should evolve who had this freedom, and thereby allowed the possibility that they might challenge his purposes and depart from his intentions. To be consistent, we must go on to assume that God had some overarching intention which made this risk worth taking."[43]

Arthur Peacocke is both a physical biochemist and a systematic theologian. An ordained priest in the Church of England, he founded the Society of Ordained Scientists. He is now professor emeritus and former director of the Ian Ramsey Centre, St. Cross College, Oxford, England. During his distinguished career, he has consistently admonished the theological community seriously to consider the points at which indisputable truths uncovered in natural science require revision in theological outlook.

Peacocke celebrates the self-organizing character of nature's history. Natural selection is the way in which life makes itself. Creativity within nature is made possible by the ongoing creativity of nature's creator, God. On the one hand, God seems to be passive while the world creates itself. "What we see as the operation of chance in a law-like framework [is] a mode of God as Creator," he writes.[44] On the other hand, God seems to be actively creating. "God is continuously creating, continuously giving existence to, what is new; God is *semper Creator*, and the world is a *creatio continua*. The traditional notion of God *sustaining* the world in its general order and structure now has to be enriched by a dynamic and creative dimension. . . . God indeed makes 'things make themselves,' as Charles Kingsley put it."[45] God is immanent to the creative activity of the natural world; therefore, Peacocke does not look for extra supposed gaps or mechanisms whereby God might act external to the world process. The processes of the natural order are themselves divine creativity at work.

Just what does "chance" mean? It refers to contingency and randomness and unpredictability in natural events, such as mutations in DNA. That mutations in organisms will occur is predictable; precisely which mutations will occur is unpredictable. Peacocke refines the idea of chance. First, we use the term "chance" when we lack the knowledge to predict natural events. For example, we are unable to determine accurately the microparameters of initial conditions that will determine macroevents. We simply do not know what the conditions are that precipitate a given DNA mutation at the microlevel, yet that mutation may have a significant effect on the organism or person at the macrolevel. Not only might we be unable to know the initial conditions, but also some natural events result from the intersection of two causal chains. The crossing of causal chains could result in unpredictable natural events whether we know initial conditions or not.

Peacocke's second refinement of the idea of chance appeals to Heisenberg's uncertainty principle. The unpredictability of events at the microlevel—in Heisenberg's case, at the microlevel of subatomic activity—still yields to lawlike activity at the macrolevel. Random mutations at the microlevel make changes in the cells of an organism; but the new gene expression in the cell obeys known natural laws. The new cell activity affects the phenotype of the organism, and it also affects the ability of the organism to maneuver in the environment and to produce progeny. At this macrolevel, the law of natural selection takes over. Some mutations survive to the next generation; others do not. What began as a random change at the molecular level in DNA may eventually become a statistically analyzable factor in species development.

Neither chance alone nor law alone describes nature. It is the interplay of chance and law that allows new forms to emerge and evolve. "It is chance operating within a law-like framework that is the basis of the inherent creativity of the natural order, its ability to generate new forms, patterns, and organizations of matter and energy."[46] Peacocke goes on to attribute the origin of this dialectic of chance with law to God's creativity. Startling here, when we compare Peacocke with classical theism, is that God's nonaction through permitting chance, rather than God's direct action to govern events, becomes the way in which God creates. God allows randomness and unpredictable events to contribute to the world's self-organization and self-development, and this constitutes God's continuing creative work in the world. "For a theist, God must now be seen as acting to create in the world *through* what we call 'chance' operating within the created order, each stage of which constitutes the launching pad for the next."[47] God is the primary cause making chance possible; chance then becomes the secondary cause, so to speak, leading to the actual forms that ongoing creativity leads to.

As each stage launches the next, we might ask whether direction or purpose or progress is discernible in evolution. Peacocke nods respect toward those evolutionary biologists who vehemently deny directionality or teleology. He acknowledges that images such as the evolutionary tree of life modeled after a Christmas tree with the human species as the crowning angel at the top fail to depict accurately what evolutionary theory is trying to say. He acknowledges that the image of the bush is better, where *homo sapiens* are but one random branch sticking out like all the others.

Despite these acknowledgments, Peacocke tenders a modest notion of trends or propensities in the growth of the human branch or twig on this bush of life. Peacocke sees potentials built in to the natural process, potentials we can see now from their state of actualization and looking backward. Like Teilhard and others, for example, Peacocke believes nature is destined to become increasingly complex. The human brain is the most complex thing we know of in nature, and the process of complexification seems to have been leading up to it. For brains to advance in complexity, they need to develop information processing along with self-consciousness and language. All these are classified as trends in nature. Peacocke adds to this list of trends the increase in pain and suffering. The ability to experience pain constitutes the necessary biological warning signal of danger and disease, an information processing advantage natural selection has conferred on human consciousness.

This is not a moral evaluation; it is an evaluation according to the measure of reproductive advantage. Complex, pain-suffering beings gain a reproductive advantage, so natural selection favors them.

> In the context of natural selection, pain has an energizing effect and suffering is a goad to action: they both have survival value for creatures continually faced with new problematic situations challenging their survival. In relation to any theological reflections, it must be emphasized that pain and suffering are present in biological evolution as a necessary condition for survival of the individual long before the appearance of human beings on the scene. So the presence of pain and suffering cannot be the result of any particular human failings.[48]

The Oxford scholar is rejecting the idea that a historical fall attributed to Adam and Eve is responsible for introducing pain and suffering into the world, and he is affirming the positive value of pain and suffering for reproductive survival and evolutionary progress.

Death is natural, not sinful, according to Peacocke. New life requires dying life for nourishment. The suffering of prey in the teeth of the predator is necessary. "So there is a kind of *structural* logic about the inevitability of living organisms dying and preying on each other. . . . The statistical logic is inescapable: new forms of matter arise only through the dissolution of the old; new life only through death of the old."[49] Peacocke proceeds to revise Christian systematic theology according to these commitments. He rejects the sequence of Fall followed by redemption on the grounds that no original pre-Fallen righteousness ever existed. By rejecting a historical Adamic golden age or paradise, Peacocke places our image of perfection in our imaginations as a goal toward which we aspire. By normalizing suffering and death, Peacocke rejects the notion of sin applied to the natural world. Death can no longer be thought of as the wage of sin; rather, it is a natural process, even a good insofar as it contributes to evolutionary advance. Peacocke recommends that we revise our classical theories of atonement to incorporate a humanity in process, a human nature that is still in the process of becoming.

What Peacocke perceives as revisions in the understanding of God required by natural science provides us with an example of a free-will theodicy. Peacocke's point of departure is God's self-limitation in omnipotence and omniscience. In contrast to Whiteheadian process panentheism, for whom God's limitations are metaphysically required, Peacocke is a classical theist who holds that God is all powerful. Any limitation on God's power is the result of God's free decision, not a requirement by anything external to God. God is free to self-limit, and this is exactly what God does when permitting a material world to engage in self-organization and self-development. And by limiting omniscience, future events can be genuinely unpredictable.

Divine self-limitation is the condition that makes the eventual development of human free will possible. Human freedom is assumed here to be an intrinsic good, even when it makes sin possible. By freely choosing to permit evolutionary history to produce free human beings, God is expressing love to the creation. "This self-limitation is the precondition for the coming into existence of free self-conscious human beings, that is, of human experience as such. This act of self-limitation on behalf of the good and well-being, indeed the existence, of another being can properly be designated as being consistent with, and so exemplifying the ultimate character of, *God as Love*."[50]

This free-will defense has two implications, one for evolutionary theory and one for theology. The self-limitation of God permits or even encourages pain and suffering and death in natural history because it is the unavoidable means necessary for the development of life, consciousness, and human freedom. Yet, theologically, self-limitation does not mean God is absent. Peacocke claims to be a theist, not a deist. This means God is involved in the world process. But how? Peacocke's answer: God shares in the world's sufferings. What we find revealed about God in the cross of Jesus Christ is that God in Godself is present to the pain, suffering, and death of all creatures in nature. "*God suffers in, with and under the creative process of the world* with their costly, open-ended unfolding in time."[51]

Thus, God is present experiencing the suffering of creatures within the world. Yet we still ask: Does God act in the promotion of the evolutionary process? We have seen that for Peacocke God acts in the world by setting up the dialectic of chance and law and then steps back to permit the world to follow its own propensities. We must see this as a theology of passive action on the part of a self-limiting God, a way of letting the natural processes follow their own uninterrupted course. Now, in light of what will come later in this chapter, we need to ask, does God take any direct action? In contrast to Robert John Russell, whose contribution to theistic evolution we will look at shortly, Peacocke locates divine direction and purpose at the macrolevel of natural selection. He does not appeal to the microlevel of quantum mechanical activity. Peacocke avoids postulating any direct action of God at the microlevel to ensure that persons eventually emerge on earth; he is satisfied with the role natural selection plays at the macrolevel in guiding the propensities mentioned above. Peacocke has no need of Russell's bottom-up hypothesis for specifically directed events; if anything, Peacocke would appeal to a top-down or whole-part action on God's part in evolutionary history.[52]

Interlude: The Theology of the Cross

One of the logical problems with the free-will defense of God in the face of suffering and death in the created order is that the question can rightfully be raised, is human freedom worth the price? As Charles Darwin surveyed the dismal history of nature with the extinction of species and the suffering of sentient beings, his considered judgment was that this is "waste." Such waste was, for Darwin, unredeemable. Free-will defenders of theism presume that the waste finds its redemption at the arrival of human consciousness and moral freedom. Can the case be made that human freedom is so valuable that it is worth the price of all of nature's sacrificial suffering on its behalf?

This leads to a second logical problem for theologians: The achievement of freedom is frequently said to be the precondition of sin. A true sin is a truly free act, free-will theologians such as Peacocke presume. The arrival of freedom establishes for the first time what believers in the Adam and Eve story know as the Fall—that is, human beings as finite nature introduce evil into an otherwise good creation. Freedom makes suffering and death possible. Rather than redemption, freedom to sin characterizes the Fall. The free-will defenders we are looking at here connect the Fall with the achievement of progressive evolution. Some sort of values reversal seems to take place in the free-will defense.

A third logical problem is that free-will defenders seek to justify God for permitting eons and eons of suffering by sentient beings. God is justified because this is the price the world pays to obtain the allegedly valuable product, human freedom and moral awareness. God is justified here because the divine self-limitation both exempts God from responsibility while bestowing a blessing on creation. God's removal from natural causation is the means for bestowing this blessing. The assumption is that the less divinity the greater the blessing.

If the free-will theodicy stands alone, it justifies a self-limiting God who blesses the world by his absence. Now, to his credit, Peacocke does not leave us with only an absent God. God is still present when sharing in the world's suffering. This leads to an important consideration in the theodicy problem, one suggested by *Theology of the Cross*. This distinctive theme coming from the Lutheran branch of the Reformation begins with the revelatory character of the cross of Jesus Christ and makes two points. First, God remains mysterious even in revelation. To look at the cross whereon a dying man suffers and to believe we see here the God of life and healing is paradoxical, to say the least. More, it is puzzling and disorienting. What we expect and hope for in God is not what we see in the revelation of the cross. We want to see a God of power and eternity, yet what we see is a God present in weakness and death. The God revealed in the cross of Jesus is not the God we would expect or desire to have if we went god-shopping. A God who participates with us in suffering and death hides what we want to see, namely, the power of healing and life. Second, entailed in what was just said, God is a victim of suffering and evil, not the author or perpetrator. God shares in the victimization of us mortals who face pain, agony, loneliness, and separation from life. In fact, God shares in the suffering of every creature in this creation.

Physicist and pastor George Murphy applies the Theology of the Cross to evolution and interprets suffering in nature as victimizing God. In natural selection,

"God is not understood as a deity who forces millions of generations through suffering and extinction without himself being affected by the process, but rather as a God who participates in the processes and shares in the suffering and death of the world. The price for the development of life is paid not only by God's creatures but also by God himself."[53]

Rather than self-limiting to permit suffering and death, God limits his eternity to enter into time, limits his infinity to become finite, limits his divine life to enter into creaturely death, limits self to ingress into the other. Rather than an absent omnipotent God, the Theology of the Cross points to a present God who is at one with our weakness. Rather than bless "survival of the fittest," in the cross God becomes one with the unfit, with those who do not survive. Divine identification with the unfit becomes the key that unlocks the door to true life, eternal life.

As we turn to the theistic evolutionary thought of Denis Edwards and John Haught, we will witness a growing appeal to divine relationality and the invocation of the Theology of the Cross.

The God *of* Evolution
Denis Edwards

The Theology of the Cross conveys that God the creator is also the fellow sufferer who shares in the very life of the creatures, including the negativities of this life. Two recent Roman Catholic theologians—Denis Edwards and John Haught—are invoking divine empathy as revealed in the cross with illuminating power as they incorporate evolutionary biology into their doctrines of creation.

By using "of" in his book's title, *The God of Evolution*, Denis Edwards affirms that the scientific theory of evolution provides actual knowledge about the way God works in nature to achieve divine purposes. "There is every reason for a Christian of today to embrace both the theological teachings of Genesis and the theory of evolution. But holding together the Christian view of God and the insights of evolutionary science does demand a rethinking of our theology of the trinitarian God at work in creation."[54] Is purpose discernible in evolution? Yes, indeed; it is God's purpose.

The God of evolution for Denis Edwards—who teaches systematic theology at the Adelaide College of Divinity in Australia—is a trinitarian God interpreted almost panenthesistically. Following Richard of St. Victor, Edwards says, "the foundation for a theology that takes evolution seriously can be found in the trinitarian vision of God as a God of mutual relations, a God who is communion in love, a God who is friendship beyond all comprehension."[55] Edwards wants to go beyond the description of God as merely self-giving; God is also relational. Internal to the Trinity, the three persons mutually affirm one another. External toward the world, God acts as a friend would act, namely, personally involved. What happens in the created world affects the internal life of God. Allowing God to be affected by the world brings Edwards close to a Theology of the Cross.

Now that Edwards has taken evolution—evolution complete with deep time, natural selection, and common descent—so fully into the divine life, we need to pose the theodicy problem. Edwards tries to solve the problem of theodicy by making two moves. The first is a verbal finesse. Like Kenneth Miller, Edwards says natural selection is not cruel and animals do not universally suffer. To say natural selection is "cruel" is to anthropomorphosize nature, to impart personalized values to an impersonal natural process. Nature, both scientifically and theologically understood, says Edwards, is impersonal and resistant to anthropomorphocizing. And, by distinguishing "suffering" from "pain," Edwards acknowledges that animals have pain but not the long-term suffering reserved for self-conscious human persons. In other words, natural selection is not as cruel as we might first think.[56]

Edwards's second move is to affirm self-limitation on the part of God. By self-limiting the divine self, God's self-restriction of divine power makes creation possible. Further, as numerous contemporary theologians argue, God makes contingency and freedom and thereby creativity within creation possible; and this in turn makes pain and suffering possible. Edwards grounds this self-limitation in the divine kenosis in the cross. Then he applies kenosis to creation so as to affirm God's self-shedding of omnipotence: "Omnipotence, understood in light of the cross, is the supreme power to freely give one's self in love. In light of this, the divine act of creation can be understood as an act of love, by which the trinitarian Persons freely make space for creation and freely accept the limits of the process."[57] Edwards employs the symbol of the cross to explicate his notion of divine self-limitation. Because in this scheme self-limitation to make space for creation is a free divine decision rather than something ontologically forced upon God's being, Edwards remains within the theist rather than the panentheist camp.

Edwards recognizes that Christian theologians have long wrestled with the knotty question about human freedom and divine power. Now this concern for human freedom slides over and is applied to natural processes that include random mutations, natural selection, and evolutionary development. By distancing the divine self from creation, humans can be free and nature can be governed by randomness and chance. "God, in creating, accepts the limits of physical processes and of human freedom."[58]

Here we see again the logic that goes like this: If God would exert omnipotence, then nature would be determined and human freedom would not exist. So, if God limits divine power, a space is opened up to permit random chance in nature and free will in humanity. The divine withdrawal from involvement makes God absent so that creation can be contingent and free. "Creation can be understood as the self-expression of the Trinity, whereby the divine Persons-in-Relation make space for what is not God within the divine life."[59]

Yet Edwards does not stop here. He wants to add that God's purpose is achieved through nature. "I would want to argue that God is not to be understood as another factor operating alongside natural selection, or in addition to it, but is rather to be understood as acting through it."[60] Is this consistent? It would seem that God is either present or absent. Can Edwards have it both ways?

The difficulty here is not unique to Edwards. We find it emerging frequently in contemporary discussions of the relation of God to the world. The fallacy in the divine self-limitation argument is that it presupposes a conflict between divine power and creature power; whereas the classic Christian view, we contend, emphasizes that God's power empowers and thereby liberates God's creatures. The fallacy presupposes a fixed pie of power. According to the fixed pie image, if God gets a big slice then creation gets a proportionately smaller slice. If God would be all powerful, then creation would be totally powerless. Now, the fixed pie image may apply to human affairs such as the class struggle, wherein economic or political power concentrated in the upper class correspondingly denies power to the working class or to the marginalized populace.

But, we ask, does this fixed pie apply to God? No, at least not when God is acting graciously. When the God of Israel acted with a "mighty hand" and an "outstretched arm" to rescue the Hebrew slaves from Egyptian dominance, the Hebrews experienced God's power as liberating, as making freedom possible. When God raised Jesus from the dead on the first Easter, Christians began to put trust in God's power to raise us into a new and transformed creation. The exertion of God's power is redemptive, salvific, liberating, empowering. When we cry out to God for redemption and liberation, the last thing we want to hear from heaven is that God has decided to be self-limiting.

Natural selection, according to evolutionary theory, favors the strong over the weak. It favors those members of a species genetically equipped to bring their own progeny to reproductive age and to exploit, if not dominate, others. What could a doctrine of the self-limitation of God in favor of natural selection mean other than to give theological blessing to the strong to dominate, if not destroy, the weak? How could such a theological blessing avoid social Darwinism? How could it avoid reinforcing the power of the powerful classes over against the working classes and the marginalized? The doctrine of God's self-limitation on behalf of evolution would leave us with a Christian faith without hope.

Does Denis Edwards want to draw out the implications of his commitments to the "God of evolution" in this manner? By no means. The trinitarian God Edwards reveres is a God of love and friendship. The God of love and friendship identifies with those who suffer in nature. Yet the problem of consistency must be posed to Edwards and to all those making the free-will defense: If God is absent due to self-limitation, then how can God be present to share the suffering, let alone the redemption?

143

Suffering with Nature's Sufferers
John Haught

Georgetown University systematic theologian John Haught has sought to answer this question with one of the most carefully thought-through theories of theistic evolution to date. Haught more than any other faces the darkness of the theodicy problem with the terror of deep time and the immeasurable suffering that predation and selection require of both those creatures who survive and those who do not. He illumines the problem with the light of the cross.

> Reflection on the Darwinian world can lead us to contemplate more explicitly the mystery of God as it is made manifest in the story of life's suffering, the epitome of which lies for Christians in the crucifixion of Jesus. In the symbol of the cross, Christian belief discovers a God who participates fully in the world's struggle and pain. . . . Evolutionary biology not only allows theology to enlarge its sense of God's creativity by extending it over measureless eons of time; it also gives comparable magnitude to our sense of the divine participation in life's long and often tormented journey.[61]

The God Haught believes it is "both *kenotic love* and *power of the future*."[62] Haught connects this God with a nature that is autonomously creative. For nature to be both autonomous and creative, it requires divine absence. What God makes absent is his power; yet God still seeks to guide the world by luring or coaxing it toward increased beauty, toward perfection. God engages in self-restraint, self-removal. This is creation through letting-be. Haught places this divine activity in the category of kenosis or divine self-emptying, and he applies it to God's creative relationship to the world. He also applies it to the concept of grace by saying that God graces the world by withdrawing and allowing creative self-organizing to develop through natural selection. Divine self-restraint is the way in which divine self-giving love is manifest in the natural world.

> It is the "self-withdrawal" of any forceful divine presence, and the paradoxical hiddenness of God's power in a self-effacing persuasive love, that allows creation to come about and to unfold freely and indeterminately in evolution. . . . The arena into which God "withdraws" in order to allow for the relatively autonomous self-creation of evolution is that of the unavailable but infinitely resourceful future.[63]

What constitutes divine action in the world for this Roman Catholic theologian is the impartation of information. Informational patterning is a metaphysical necessity. It is required for one thing to be distinguishable from another thing or no-thing. Evidently, information is noncoercive yet alluring. How does impartation of divine information fit with evolution's self-organization? Haught holds that self-organization is spontaneous, but God integrates particular evolutionary achievements into more comprehensive wholes of meaning. "Information 'works,' we can say at the very least, only by *comprehensively* integrating particulars (atoms, molecules, cells, bits, and bytes) into coherent wholes."[64] Rather than emergence from below, Haught advocates integration from above. From this one might conclude that the future reinterprets the past—that is, future comprehensive wholes draw past particulars into new patterns of coherence.

In fact, Haught relies upon a strong doctrine of eschatology and asserts that it is the divine promise of future renewal that opens the present moment up to creative advance. At times Haught seems to waver. In attempting to explain novelty in natural history, he occasionally flirts with Whiteheadian metaphysics, a philosophical system that precludes a consummate eschatology. Yet, at other crucial junctures, he sees the role that a transformatory future plays in opening every present reality toward creative advance. "It is the arrival of the future, and not the grinding onward of an algorithmic past, that accounts for the novelty in evolution. . . . It is not the occurrence of contingency that brings about the future; rather, it is the arrival of the future that allows events to have the status of contingency, that is, to be more than just the inevitable outcome of past deterministic causes."[65] The power of God's future is the ultimate metaphysical explanation for the physical reality of which we are a part. "I would argue that it is precisely the implied metaphysics of the future that can best account for the three cosmic qualities—chance, lawfulness, and temporality—that allegedly provide the raw stuff of biological evolution."[66]

God's future, for Haught, is what is eminently real. It is the reality toward which all is being drawn. The future shows up after every present moment has run its course and slipped into its past. The future is also the dimension from which God comes to renew the creation. Because God's future grounds metaphysical reality, it must apply to physical reality as well. At minimum, we have a uniformitarian understanding of divine action. But, because of the dynamism of the interaction of the future with the present, Haught most likely belongs with the noninterventionists. Remaining to be explained is whether the eschatological renewal of creation will be due to an interventionist or noninterventionist divine action.

Does evolution have a direction, a built-in purpose? Recall, its self-organization is autonomous for Haught. This means that whatever purpose evolutionary creativity has derives not from an embedded entelechy, but rather from its future place in the comprehensive renewal of creation. "Rather than attributing to God a rigid 'plan' for the universe, evolutionary theology prefers to think of God's 'vision' for it. Nature, after Darwin, is not a design but a promise. God's 'plan,' if we continue to use the term, is not a blueprint but an *envisagement* of what the cosmos might become."[67]

What we embrace as John Haught's most valuable contributions to theistic evolution is the decisive role he gives to eschatology and his dramatic treatment of the theodicy problem in light of the Theology of the Cross. What we are less sanguine about is his free-will defense. Our criticism of free-will defense theologians has been that they want their cake and to eat it too. They want to remove God through self-limitation yet still keep God involved in the world and in some cases even to suffer with the world. This is an internally inconsistent position, even though some of the most thoughtful theistic evolutionists advocate it. John Haught exemplifies the double commitment: "God's will is that the world become more and more independent, and that during its evolution its own internal coherence intensify, not diminish. But this *absent* God is *present* to and deeply united with the evolving world precisely by virtue of selflessly allowing it to achieve ever deeper autonomy—which occurs most obviously in the evolutionary emergence of human freedom."[68] Now, which is it: Is God absent or present?

Evolution Has Determined That We Would Be Free
Philip Hefner

Like John Haught, Philip Hefner appeals to God's promise of eschatological newness for both nature's purpose and the divine contribution to novelty in the evolutionary process. And, like Teilhard de Chardin, Hefner paints a picture of a grand evolutionary epic through which God celebrates human achievement and envisages still greater fulfillment yet to come.

For Philip Hefner, science is an essential component to theology. Hefner is an emeritus professor of systematic theology at the Lutheran School of Theology at Chicago, former director of the Zygon Center for Science and Religion, and editor of the journal *Zygon*. Hefner pursues Christian theology within the matrix of evolution. Hefner's theological picture includes deep time, natural selection, common descent, divine action, and a resolution to the theodicy question. He understands "evolution as the work of God to allow for the emergence of that which is necessary for human fulfillment of God's intentions."[69]

Hefner offers us something that, at first, seems paradoxical: Evolution has determined that we would be free. Hefner more astutely than others avoids the misleading dichotomy between determinism and freedom. They can fit together, if rightly understood. "Freedom, as it has arisen among human beings within the evolutionary context, seeks to be in harmony with the determinist course of evolution in which humans find themselves."[70] Or, a bit more paradoxically: "We are deterministically defined as free."[71]

Freedom is the goal, the end, the *telos* of the long epic of evolution. Hefner is referring specifically to human freedom. With our human freedom comes creativity and the responsibility of continuing God's creative work in the world. Key to this Lutheran theologian's anthropology is describing the human being as

God's *created co-creator*. When asked if evolution has purpose, Hefner answers with a resounding affirmative: *"The freedom that marks the created co-creator and its culture is an instrumentality of God for enabling the creation (consisting of the evolutionary past of genetic inheritance and culture, as well as the contemporary ecosystem) to participate in the intentional fulfillment of God's purposes."*[72]

However, freedom is tied to eschatology for Hefner, just as it is for Haught. Hefner is careful to show that the divine purpose is not intrinsic to the natural process, not available for scientific perception. Purpose is discernible in light of God's future, not from reviewing evolution's past. Rather than posit a *teleology* intrinsic to nature then, Hefner speaks of *teleonomy*, according to which he can posit an eschatologically appointed purpose that is consistent with natural structures but cannot be derived from them. ("Teleonomy" ordinarily refers to natural phenomena that appear to have purpose but do not in fact have purpose, only function. Hefner's use of this term extends its meaning.) The newness adhering to God's promised eschatology refers to new possibilities and new futures without destroying the life-giving continuities with our evolutionary origins. Both freedom and purpose within nature now derive from the promised newness of God's still-outstanding eschatological future.

For Hefner, evolution is not merely biological. It includes culture. His inclusive framework is biocultural evolution. Free human beings express themselves symbolically, and symbols create culture, and culture evolves. In fact, in our epoch of natural history, genes and culture together are responsible for the next stage of evolution. "*Biocultural evolution* refers to (1) the emergence, within the physical realm, of biological processes of evolution that themselves generate the phenomenon of culture; and to (2) the distinctive, non-Darwinian, dynamic processes by which culture proceeds. . . . Culture is defined as learned and taught patterns of behavior, together with the symbol systems that contexualize and interpret the behavior. The single most critical product of human culture today is technology."[73] In the opinion of the *Zygon* editor, we human beings have a moral obligation to use our advanced technology in ecologically responsible fashion to better our planet and the lives of our fellow creatures.

Of particular interest to Hefner is picking up where sociobiologists such as E. O. Wilson leave off in explaining altruism. As a Christian who recalls Jesus' admonition that we should love our enemies and not just our families, Hefner probes into our moral responsibility for loving persons beyond our genetic kin. If we are genetically determined to limit altruistic behavior to only those who are genetically proximate in order to ensure the reproductive survival of our selfish genes, then what would permit trans-kin altruism? Hefner answers, culture. Culture is an emergent property that transcends our genetic history while maintaining continuity with that genetic history. "Trans-kin altruism cannot be accounted for on grounds of genetic evolution alone. . . . Culture is the stream of information that enables trans-kin altruism. . . . Culture functions as a set of epigenetic rules that comprise a sort of game in which humans form cultural strategies that override the biological information of selfishness."[74] It is God's will that we, as created co-creators, engage in trans-kin altruism. That is our purpose.

What all this means, according to the Chicago professor, is that nature has the character of a project. What this project is has been revealed in the human being. Our species, at least for the present chapter in the evolutionary epic, is now burdened with responsibility for the next stage in this grand project. Furthermore, "the Christian faith proposes that nature's project is God's project."[75]

Is this project flawed? When Hefner faces the theodicy problem in light of the selfish gene and natural selection, he turns not to Darwin, but to Genesis and God's declaration that the natural world is "very good." First and foremost, he emphasizes that the creation is good. At our present stage in evolution's epic, however, we human beings are not what we are called and created to be. We live in deviation from our own essential character. This renders what we know to be original sin along with evil as secondary to nature's status as declared by God. "Evil is a phenomenon that occurs after the initial articulation of the essential goodness of Creation, and it is a phenomenon that will be transmuted into goodness eternally."[76] Even though Hefner is clear that he wants to make a logical or ontological claim that goodness is primary and evil is secondary, what is not clear is just how this is the case. When and where do we find this goodness? He cannot place it in an historical Garden of Eden in our archonic past. Nor can he locate it in an eternal depth, an unreachable essence from which we are estranged. What is left is locating it in the eschatological future, a future that redeems while it creates. Rather than leave it that we simply are not what we ought to be, perhaps it would be better to say we are not yet what we ought to be. The "human being was created with a high destiny toward which it is tending."[77]

The Sacred Depths of Nature
Ursula Goodenough

Although her work does not fit exactly into the category of theistic evolution, Ursula Goodenough's contribution to our discussion is akin to that of Philip Hefner. Both frame their theological views within what is becoming known as the "Epic of Evolution."[78] Goodenough is a cell biologist at Washington University who embraces a noninterventionist religious naturalism, placing her on both our divine action spectrum and causal explanation spectrum between deism and materialism. She is a materialist who celebrates mystery.

A scientist with sensibilities for the sacred, Goodenough finds herself awestruck by the sense of mystery evoked by the vastness of the universe and the development of complex life over deep time. She constructs her naturalism on the Steven Weinberg dictum—"the more the universe seems comprehensible, the more it seems pointless." Then she proceeds to place atop Weinberg's bleak emptiness a more poignant nihilism by celebrating nature as mystery. She discovers lurking in both the infinite and the infinitesimal a set of mysteries that she mines for building materials. She is struck by what Paul Tillich has called the question of ontological shock, namely, "Why is there anything at all, rather than nothing?"[79] This shocking thought is the origin of all ontological speculation. It is the question of being itself. It is a puzzling question because asking about anything that is is derived from it. Yet being itself cannot be derived from anything else. Goodenough is aware that this is a question to which the cosmologies of the world's religions provide their respective answers.

Of those questions that derive from the ontological one she asks: From where did the laws of physics come? Why does the universe seem so strange? These questions are the locus of mystery for Goodenough. Deists and creationists and theistic evolutionists all have answers, namely, God is the source of the very existence of the universe, the laws by which it is governed, and the author of its mystery and magnificence. Goodenough gives consideration to the mildest form of divine creation, the deistic form; and she decides that this requires too much belief in God. Even the God of deism, to Goodenough's reading, appears like an enlarged human creator; "and the concept of a human-like creator of muons and neutrinos has no meaning for me. But more profoundly, Deism spoils my covenant with Mystery. To assign attributes to Mystery is to disenchant it, to take away its luminance."[80] And so where deism would place God, Goodenough places the very mystery of nature itself prior to assigning to it any anthropomorphosized attributes.

For Goodenough, the Epic of Evolution is a story "beautifully suited to anchor our search for planetary consensus, telling us of our nature, our place, our context."[81] She begins this epic story with the origin of the universe and then moves to planet earth with the origin of life. Life grew from nonlife. It is important to her that this origin be explained solely as the result of chance. No divine intervention has explanatory place here; it is chance that leads to emergence and the regularities of life's laws. "A system got thrown together, apparently quite by chance, that allows biomolecules to be synthesized by a sunlight-driven chemistry. . . . New life-specific functions are referred to as emergent functions."[82] Thus, Goodenough responds "to the emergence of Life not with a search for its Design or Purpose but instead with outrageous celebration that it occurred at all. I take the concept of miracle and use it not as a manifestation of divine intervention but as the astonishing property of emergence."[83]

This cell biologist thinks of her own body in materialistic terms. "My body is some 10 trillion cells. Period. My thoughts are a lot of electricity flowing along a lot of membrane. My emotions are the result of neurotransmitters squirting on my brain cells."[84] Yet this former president of the Institute on Religion in an Age of Science (IRAS) also has an affinity for mystical experience. She honors mystical reports from the world's religions. She appreciates the bond with wider nature that mysticism affords. So, she interprets mysticism within the framework of her naturalism. "As a non-theist, I find I can only think about these experiences as wondrous mental phenomena."[85]

Goodenough professes a faith in the sacredness of life as a tenet to her religious naturalism. What reverence she finds she can offer to anything she offers to nature. Her awareness of nature's complexity and beauty, combined with her human ability to apprehend it, "serves as the ultimate meaning and the ultimate value." Because life takes on sacredness due to its ultimacy, she advocates an ethic of "continuation." Life should continue, and an ecological ethic that fosters life's continuation follows from this sacred commitment. Yet she insists on pursuing her nature spirituality without God. "The continuation of life reaches around, grabs its own tail, and forms a sacred circle that requires no further justification, no Creator, no superordinate meaning of meaning, no purpose other than that the continuation continue until the sun collapses or the final meteor collides. I confess a credo of continuation."[86]

Goodenough has no trouble taking on board deep time, natural selection, and common descent. What she eschews is divine action because she eschews belief in the kind of God who could take action. With no such God, no theodicy problem arises. Suffering in the world can only be natural, therefore morally neutral. Goodenough is an evolutionary naturalist, not a theist.

One of Goodenough's colleagues in IRAS is Karl E. Peters, former editor of *Zygon*. Peters, too, follows the naturalist trail leading from Darwinian evolution to an acceptance and even celebration of nature as it comes to us. Yet Peters still believes God-language is appropriate. "Darwinian evolution portrays nature as constantly dancing—dancing with no one leading but all participating and mutually [influencing] one another," writes Peters: "This creativity that continually gives rise to new structures, new life forms, new thoughts and practices in a society, can be called the 'dance of God.'"[87]

"Evolution Is the Way God Did It!" Robert John Russell

"Evolution is the way God did it!" exclaimed Robert John Russell when being interviewed by Margaret Wertheim for a 1997 television documentary, "Faith and Reason." Note that God is the subject of this sentence, and the past tense verb is in the active voice. Evolution is something God does, or has done. More than simply allowing evolution to happen as we find the free-will defenders saying, Russell says, God plays an active role in evolutionary history. This places Russell between Arthur Peacocke or John Haught, on one end, and Philip Hefner along with Teilhard de Chardin, on the other. Because God actively creates through evolutionary processes, this places Russell on the evolutionary worldview side of the free-will defenders; but because Russell denies that eschatology is an extension of already-operative evolutionary principles, he remains closer to the middle of our subspectrum than Teilhardianism.

Robert John Russell is founder and director of Center for Theology and the Natural Sciences, an affiliate of the Graduate Theological Union in Berkeley, California. An ordained minister in the United Church of Christ with a Ph.D. in physics plus a M.A./M.Div. in theology, Russell has lifted up and institutionalized his vision for advancing the dialogue between science and religion. What Russell inherited when he began his scholarly work in the late 1970s was the two-language view, the view that science and faith speak separate and untranslatable languages. Unsatisfied with this separation, Russell has pressed his method, which he dubs the "creative mutual interaction" model. Creative mutual interaction goes beyond mere dialogue because it requires that theologians consider revising their views if science compels it, and it requires scientists to consider theological claims as prompting hypotheses for research programs. Russell stops short of projecting a single worldview inclusive of science and religion; yet he presses for the kind of mutual interaction that could eventually lead to consonance if not integration.

Russell begins a tightly packed summary of his theistic interpretation of evolution with a strong trinitarian commitment: "*Systematic theology speaks of the Triune God as Creator,*" he writes; "*the absolute source and sustainer of an intelligible and contingent universe* (creatio ex nihilo), *and the continuing Creator who, together with nature, brings about what science describes in a neo-Darwinian framework as the biological evolution of life on earth* (creatio continua). *Thus the 3.8 billion years of biological evolution on earth is God's way of creating life (theistic evolution).*" Russell then adds, "*Thus God not only creates but guides and directs the evolution of life towards the fulfilling of God's overall, eschatological, purposes.*"[88]

The domain in which Russell wants to work is quantum mechanics and its influence on genetic variation through mutation. The life of the cell, with its DNA, as the biologist studies it is constrained by the laws of physics, which come prior. Nothing can happen in chemistry or biology or psychology that the prior laws of physics have not made possible. Russell's is a bottom-up approach. Russell is clear that the processes and properties described by chemistry, biology, or psychology cannot be reduced to physics; so he takes a bottom-up approach without being reductionistic.

Russell asks, what if Werner Heisenberg was right in pointing to a fundamental ontological indeterminacy in physical nature? If the properties of the most fundamental physical entities—waves or particles of electrons—are indeterminate until they are measured, then all of the laws of the natural world point to a foundation of ontological indeterminacy. Russell's ontological indeterminism is his philosophical interpretation of what the physicists are saying about quantum mechanics.

Even though electron behavior is statistically calculable, what any individual electron will do is not fully determined by nature nor predictable by the laws of quantum mechanics. If we would take a chunk of uranium, for example, we could predict through statistical methods how, over time, a certain number of atoms would decay into thorium; but we could not predict when any one particular uranium atom decayed while its neighbors did not. Such quantum mechanical indeterminacy applies as well to "the making and breaking of covalent bonds in molecules, to the tunneling of electrons in transistors, to the absorption and emission of photons by atomic electrons, and so on."[89] This underlying indeterminacy appears in physical events as chance or contingency; and in conscious beings such as humans it provides the possibility to act freely.

Here, at the moment prior to the determination of a particular quantum event, Russell locates the consequences of divine action. God acts with nature to make the indeterminate determinate. Quantum physics has shown that nature's causal nexus makes room for divine action without upsetting nature's laws. If Heisenberg's interpretation of indeterminacy is correct, opines Russell,

> we can view nature theologically as genuinely open to God's participation in the bringing to actuality of each state of nature in time. Where science employs quantum mechanics and philosophy points to ontological indeterminism, faith sees God acting with nature to create the future. This is neither a disruption of the natural process nor a violation of the laws of physics. Instead, it is God fulfilling what nature offers . . . specifically in all events, moment by moment.[90]

Russell refers to his theory as describing noninterventionist objective divine action, meaning that God acts in nature but, in contrast to miracles, does not intervene to abrogate a natural law.

In a manner complementary to Russell, Nancey Murphy describes the predeterminate situation of the electron by comparing it to Buridan's ass. Paris philosopher John Buridan (c. 1292–1358) imagined a donkey tied equidistant between two bales of hay, both of equal size and delectability. The donkey died of starvation, said Buridan, because it could not find sufficient reason to prefer one bale over the alternative. Similarly, applied to electrons, "there is no sufficient reason either internal or external to the entities at this level to determine their behavior."[91] What is responsible for the electron's behavior that makes it determinate? Murphy answers: God. God activates one or another of the quantum entity's innate powers at a particular instant. "To put it crudely, God is the hidden variable."[92]

Moving from physics to genetics, Russell argues that what we see as random mutations in our DNA are the results of divine action at the prior quantum level. "God's action in genetic mutations is a form of objectively special, noninterventionist divine action. Moreover, since genetics plays a key role in biological evolution, we can argue by inference that God's action plays a key role in

152

biological evolution."[93] By moving up the physical ladder from subatomic activity through genetic variation by mutation and through natural selection, Russell has provided a bottom-up description of God's influence on evolutionary change. Randomness and chance can still be studied by science and still be subject to strictly naturalistic explanations; yet by faith we can posit that in, with, and under this randomness and chance God is at work.

Ian Barbour is uneasy with Russell's proposal and others like it. "A possible objection to this model is that it assumes *bottom-up causality* within nature once God's action has occurred, and thus seems to concede the reductionist's claim that the behavior of all entities is determined by their smallest parts (or lowest levels)."[94] Russell would not concede that this is a valid objection. Russell locatesto bottom-up influence. He makes room at levels of consciousness for top-down and whole-part causation as well.[95]

Paul Davies raises two objections to Russell's program, answering one immediately and leaving another to linger a bit. Davies's first objection is that what Russell is proposing sounds like a "traditional God-of-the-gaps theme." "But," Davies goes on,

> this objection can be easily met, since in this case the gaps are not explanatory gaps due to human ignorance, but physical gaps inherent in the structure of nature itself. A second, stronger objection that if God were to act repeatedly in this way on a specific physical system (e.g. on a particular atom) then the spirit, though not necessarily the letter, of the statistical laws of quantum physics would be violated.[96]

This nonintervention could then begin to look like intervention; and the statistical variability of quantum activity would begin to look like divine determinism. Yet this objection need not be decisive either. Davies, sympathetic to Russell and others who hold this position, imagines God as loading the quantum dice slightly across the universe. Indeterminacy would continue but within parameters that would guide natural history toward divine ends. God could pick the choices so as to respect the statistical laws. Finally, for Davies, although the objections are worth entertaining, neither stands.

We need to amplify the relationship between physical activity at the fundamental quantum level and what actually happens in the evolution of life. The latter cannot be reduced to the former, even if it is constrained by the former. What we observe with the development of life-forms is self-organization and creativity within nature. Quantum indeterminacy makes this possible, but the emergence of complex life-forms adds something. "God's choice of chance bestows an openness—a freedom—upon nature that is crucial for its impressive creativity, for without chance the genuinely new could not come into existence and the world would be reduced to a pre-programmed machine," comments Davies. Then he goes on: "Thus the laws of physics produce order—the order of simplicity—at the micro-, reductionistic level, while the felicitous interplay of chance and necessity leads to the emergence of *a different sort of order*—the order of complexity—at the macro-, holistic level. It is this *specific* view of chance, which acts as a prerequisite for emergence."[97] What happens at the level of life requires quantum openness; yet its creativity leads beyond toward the emergence of new levels of complexity.

Russell claims to be a noninterventionist, but how does this differ from uniformitarianism? A revealing question is this: Does God act in all quantum moments or only selectively in some? Russell first tips on the side of divine action in all quantum events, but then he distinguishes between preconscious and conscious natural entities:

> We may think of God as acting in all quantum events in the course of biological evolution until the appearance of organisms capable of even primitive levels of consciousness. From then on, God may continue to work in terms of the quantum-genetic domain, but God may then abstain from acting in those quantum events underlying bodily dispositions, thereby allowing the developing levels of consciousness to act out their intentions somatically.[98]

Russell contends that God has acted in all quantum events through evolutionary history. This implies that God did not self-limit omnipotence in order to free nature to pursue its own course, at least in the manner we have seen proffered by previous free-will defenders. When it comes to somatic events in the bodies of creatures with minds and consciousness, God now refrains from acting at the quantum level so that these creatures can enact their mental decisions.

Russell is not a deist, for whom God sets up the dialectic of law and chance at the original moment of creation and then abandons the natural world to operate on its own. Russell still believes in divine providence operative within the continuing creation. He believes each quantum event throughout the history of evolution is due in part to nature and in part to objective divine action. Some of these events are amplified and result in what we would call *special divine acts* at the macroscopic level. But when it comes to the actions of sentient creatures, he believes that God's self-restraint permits consciousness to act top-down in the quantum events that make bodily action possible.

As we have seen, Russell takes on board deep time, all 3.8 billion years of life development. His focus is on genetic variation and natural selection. On the one hand, he admits that random genetic mutations are the result of chance and not subject to any scientifically discernible teleology; yet, on the other hand, the divine hand is invisibly at work at the quantum level determining what direction those mutations might follow. Common descent of all life-forms is simply assumed by Russell without question.

Russell is acutely aware of the theodicy problem and addresses it courageously. By placing God so intimately involved at the level of gene activity, does this not make God "responsible for the disease, pain, suffering, and death brought about by these genes"?[99] Yes, but indirectly. Russell suggests that the eventual appearance of moral agents was in the divine mind before evolution began. God originally brought the creation into existence, with the evolution of moral agents as part of the divine plan. Suffering and disease and death were simply the price God would have to pay in order to purchase what would eventually become human freedom and moral development.

Russell's position is distinguishable from that of other free-will defenders who accommodate the Christian doctrine of creation to the eons of suffering over deep time. Russell does not stop with creation. He proceeds to draw redemption into the picture. The theodicy problem cannot be resolved in the doctrine of creation; it requires the doctrine of redemption. He starts with "the central biblical insight that the God who creates is the same God who redeems."[100] Then he looks for redemptive components in the evolutionary process.

> Evolution must somehow provide the occasion, albeit hidden, not only for creatio continua but even more profoundly for healing, cruciform grace to continuously redeem creation and guide it along with humanity into the new creation. . . . The long sweep of evolution may not only suggest an unfinished and continuing divine creation but even more radically a creation whose theological status as "good" may be fully realized only in the eschatological future.[101]

Our Spectrum

Where have we been? On one end of the divine action subspectrum of theistic evolutionists we place B. B. Warfield, the Princeton theologian revered by American fundamentalists and evangelicals. Reluctantly yet with considerable investment in studying thoroughly the claims of Darwinian theory, Warfield could admit into the Christian doctrine of creation deep time and transformationism. He rejected natural selection as an exhaustive explanation for speciation, and he was slow to accept common descent of humans with apes. We asked Warfield to represent the least enthusiastic form of theistic evolution, a grudging acceptance of scientific truth on the grounds that all truth rightfully demands admittance to the Christian understanding of reality. With his concept of *concursus* and secondary causation, Warfield affirms divine action in evolution and places himself among the theists.

Next door we locate Kenneth Miller. Whereas theologian Warfield had to work to admit science into this theology, scientist Miller works diligently to make some sort of room for religion. Miller cannot incorporate religion into his science. So he assigns claims about God to a nonscientific domain, namely, the domain of nonmaterial spirit. To a scientific materialist, natural selection is sufficiently comprehensive to explain every significant component to evolution.

No theological claims for divine action can affect the already-exhaustive scientific explanation. Miller believes in the biblical God shared by Jews, Christians, and Muslims; but this God has no demonstrable directing or guiding effect on evolutionary history. Even though Miller claims to be a theist, he *de facto* places himself in the deist camp.

As we move more toward the middle of our spectrum, what we find shared among a number of theistic evolutionists is a retrieval of the classic free-will defense of God. The free-will position applies to both creation and theodicy. As creator, God self-restricts the exertion of divine power in the world; and this allegedly opens up space within creation for contingency, chance, and self-organization. This openness due to God's self-withdrawal also makes human freedom possible. With regard to theodicy, God's self-withdrawal exonerates God from creator's guilt for the presence of evil and suffering in the world. God is not responsible. What we know as evil and suffering in the natural world are due to the way in which nature self-organized. What we know as human sin is due to human freedom, not divine determinism. Allowance of the possibility of evil and suffering in evolution is the price God paid in order to achieve the indirect goal of coaxing human existence to the present point in evolutionary history.

Few make the free-will defense argument more forcefully than Arthur Peacocke. By withdrawing from creation and presenting creation with the dialectic of law and chance, God permitted and encouraged the ongoing creative advance of the natural world. Although Peacocke considers himself a theist, and even on occasion a non-Whiteheadian panentheist, leaving the creation to the destiny bequeathed by law and chance signals a tacit deistic component within his doctrine of God.

Beyond Peacocke, we come to Denis Edwards, for whom evolution is the instrument by which God actively creates the human race. Edwards emphasizes that within the Holy Trinity the three persons relate to one another as friends. God's friendship with the world consists in a self-limitation of divine power in order to make room for a contingent creation and human freedom.

Beyond Edwards, we come to John Haught. For Peacocke, Edwards, and also for Haught, we see the schizoid combination of divine self-withdrawal to permit natural self-organization combined with claims that this is the manner by which God continually creates the world. It is schizoid because, on the one hand, God is passive while the world creates itself; and, on the other hand, this is a God of theism who they claim actively engages the world through creation and providence. Shifting from creation to theodicy, what we see dramatically in Haught that was just hinted at in Peacocke and Edwards is the Theology of the Cross—that is, God enters the physical world and shares in the suffering and evil that all sentient creatures undergo. The negativities of evolutionary history enter the divine life proper.

Robert John Russell begins where Peacocke, Edwards, and Haught leave off by adding two things: a more detailed description of God's active participation in the world and an appeal to redemption. God actively participates in the world's creativity at the quantum level, says Russell, not merely by setting up the dialectic of law and chance, but also by determining the direction taken by specific quantum events. This is clearly active theism, not passive deism. In addition, Russell recognizes how creation, as we understand it in evolutionary terms, necessarily has suffering and death built into it. Suffering and death are natural—natural today, at least, but not necessarily tomorrow. Russell looks forward to an eschatological new creation, wherein God will act to redeem the present order from suffering and death and from its history of evil.

With Philip Hefner we are moving closer to a theologically baptized evolutionary worldview. Evolution is the matrix for theology, and theology paints a picture of reality as the epic of evolution. Hefner shares with the free-will defenders the high value placed on human freedom, so high that it becomes the goal toward which evolution has been directed. He shares with Haught and Russell a strong role for eschatology, for the effect that the new has on the old in opening up the old for change and novelty. He shares with Ursula Goodenough and with Teilhard de Chardin the *Epic of Evolution* as the inclusive matrix for the theological doctrine of creation.[102]

Finally, occupying the far end of the subspectrum, we find Teilhard de Chardin. For this French Jesuit evolution is the story of God's creation, a story still unfolding. Eschatology becomes collapsed into evolution, so the future becomes a future chapter of nature's unfolding *telos*. What others have celebrated as the achievement of human freedom, Teilhard sees as a mere stepping stone to the *noosphere* and a yet-to-be-enjoyed sharing of mind. Finally, at Point Omega, we will see the rise of God and the full integration of matter and spirit.

As we turn now to chapter 7 and our own constructive proposal, we acknowledge our indebtedness to the theistic evolutionists we have explicated here. The challenge to relate, let alone integrate, biological evolution with a theological understanding of creation and redemption is daunting. Yet the challenge cannot be avoided. It may even be greeted with relish.

CHAPTER SEVEN

THEISTIC EVOLUTION: A CONSTRUCTIVE PROPOSAL

We have placed the phrase "from creation to new creation" in our book's title for a reason. God's creative work is not done yet. It is still going on. From our perspective at the present moment, God's future work will appear to us as something new, a new creation.

We find two weaknesses in most versions of theistic evolution proposed to date. First, they drop creation into the theory of evolution, almost neglecting the doctrine of redemption. Oh, yes, a few of the theistic evolutionists reviewed in the previous chapter could see that the theodicy problem warrants appeal to redemption. Yet we wish to argue that evolutionary history gives evidence that this creation is still underway, not yet complete, not yet what God in Genesis would deem "very good." Creation requires redemption. Second, the tendency among theistic evolutionists to collapse the theodicy problem into natural processes—to see violence, suffering, and death as merely natural and hence value-neutral—represents a failure of theological nerve. It is a sellout to naturalism and a loss to theism. The biblical view is that death is the wage of sin; or, to put it another way, God has promised that death is going to be replaced by resurrection, and suffering will be no more. From the theological point of view, we simply cannot let science alone define what is natural or, worse, redefine violence, suffering, and death as value-neutral.

Still, there is admirable strength in the honesty with which theistic evolutionists struggle to incorporate the apparent directionlessness of natural selection.

Out of respect for science, they simply accept the insistence by evolutionary biologists that a built-in purpose or inherent *telos* must be expunged from natural processes. For scientists to pursue their research, they must work with the absence of *telos* as their assumption. Some theologians, wishing to honor science as scientists themselves see it, conscientiously take randomness and chance and purposelessness into their doctrines of creation. These theologians gulp and force it down, like a cod liver oil pill too large to swallow, into their intellectual systems.

On the one hand, Charles Darwin did theologians a favor by expunging purpose from natural selection. The contextual milieu, which included his own grandfather, Erasmus Darwin, would have us believe that evolution has a direction, and we can measure its progress. Evolutionary biology, in this case, would look like technological progress. In fact, the popular mind associated evolution with progress and still does even today. Thinking of evolution as progress has led to horrendous moral problems, such as providing scientific justification for a naturalistic ethic that supports robber baron capitalism, racism, eugenics, and militarism. A restricted Darwinian approach to biology minus progress serves to undercut the social misuse of what scientists discover about nature. This is something theologians need to applaud.

On the other hand, Charles Darwin's decision to expunge *telos* was a form of dogmatism, an arbitrary ideological intrusion into the scientific research program. Rather than expelling purpose, Darwin could have left the question open. Scientists in principle could have opted to ask: Does nature reveal a purpose or direction? Rather than close the door in advance, the door could have been left open for future discovery.

Regardless, a nature without purpose is a difficult pill to swallow for theologians in the biblical tradition. One temptation is to cheat a little bit, to spy out some theologically visible *telos* within nature that scientists allegedly cannot see with their microscopes and telescopes. Another temptation is to celebrate the consequent—that is, to take a look at where the human race is today and then interpret the entire epic of evolution as leading to our present threshold of complexity or human freedom. A third temptation is to romanticize nature, to reorient human values around natural processes such as survival of the fittest and then acquiesce to violence, suffering, and death.

In the version of theistic evolution we propose here, in contrast, we wish to accept the Darwinian interpretation of nature as devoid of inherent *telos*; and we still plan to work around the temptations mentioned above. We will not attempt to locate purpose or direction or even value *within nature* itself; yet we affirm a divine purpose *for nature*. We plan to look for this divine purpose where it belongs, namely, in God. The purpose for the long history of nature over deep time is not a built-in *telos*; rather we prophesy that it will be retrodictively imparted by God in the eschatological consummation.

Purpose comes from the end looking backward, not from a potential lying in wait at the beginning. In fact, the Greek word for end, *telos*, means end both as final state and as purpose or goal. It is the divine act of redemption that determines what previous creation will have meant, and this can be discerned only eschatologically. It is omega that determines alpha.

From Creation to New Creation

Our ontology is based on Genesis 1:31—"God saw everything that he had made, and indeed, it was very good"—along with Revelation 21:1—"Then I saw a new heaven and a new earth." Our epistemology is based on 1 Corinthians 13:12—"Now we see in a mirror, dimly." What do we mean by this?

God creates from the future, not the past. God starts with redemption and then draws creation toward it. Or, perhaps better said, God's ongoing creative work is also God's redeeming work. Only a redeemed creation will be worthy of the appellation "very good."

The first thing God did for the creation at the moment just prior to the Big Bang was give the world a future. God gave the world a future in a double sense. The first sense of the future is openness. The gift of a future builds into physical reality its dynamism, openness, contingency, self-organization, and freedom. The bestowal of the future is the bestowal to reality of the possibility of becoming something it had never been before; it is the condition that makes ongoing change possible. This openness that characterizes futurity is what the free-will defenders among theistic evolutionists wish to preserve; but we view this not as a divine self-limitation, but rather as an expression of divine power in creation. The second sense of the future is fulfillment. God gave the world a promise that, in the end, everything would be "very good." God provides the final cause, so to speak, at least in a qualified sense.

Future-giving is the way God creates the world and redeems the world as well. The world in which we live is still being created; and when it is finally created, it will be redeemed.

As the reader can see, we do not confine the concept of creation to a single act back at the beginning, back at the Big Bang. We do not follow the deist path, according to which God creates the world and then goes on vacation to let the world run on its own. Rather, the essential creative act of imparting an open future is an ongoing one. We certainly affirm creation from nothing, *creatio ex nihilo*, to be sure. Yet, we also affirm that the creative power by which God brought being out of nonbeing continues to sustain the world, and more. Each moment God imparts openness to the future that releases the present from bondage to past causes. God's creative activity is never ceasing; each moment the entire physical universe is given its existence in such a way that it is open toward what comes next. This ceaseless future-giving by God explains why the laws of nature cannot grip nature in a rigid determinism. What we see as contingency or chance is the result of God's liberating gift of an open future.

The abiding divine activity of continuing to provide the world with an open future we refer to as continuing creation, *creatio continua*. Theologians of previous generations have not necessarily used this vocabulary. Presuming that the act of creation was a completed act in the distant past, theologians have traditionally employed different terms for God's sustaining of the universe and providential care. *Preservatio* or preservation refers to God's sustaining of existence. God preserves the world's existence by preventing it from dropping back into nonbeing. If we think of God's creation from nothing as the act prior to time that makes time and space possible, then we need a separate concept to identify God's activity within the temporal stream. *Conservatio* or *concursus* provides this. It refers to God's ongoing activities within time and space, concurrent with the activities of creatures such as ourselves. *Concursus* does not obviate the independence of creaturely activity; rather, it simply places God's activity within the world's temporal flow. *Gubernatio* or governance indicates that God's providence is not without purpose. God works with a promise or aim or goal. For God to achieve the divine aim, we can expect further activity such as purifying, delivering, reconciling, and consummating the created order.[1] Theologians working with such distinctions did not intend to sever the tie between God's creating and sustaining work, to be sure; in fact, the latter was seen as an extension of the former.

Our plan here is to account for these traditional theological concerns within the rubric of continuing creation. The act of drawing the world from nonbeing into being is not limited to a once-for-all event in the past. God is doing it right now. Without God's vigilant activity as what we call the primal cause, the world would immediately cease to exist and we would never know the difference. Moment by moment in a continuous temporal flow, God is drawing the world into being and protecting it from falling into nonbeing; and this accounts for what previous theologians thought to be God's sustaining or preserving work. Rather than as preserving a creation already complete, we view God's creative work as ongoing. It is yet to become complete in the eschatological future. Right now, we creatures are on the way to becoming who we will be. So also is the entire creation still under construction, so to speak, yet to be completed and yet to be judged "very good."

New Creation As an Emergent Whole

On the one hand, God's gift of futurity to the physical world provides openness to change and self-organization. On the other hand, God's eschatological future embodies an aim, namely, the harmony and benefit of all God's creatures.

In his commentary on Genesis 1:1, Basil of Caesarea says, "The world was not created by chance and without reason, but for a useful end, and for the great advantage of all beings."[2] Neither alpha nor omega belong to chance, even if much of what happens in between does.

Key to our understanding of creation is the concept of epigenesis. We do not use the term as sociobiologists do to refer to the genetic leash on cultural creativity. Rather, we use it to refer to the transformative dynamism in cosmic and evolutionary history. Coming from the Greek, *genesis* means "to create or generate," and *epi* means "again" or "on top of." Thus, *epigenesis* refers to ongoing creativity.[3] Its antonym is *archonic* creation, from the Greek *arche*, meaning both "beginning" and "governance." Rather than assume that everything is governed by the way the world began, we affirm epigenetic newness as every day's new possibility.

With epigenesis comes the possibility, though not the necessity, of emergence. Specifically, we refer to the emergence of new wholes. According to holistic thinking, the whole is greater than the sum of the parts. Evolutionary history has witnessed the emergence of living creatures, which, as organisms, constitute wholes that reorganize and give new meaning to the chemical parts that make them up. No organism can be reduced to its chemical components and retain its identity as a living creature.[4] Such holistic achievements in the history of nature demonstrate epigenesis at work.

New wholes transform past parts. Integration into new, more comprehensive unities preserve while renewing what came before. This holistic complexification process is nonlinear. Adding a new whole changes an entire situation in a significant way. The degree of transformative effect renders redemption possible. By analogy, we apply what we have observed as emergent holism to God's eschatological promises to see if this method yields increased understanding.

The new heaven and new earth prophesied by the biblical Apocalypse will transform, yet preserve, the entire history of cosmic creation. What God did at the beginning to draw the physical world from nonbeing into being, along with God's continuous sustaining of the natural order during its period of self-organization, will be taken up into the consummate eschatological new creation. God's creative activity within nature and within human history is derivative from his eschatological act of redeeming the whole of the cosmos. Where we find ourselves today is looking back to alpha, to *creatio ex nihilo*, and looking forward to omega, the new creation *ex vetere*, out of what has come before.[5] The new creation will be the result of what God's Spirit does to the present creation.

The new creation will be a physical creation, even if it is pervaded by the divine Spirit. "Death will be no more; mourning and crying and pain will be no more, for the first things have passed away" (Rev. 21:4). The violence, suffering, and death so inescapable in Darwin's world will become only a past memory. This is the component of redemption in the new creation. What we have accepted as the laws of nature to date will have to undergo modification. The new creation "can be free from suffering," writes John Polkinghorne, "for it is conceivable that the divinely ordained laws of nature appropriate to a world making itself through its own evolving history should give way to a differently constituted form of 'matter,' appropriate to a universe 'freely returned' from independence to an existence of integration with its Creator."[6] Exactly how the laws of nature could be modified to eliminate the suffering of sentient beings is difficult for our scientifically informed imaginations to conceive, because now we only see through a mirror dimly.[7] Yet, nothing short of this is the divine promise. Figuring out how to accomplish it will be up to God's imagination.

We can see that the arrival of the new heaven and new earth will not signal the abandonment of the old heaven and old earth. The new creation will consist of refashioning the present creation, a weaving of the divine thread throughout the fabric of physical reality. God's grace will clothe every creature, and every creature will freely don its redemptive garments. God's spirit will imbue everything bodily while everything bodily will retain an enhanced self-identity. The creation will constitute a single, all-encompassing sacrament. Although we consider ourselves theists, we can imagine embracing an eschatological panentheism.

Certainly the reader can see that we have no sympathy for the school of thought that tries to collapse the Christian understanding of creation into the so-called *Epic of Evolution*. We believe it should be the other way around: Evolutionary history should fit within the broader story of God's creative and redeeming work.

Perhaps the reader can also see that we have considerable sympathy for Teilhard's grand vision of cosmogenesis. Anticipating the emergence of a divinely imbued cosmic harmony provides our orienting vision. Yet we differ from Teilhard on one important point. Whereas Teilhard locates *telos* as a Christification principle within the evolutionary process, we locate it in God's eschatological act that will retroactively consummate all that has gone before. What will emerge as the omega of creation will involve more than the world's autonomous self-organization; it will involve a new divine act of giving the world a unifying future, an eschatological and redemptive future.

How Should We Read Genesis 1:1–2:4*a*?

In the beginning, God created by uttering the Word. Actually, God's Word is not limited to the beginning. God's Word is eternal; and it is also incarnate in Jesus Christ. And we receive God's Word in the form of promise. God plans to keep his Word.

Might we think of the opening account of creation in Genesis 1:1–2:4*a* as describing not merely a beginning, but also the present time? Could we think of the creation week of seven days as inclusive of the entire history of the creation from Big Bang to whatever will become of the universe in the future? Could evolutionary history constitute one small episode in the divine *Epic of Creation:* "Let the earth bring forth living creatures" (Gen. 1:24)? Could we see ourselves today standing between the initial moment when God opened his divine mouth to say, "Let there be," and the final moment when God declares that, behold, it is "very good"? Could we still be looking forward to the Sabbath day, to God's first day of rest yet in the future?

Augustine nearly approached such a schematization when wrestling with the question: Does creation out of nothing take place in time or in eternity? Regardless of his answer, the tantalizing thought raised by this asking is that God's eternal Word might be inclusive of the entire scope of evolutionary and even cosmic history. God's "word is spoken eternally, and by it all things are uttered eternally. It is not the case that what was being said comes to an end, and something else is then said, so that everything is uttered in a succession with a conclusion, but everything is said in the simultaneity of eternity. Otherwise time and change would already exist, and there would not be a true eternity and true immortality."[8] What we can take home from Augustine's musings is that the Word by which God drew being from nonbeing, drew a physical world out of a nothing that preceded it, is the very same Word by which all of reality is presently sustained and will be consummated. What we are adding here is that we consider that future consummation the crowning conclusion of creation, a single inclusive divine act whereby what comes into existence is perfected in its existence.

Deep Time

Now we turn those five credential questions we asked of other theistic evolutionists toward ourselves: deep time, natural selection, common descent, divine action, and theodicy.

We will start with the question posed to theologians by the commitment in evolutionary biology to the concept of deep time. Charles Darwin was anxious about attempts to keep short the period of time estimated between life's beginnings and today's kaleidoscope of life-forms. If the biblical creationists of the nineteenth century would be right that the earth had been created in 4004 B.C., then a separate creation for each species would be required, and the slow process of descent with modification would be obliterated. Darwin rejected this view of time out of hand, of course. He even got nervous when Lord Kelvin estimated that the earth had been in existence for 100 million years. This would still not be enough time for descent with modification to make transitions from one species to another, feared Darwin. Time, time, he needed more time. Current estimates at 4.5 billion years of earthy history allow today's Darwinists to sleep soundly at night.

What about today's theologians? Theistic evolutionists do not answer like young earth creationists on the question of time. Theistic evolutionists have had no difficulty taking deep time on board, as we have seen. Even the most conservative B. B. Warfield finds no distinctively theological grounds for mandating either a young earth or an old earth. This is for science to decide. We, too, will leave the question of chronicling the geohistory and biohistory of our planet to scientific reasoning.

Perhaps what makes this relatively easy is the awareness within Christian consciousness that our experience of time is so much a matter of perspective. The meaning of history and the meaning of our individual lives is perspectival; and Christians treat this with near humor in order to avoid the tragedy of overestimating the importance of our particular place in the larger temporal flow. Biblical allusions and metaphors border on the humorous when comparing God's eternity to our experience with temporality: "For a thousand years in your sight are like yesterday when it is past" (Ps. 90:4) or "with the Lord one day is like a thousand years, and a thousand years are like one day" (2 Pet. 3:8).

More important than chronological calendar time (*chronos*) is the *kairos*, or the moment of time's fulfillment. Such a moment can refer mundanely to a definitive time in one's destiny. "For everything there is a season, and a time for every matter under heaven" (Eccles. 3:1). Such a moment can also refer to a temporal decision with eternal significance. Jesus announces, "The time is fulfilled, and the kingdom of God has come near; repent, and believe in the good news" (Mark 1:15). Finally, such a moment marks a cosmic threshold. God has a plan for the "fullness of time, to gather up all things in him [Christ], things in heaven and things on earth" (Eph. 1:10). The simple flow of calendar time or even geological time, regardless of how many billions of years may be involved, is less important to Christian consciousness than the *kairos* moment, which becomes the lens through which all other times are interpreted and evaluated. What we look forward to now is the future new creation, the advent of the *kairos* that will reinterpret all previous *kairoi* as well as chronological time throughout cosmic history.

Even so, the concept of deep time corroborated by biology, geology, and cosmology leaves an impression on human consciousness. Our individual lifetime is so short compared to nature's duration. Our historical era is so minute compared to the eons of cosmic history. So much has happened in the epic of life's story on earth that has never been told nor could be; yet all that has happened coconstitutes the reality of which we are a part and for which we believe God finds meaning. And projections for nature's future stretch out for eons even longer, confounding our minds with our inability to gain a sense of proportion.

We had become used to thinking of God as mysterious, used to thinking of transcendent reality as infinite and beyond the ability of our finite minds to comprehend. Now, thinking about the finite natural world elicits the same kind of thinking. Deep time in biological history, let alone cosmic history, catapults our thoughts into a yawning canyon of unfathomable temporal duration. Although certainly unintended by Darwin who simply sought to make temporal room for common descent with modification, deep time indirectly elicits a sense of the divine Creator's majesty.

> Lord, you have been our dwelling place
> in all generations.
> Before the mountains were brought forth,
> or ever you had formed the earth and the world,
> from everlasting to everlasting you are God. (Ps. 90:1-2)

Here in our constructive proposal for theistic evolution, we do not, by implication, incorporate into theology a Newtonian view of time as an empty container to be filled up with a chronicle of historical events, even a large number of events. We are not looking at our calendar with a bunch of empty future dates and wondering just when the new creation will arrive. We are not looking for signs of the apocalypse, an activity Jesus had warned us against (Mark 13). Rather, we see the eschatological new creation as the next moment, the future of the very moment in which we now find ourselves. It is the eschatological pull of God's future right now that is drawing the present out from its past and relieving us from slipping either into nonbeing or into the grip of past determinisms. The divine power of renewal and liberation is the very power by which the world is continually being created. The new creation is the retroactive source of the present creation. Fulfillment is as close to us as the next moment, and it is influencing us now. The fragmentary ways we realize the goodness of creation now are proleptic anticipations of the eschatological completion of the creative process yet to be consummated. Whether in the context of deep time or brief time, the influence on all time by God's promised new creation is where we direct our vision.

Natural Selection

It is not hard to imagine the reaction of Victorian society upon hearing Darwin's proposal—all of the life that we see around us is the result of a force called natural selection, by which those less fit do not reproduce. The cold impersonality and raw violence of this new force of nature seemed to be captured in a verse penned in 1850 by Alfred, Lord Tennyson:

> "Who trusted God was love indeed
> And love Creation's final law—
> Tho' Nature, red in tooth and claw
> With ravine, shriek'd against his creed—"

While this was written almost a decade before the publication of *Origin of Species*, the lines have come to symbolize the starkness of the evolutionary model.

Certainly, a part of the reaction of those opposed to the Darwinian paradigm comes from a revulsion with a world in which such a principle could rule, a conviction that a loving God would not let this be the case. We come below to the issue of theodicy that this raises. For now, we must ask ourselves, as theistic evolutionists, how we answer the question: Can we accept the force of natural selection as a reasonable explanation of how life evolved?

The question goes beyond the bloody picture that confronted the Victorians. The neo-Darwinian model also throws the concepts of chance and randomness into the equation. Thus, the current form of the model includes the absence of purpose and design in the process, the lack of any inner *telos*, as we have defined it earlier.

Like the theistic evolutionists we met in the previous chapter, we accept the science of evolution as it is embodied in the principle of natural selection. We admit that, within the bounds of the scientific method, no purpose or design can be discerned for this process. We see no *telos* within the process of evolution. However, in our broad eschatological argument we can certainly see a purpose *for* natural selection within the epic of creation. We agree with the position that the contingency found in nature is a reflection of the freedom inherent in creation. However, we do not wish to rely upon the free-will argument to supply the reason for this contingency.

We recognize that the scientific enterprise constructs conceptual models of the natural world. Our critical realist view leads us to the awareness that these models are an approximation of reality. One way in which this approximation is arrived at is by a retrospective analysis of systems. The Darwinian model is one such retrospective or historical account. Given the self-imposed limitations of its method, science can only view creation in process, not in its origin or its final state.

As a result, we argue that natural selection and the contingency by which variations arise are features of an ongoing creation (*creatio continua*) that permit the arrival at the end point. Without this randomness the possibilities are eliminated and the end point is known from the beginning. In a mathematical sense, we can say that maximizing the number of degrees of freedom in the system gives it the greatest potential. The alternative is a deterministic view that belies the continuing creative power of God and restricts us to just one path. Our eschatological argument is such that all possible paths must be available for creation; and earth's self-organizing history contributes the material content of creation's fulfillment. It is to this evolutionary history that God can finally look back and say that it is "very good."

Common Descent

The incredible variety of living things made Darwin's conclusion of descent with modification from a common ancestor seem completely counterintuitive. How could this be? What evidence would convince us of the logic of this statement?

Unlike the scientific creationists, we accept the interpretation of the data of evolutionary biology as the marks of common descent rather than separate creation of individual kinds. The arguments from the fossil record and from DNA sequence analysis converge into a theoretical framework, which, as Pope John Paul II has said, makes this more than a hypothesis:

> Today, almost half a century after the publication of *(Humani Generis)*, new knowledge has led to the recognition of the theory of evolution as more than a hypothesis. It is indeed remarkable that this theory has been progressively accepted by researchers, following a series of discoveries in various fields of knowledge. The convergence, neither sought nor fabricated, of the results of work that was conducted independently is in itself a significant argument in favor of this theory.[9]

Therefore, since we accept common descent as the most likely explanation of the data, what effect does this have on our position as theistic evolutionists? The scientists and theologians we have encountered in chapter 6 all embrace common descent as a pivotal feature of the Darwinian model. Their theological reflection focuses on the unity of the created living world. We, as a part of that world, share a common history, as evidenced in the molecular mechanisms that operate within our cells. This awareness approaches, in a sense, the cosmological understanding of American Indians, for whom the entire universe is connected and conscious.[10]

There are two aspects to this awareness. First, the ecological implication of the unity of creation places us in a position of stewardship or, in the American Indian view, relationship to the rest of the cosmos. Therefore we are called to live in this unity, to be a responsible part of the whole. The outdated translation of Genesis that gave us "dominion" over the earth no longer justifies a strictly utilitarian exploitation of nature when we see ourselves as part of the continuum of life.

Second, the common descent of humanity emphasizes the unity of our species. This flies in the face of racial distinctions that have been used to set social policy. We have discussed, in chapter 3, the uses of the Darwinian model in this regard. Social Darwinism and the eugenics programs that derived from it were failed uses of the biological data to justify the supremacy of one racial group over others. The contemporary fields of sociobiology and evolutionary psychology, though admirable in their attempts to emphasize the common features of our species, still harbor the possibility of such divisive uses. As theistic evolutionists, we reject the use of the evolutionary model to separate us, one from another. Common descent seems to provide physical corroboration for spiritual unity as Paul described it in his first letter to the Corinthians, in which he wrote, "For in the one Spirit we were all baptized into one body—Jews or Greeks, slaves or free—and we were all made to drink of one Spirit" (1 Cor. 12:13).

However, as theists, we also have a conviction that humans are more than just the sum of their physical parts. While the body plan we have, in the form of our DNA, descends from a common ancestor shared by all living things, our spiritual side is somehow different from that of other life. Therefore, we need to confront the concept of the human soul. Here we must rely on our critical realist view of the biological data. We understand that science is not, by its very nature, equipped to observe the nonmaterial. We hold that this self-limitation of the method cannot be used to argue that the nonmaterial does not exist. We hold that the human soul is a special creation of God. Even if the soul is an emergent phenomenon not requiring an interventionist interpretation of divine action, the soul still constitutes a level of creative transcendence beyond our mere physical past. We do not see theological judgments such as this to be a violation of the natural order as measured by the scientific method.

Why do we need to posit the existence of a human soul with such distinct properties? Our eschatological perspective relies upon the soul as the link between our future resurrection and our present anticipation of renewal beyond death. The concept of the soul is a place marker, so to speak, that points to the relationship we have with God. We are temporal beings pondering a divine promise for everlasting life, and our soul marks the dimension of the eternal within the ephemeral.

Is the soul connected to what is conscious, to the mental, the rational, the reflective? Yes. Although human beings may not be the only sentient life with the ability to be reflective, we would argue that our consciousness must be of a distinct kind. Clearly our genetic potential, our nervous system, and our complex brains are products of our evolutionary history; and our consciousness is somehow intimately connected with the resulting physical structure. Perhaps our complex evolutionary history has made possible the rise of the soul; and perhaps our biological history has conditioned the operations of our mental processes. Yet the soul is more than the body. The human soul operates out of or through our physical structure, to be sure; yet it is not reducible to this structure.

As theistic evolutionists, we still need to reconcile our concept of the soul and our conscious confidence in the divine promise of resurrection with the scientific description of nature we wish to respect and celebrate. Within the scope of what empirical science can explicate, nothing can be said about a future reality such as resurrection; nor can anything be said scientifically about consciousness within the human soul. Where, then, derives the relationship between the physical and the spiritual? How can we open the discourse between these apparently disparate concepts? We use the idea of epigenesis that allows continuing creation to result in the emergence of properties that are more than the sum of the previous parts. In this view, consciousness itself is seen as just such an emergent property. Therefore, we attempt to avoid the dualistic trap and to embrace a position that sees the intimate union between what is spiritual and what is physical.

Divine Action

> In the beginning when God created the heavens and the earth, the earth was a formless void and darkness covered the face of the deep, while a wind from God swept over the face of the waters. Then God said, "Let there be light"; and there was light. (Gen. 1:1-3)

Thomas Aquinas, using the then-current Aristotelian system of understanding the natural world, realized that *creatio ex nihilo* requires a cause that is different from the causes that describe the nexus of already-created things. This means that the universe, all that is, cannot come into existence by itself. Therefore, the second of Thomas's five ways of coming to the existence of God is the argument of a first efficient cause.[11] Recall that, for Aristotle and Thomas, the efficient cause of a thing is synonymous with the agency that brings the thing about. Thomas argues that no thing can be its own efficient cause, since this would require that it pre-exist itself. He concludes that there must be a first efficient cause, which he says can be called God.

This first efficient cause is also called the primary cause. All other causes follow this one and are therefore called secondary causes. Science, by its own self-defining methodological and philosophical limitations, deals with secondary causes. Admittedly, this metaphysical language has fallen into disuse, so much so that in a recent E-mail exchange with a scientific colleague, the use of the terms primary and secondary causation were termed by him "medieval theology." Nevertheless, we contend that the laws of the universe as science comes to know them are secondary to the action of God.

This is an important point for us as theistic evolutionists and deserves more definition. Let's consider how it is that science can only examine secondary causes. The scientific method consists of a series of prescribed steps. One formulation of it is as follows:

1. Observation
2. Hypothesis formation
3. Experimentation
4. Revision of hypothesis based on experimental results
5. Reiteration of this process
6. Formulation of a theory or law

Notice that the process begins with the observation of something that exists or occurs in the physical world. In fact, this restriction on observation to the material was a part of the method from the beginning and was placed into firm philosophical context by David Hume. After defending his skeptical stance and arguing against cause and effect in favor of temporal sequence, he then went on to place limits on the proper objects for scientific inquiry: "It seems to me, that the only objects of the abstract science or of demonstration are quantity and number, and that all attempts to extend this more perfect species of knowledge beyond these bounds are mere sophistry and illusion."[12]

Thus, science is limited to measurements that can be made on physical systems. And so, observations in the scientific method are restricted to physical things that exist and, therefore, are the effects of a primary or secondary cause or are themselves secondary causes. For this reason we, without being critical of science, argue that science is blind to primary causation.

Of course, this does not inhibit some scientists from surmising that primary causation does not exist. The denial of primary causation is unwarranted by scientific observation, to be sure. Yet we see those arguing the case for ontological materialism and atheistic interpretations of Darwin's model as making this unwarranted move. As theistic evolutionists, however, we take the strong position that Darwinian theory, as a product of the scientific method, can only be about secondary causes. This reserves to our theological reflection the place for primary divine action in creation.

As we have seen, Thomas did not just consider *creatio ex nihilo*, but also argued for the continuing action of God in creation—*creatio continua*. We hold that this divine action, which stretches over the entire historical sweep of the created order, even to its eschatological limit, is also primary cause. Our claim to this sustaining work of God distinguishes our position from that of the deist. For us, God's action in creation is constant, keeping it from devolution into nonbeing as well as calling forth the newness from the possibilities that are inherent in the very fabric of the created order.

Theodicy

Finally, the question of theodicy. One of the temptations for theologians when offering a premature reconciliation of evolutionary science with Christian theology is to concede that violence, suffering, and death are merely natural and hence value-neutral. This concession is too much. Just because such things are natural does not make them God's will. From the point of view of faith, we cannot simply sigh and say, "Oh, that's nature's way," as if this concludes an argument. Nature is not value-neutral, from the perspective of faith in the God of the Bible.

We must begin with what we do not know. What we do not know theologically is why violence, suffering, and death have had to play such a role in the creation up to this point. Job asked God about this, and Job's questioning was filled with grief, impatience, and passion. When God responded to Job from the whirlwind, the divine answer to this human question did not resolve the impenetrable mystery. "Where were you when I laid the foundation of the earth? Tell me, if you have understanding" (Job 38:4), demanded God rhetorically. God would not grant to Job a resolution to the tension, even though God would care for Job providentially. Though Job could not understand why we need to be victims of suffering, he could understand that the God of creation is also the God of redemption. "I know that my Redeemer lives," he said (Job 19:25).

With this in mind, we appeal to the Theology of the Cross as we receive it from the Lutheran branch of the Protestant Reformation (even though one of this book's authors is a Catholic and the other Lutheran). The cross of Jesus Christ comes to us as a double paradox. The first paradox is that it hides what it reveals. To view a suffering and dying man nailed to a cross is to see just the opposite of what we might expect from a God who is omnipotent and eternal and immutable; yet we say this very God of cosmic majesty is fully present under the conditions of finitude, sin, and death. In the cross we experience the revelation of God under the appearance of the opposite, *revelatio sub contrario specie*. The second paradox is that we see God participating in creaturely suffering, sharing in the suffering of all creatures in nature and history; yet this very God pronounces a curse on suffering and promises to end it. Divine participation in suffering is not a blessing of it; rather, just the opposite, it is the prelude to its overcoming. Death on the cross is the door to resurrection and eternal life.

"The cross does not bless suffering, punishment, and the rest," writes church historian Timothy Wengert; "It forces us to tell the truth that such things are curses. Suffering is not some great salvific act in and of itself. On the contrary, it is God's alien work, opposed to God's very nature. It sends humanity to the slaughterhouse. . . . Thus, the cross reveals human suffering for what it truly is—a curse—and thereby opens us up to receive God's own, proper work and blessing in the resurrection."[13] What we know theologically is that God's proper work is redemption, resurrection, and renewal.

Because God sides with the victims of suffering, our constructive proposal for a theistic interpretation of evolution cannot invoke a divine blessing on the survival of the fittest, either in ontology or ethics. That natural selection is a principle describing how over deep time some species survive while others die out is simply warranted scientifically. Yet, here in a very limited way, we side with the biblical creationists. The struggle for survival is a mark of fallen creation. We differ from the creationists, however, in temporally locating the Garden of perfection. They locate it in the past, in an original perfection from which subsequent nature has fallen. We locate it in the future, that toward which creation is rising. Our world is being redeemed while it is being created. The Easter resurrection of

Jesus Christ is for the theologian a prolepsis that anticipates the new creation yet to come. The eschatological new creation as envisioned in the New Testament will put an end to violence, suffering, and death.

Our answer to the theodicy question is not a logical one. We do not invoke twists of logic to justify God for creating a world of struggle with survival of the fittest and all its accompanying waste. Rather, we point to God's promise of resurrection and renewal. Death is not the final chapter in the story of God's drama with nature. Life is. Eternal life is. This renders theodicy a temporal problem, not an eternal one.

Theology of Nature Versus Natural Theology

Our constructive proposal belongs in the file cabinet under "theology of nature." We draw upon distinctively theological resources such as biblical revelation and history of religious thought to establish the perspective from which we view the natural world. We draw upon God's self-revelation in the cross of Jesus Christ, and we draw upon God's promise in the Easter resurrection of Jesus Christ. Such revelation provides the lenses through which we view the natural world understood by empirical research and scientific reasoning. This is the form our quadrilateral—Scripture, tradition, experience, and reason—takes.

Our method here is the reverse of what we might find in a file labeled "natural theology." Under that label, William Paley and his twenty-first-century heirs watch for design within biological processes; then they argue that design is evidence for a transcendent designer. The direction is from understanding nature to understanding God. The problem with such a natural theology, as we see it, is that the designer imagined can be nothing more than the designer of violence, suffering, death, and enormous waste. Nature does not all by itself speak the voice of grace or offer the promise of renewal.

Created Co-Creator

As we turn to theological anthropology, we find affinity with the concept developed by some theistic evolutionists such as Philip Hefner: the human being as the *created co-creator*.[14] What does this mean? We are passive when it comes to being created by God. We are created; we did not create ourselves. Yet we are also active when it comes to our influence on the ongoing evolution of the natural world. We are creative.

We have been endowed by God through the evolutionary process with capacities and opportunities to develop science and technology. As tool makers, *homo faber*, we can fabricate new physical realities. We can rearrange the elements in our environment. We can transform cotton into corduroys, stones into steel, petroleum into plastic, dams into dynamos. We can envision future possibilities that had never existed in the past. And, in some instances, we can actualize those visions.

Below we will take up the topic of genetic engineering. We find ourselves on the threshold of designing our own descendants. We can modify descent with modification by speeding up modification. We can modify natural selection by selecting the nature we design. We can modify survival of the fittest by protecting the unfit from violence by the fit. We can, in short, influence the future path of evolution.

From anthropology this leads us to ethics. We are, as the existentialist philosophers told us, condemned to freedom.[15] We are free. Whether we asked for it or not, this freedom lays upon our shoulders the mantle of responsibility. These technological capacities provide opportunities for either improvement or destruction. Whatever modifications we engineer into the human or even animal gene pool, we cannot avoid having an influence. The ethical question is: Can we in the present generation envision wholesome possibilities, make the right decisions, and take the actions that will enhance human health and global well-being?

Overcoming the Naturalistic Fallacy

With anthropology comes ethics. We human beings as created co-creators have a responsibility to shepherd the natural and technological processes over which we have an influence toward a vision of the good. The vision of the coming new creation—symbolized in Scripture as the Kingdom of God—locates the good in God's future while providing middle axioms for guiding right conduct. Right conduct consists of practical means toward a good end. This is how ethical thinking works.

The concept of the good *(tou agathou idea)* already in Plato had a transcendent component to it.[16] The good is that for which we strive because we do not yet possess it, said this ancient Greek philosopher. The biblical vision of the transcendent good is embodied in the prophetic vision of God's will for the future. The ancient divine covenant to the Hebrews for a "promised land" becomes the model for God's new covenant to us in Jesus' Easter resurrection for a promised "new creation." It is that for which the creation has been groaning in travail up until now (Rom. 8:22), that for which all things strive but have not yet attained. The good became incarnate for a moment at the Easter resurrection of Jesus, in his person; the rest of the creation now awaits its total incarnation in the eschatological advent of God's kingdom.

Not only is the good transcendent, but also it is redemptive. Any embodiment of the good would incorporate qualities not yet available to the world of nature, let alone the world of sin. Among these qualities would be exemption from violence, suffering, and death. One implication stands out: Nature, as evolution has bestowed it upon us, is incapable of exhaustively embodying what is good.

It is at this point that we run into difficulties with ethical philosophies based upon evolutionary biology. Both social Darwinism of the nineteenth century and sociobiology more recently seek to establish guidelines for moral conduct based upon survival of the fittest. By fittest here, they refer to reproductive fitness—that is, producing children whose genes survive. For social Darwinism, this meant *laissez-faire* capitalism and similar social policies would simply let the weak fall by the wayside. For sociobiology, reciprocal altruism as a means to perpetuate the genetic codes of close kin would become the social ideal. These ethical systems begin with what they find in nature and then declare this to be the good after which human beings should strive. Whether capitalism or altruism, what we *ought to do* is here based on what already *is* the case in nature. Missing in evolutionary naturalism is any appeal to a transcendent source for the good.

Philosopher G. E. Moore dubbed this type of argument the "naturalistic fallacy." "To argue that a thing is good *because* it is 'natural,' or bad *because* it is 'unnatural,' in these common senses of the term, is therefore certainly fallacious."[17] Moore criticized specifically evolutionistic ethics that maintain that the course of evolution shows us the direction in which we *are* developing and, for this reason, shows us the direction that we ought to develop. Ethical sanction gets drawn from being more developed or evolved. Yet the state of being more evolved does not in itself make it better or higher. To conflate a natural condition with an imperative—an *ought*—is fallacious. Since the work of Moore, it has become nearly axiomatic that an ethicist should avoid conflating an *ought* with what is already found in nature. We agree that evolutionary naturalism is fallacious, and we agree with Moore that "Evolution has very little indeed to say to Ethics."[18]

We would like to add the following observation to Moore's argument: To commit the naturalistic fallacy would prevent us from envisioning qualitative transformation. To conflate *ought* with *is* leads to a blessing of the status quo. Natural selection or survival of the fittest constitute what *is*, and an ethic that says this *ought* to be the good for which we strive in the future would preclude striving for transformation, preclude rescuing the weak or healing the sick or making peace among nations. No principles presently visible in evolutionary processes provide warrant for thinking that sentient creatures will ever escape the predator-prey interaction or experience life without violence, suffering, and death. No hope exists for nature that is anything but blood "red in tooth and claw." The naturalistic fallacy would remove hope from ethics as well.

Our view is that human ethics must be realistic about where nature has placed us, but our ethical visions should carry us well beyond. Ethical visions of a better life include social coexistence without violence, healing that relieves us from suffering, and at minimum acceptance of death and at maximum hope for resurrection. Politics, medicine, and faith are cultural means for us to envision directions for transformation. The redemptive renewal we envision here anticipates the good for which we strive. We advocate proleptic ethics—that is, we act now on the basis of what we anticipate God's transformative future will be.[19]

An evolutionary ethic all by itself lacks the ground for projecting transformatory visions. It could only endorse the status quo. It lacks warrant on its own to promote healing. It is not unusual for one to argue, on the basis of evolutionary naturalism, that we should refrain from caring for our young with defective genes in order to prevent them from reproducing. To die prior to reproductive age contributes positively to higher stages of evolutionary development. Such became the doctrine of eugenics, carried out ruthlessly by the SS during the Nazi period in Germany. Eugenics sought to advance evolution by restricting the reproduction of undesirable people. Eugenics was the evolutionary-based philosophy that justified the Final Solution to eliminate the mentally retarded, physically disabled, Gypsies, homosexuals, and the Jewish population.

In contrast to evolutionary naturalism, we locate the good for which we strive in a transcendent source, God. We begin with an eschatological vision of the new creation, of God's heavenly city where "death will be no more; mourning and crying and pain will be no more, for the first things have passed away" (Rev. 21:4). We consider this vision to be an eschatological one because it is not possible on the basis of law and chance as we currently witness them in nature. Such a vision will require a divine act for fulfillment. Yet, within present evolutionary history, contingency and openness and newness make possible human actions that in form anticipate this eschatological vision. Peace-making, healing, and comforting are the forms of right conduct that make the world a better place during the epoch assigned to us. Although we do not derive an ethic from evolution, we believe an eschatological or proleptic ethic fits our evolutionary past and present. To be a created co-creator is to steward our resources and opportunities in light of our vision of the coming new creation.

Our Genetic Future

Evolution has a past. We can expect it to have a future as well. One of the distinguishing features of future evolution is that it may contain a component of deliberate direction. Or, to put it another way, we in the human race cannot help influencing the direction of future evolution. Like a gardener in an established garden, whether we ignore it, weed it, or cultivate it further, what we decide will have an effect.

The neo-Darwinian synthesis described in chapter 2 shows what a decisive role the field of genetics plays in evolutionary theory. Genetics will be decisive in practical ways as well. As we gain the technical ability to intervene in the human genome and to engineer the genetic codes of future generations, what happens in evolution will feel the effect of human decision making. It will become, at least in part, a product of human freedom. The ethical question will be: By what vision of the good will we make the decisions regarding our genetic future?

This issue comes to the forefront of discussion in our time due in large part to the enormous influence of the Human Genome Project on the biological and even the social sciences. We know descriptively the stated purposes directing the Human Genome Project as originally conceived. First, its aim has been gathering new knowledge. The simple goal that drives all pure science is present here, namely, the desire to know. In this case it is the desire to know the sequence of the base pairs plus the location of the genes in the human genome. Second, its aim has been improving human health. The avowed ethical goal is to employ the newly acquired knowledge in further research to provide therapy for the many genetically caused diseases that plague the human family. John C. Fletcher and W. French Anderson put it eloquently: "Human gene therapy is a symbol of hope in a vast sea of human suffering due to heredity."[20] As this second health-oriented purpose is pursued, the technology for manipulating genes will be developed and questions regarding human creativity will arise. How should this creativity be directed?

Virtually no one contests the principle that new genetic knowledge should be used to improve human health and relieve suffering.[21] Yet a serious debate has arisen that distinguishes sharply between therapy for suffering persons who already exist and the health of future persons who do not yet exist. It is the debate between somatic therapy and germline therapy. By "somatic therapy" we refer to the treatment of a disease in the body cells of a living individual by trying to repair an existing defect. It consists of inserting new segments of DNA into already differentiated cells such as are found in the liver, muscle, or blood. Clinical trials are underway to use somatic modification as therapy for people suffering from diabetes, hypertension, and adenosine deaminase deficiency. By "germline therapy," however, we refer to intervention into the germ cells that would influence heredity and it is hoped will improve the quality of life for future generations. Negatively, germline intervention might help eliminate deleterious genes that predispose us to disease. Positively, though presently well beyond our technical capacity, such intervention might actually enhance human health, intelligence, or strength.

Two issues overlap here and should be sorted out for clarity. One is the issue of somatic intervention versus germline intervention. The other is the issue of therapy versus enhancement. Although somatic treatment is usually identified with therapy and germline treatment with enhancement, there are occasions where somatic treatment enhances, such as injecting growth hormones to enhance height for playing basketball. And germline intervention, at least in its initial stages of development, will aim at preventive medicine. The science of enhancement, if it comes at all, will only come later.

Now the question of playing God makes its appearance. The question of whether we are asking our scientists to play God derives from the naturalistic fallacy. This is the position of those who tacitly believe that the present state of nature provides the ethical ideal or the criterion of the good object to science and technology when it alters what we have received from nature. In the case of human genetics, those who tacitly treat human DNA as sacred and hence unalterable, fear genetic research and, most of all, germline intervention. Genetic engineering, from the naturalistic point of view, violates the sacred order of nature.

In contrast to naturalistic ethics, we locate the sacred in God, not in nature. And we locate our ethical vision in the eschatological vision where "mourning and crying and pain will be no more" (Rev. 21:4). Striving for creative advances in science and technology pressed into the service of improving human health and well-being is an inescapable ethical mandate, in our judgment.

Nevertheless, those who blow the whistle about playing God issue a warning we need to heed. The risk of exerting human creativity through germline intervention is that, though we begin with the best of intentions, the result may include negative repercussions that escape our control. Physically, our genetic engineering may disturb the strength-giving qualities of biodiversity that just may contribute indirectly to human health. Due to our inability to see the whole range of interconnected factors, we may inadvertently disturb some sort of existing balance in nature, and this disturbance could redound deleteriously.[22]

Socially, we risk contributing to stigma and discrimination. The very proffering of criteria to determine just what counts as a so-called defective gene may lead to stigmatizing all those persons who carry that gene. The very proffering of the image of the ideal child or a super strain of humanity may cultivate a sense of inferiority to those who do not measure up. To embark on a large-scale program of germline enhancement may create physical and social problems, and then we would blame the human race for its pride, its *hubris*, its stepping beyond its alleged God-defined limits. All this could bring disaster upon ourselves.

Yet we cannot allow our fears of unforeseen consequences to leave us with inaction. We need another way to look at the challenge that confronts us. The correlate concepts of God as the creator and the human as the created co-creator orient us toward the future, a future that should be better than the past or present. One of the problems with the naturalist argument against playing God is that it implicitly assumes the present state of affairs is adequate. These arguments tacitly bless the status quo. The problem with the status quo is that it is filled with human misery, some of which is genetically caused. It is possible for us to envision a better future, a future in which individuals would not have to suffer the consequences of genes such as those predisposing us to cystic fibrosis,

Alzheimer's disease, or Huntington's disease. That we should be cautious and prudent and recognize the threat of human *hubris,* we fully grant. Yet our ethical vision cannot acquiesce with present reality; it must press on to a still better future and employ human creativity with its accompanying genetic technology to move us in that direction.

Geneticist and ethicist James C. Peterson carefully parses questions of limited knowledge regarding the future effect of present germline intervention as well as questions regarding the autonomy and welfare of future persons we might affect. "There are multiple reasons to be concerned about our descendants," he writes, including "love for one's own children, the worth of all human beings, membership in the moral community of humanity, love of neighbor, and fear of God. . . . Actually, choices that shape future generations are unavoidable. What we can do out of respect for future persons is make changes incrementally and reversibly that are likely to increase future choice. . . . The genetic heritage we pass on to future generations should be a considered part of our current reflection as we make choices that will deeply affect our children and theirs."[23]

By our acting or not acting, what future generations receive from us will be the result of our ethical decision. Christians should greet this unavoidable moral situation as an opportunity, an opportunity to anticipate human betterment. "In the not-too-distant future," says Pope John Paul II, "we can reasonably foresee that the whole genome sequencing will open new paths for therapeutic purposes. Thus the sick, to whom it was impossible to give proper treatment due to frequently fatal hereditary pathologies, will be able to benefit from the treatment needed to improve their condition and possibly to cure them. By acting on the subject's unhealthy genes, it will also be possible to prevent the recurrence of genetic diseases and their transmission."[24] To prevent the genetic transmission of disease will take human creativity operating out of a vision of better health for future generations.

The Not-Yet Future and the Ethics of Creativity

Would a future-oriented theology of creation and its concomitant understanding of the human being as God's created co-creator provide a version of theistic evolution that could deal adequately with the ethical issues such as those posed by the frontier of genetic research? Yes. Here is why. First, a future-oriented theology of creation is not stymied by giving priority to existing nature over future persons who do not yet exist. We believe future persons make a moral claim on us now. The next generation has a right to ask that we act responsibly toward their welfare. Or, to put it in terms of ethical opportunity, a theology of continuing creation looks forward to the new, to those who are yet to come into existence as part of the moral community to which we belong.

Second, such a theology is realistic about the dynamic quality of our situation. Everything changes. There is no standing still. What we do affects and is affected by the future. We are condemned to be creative for good or ill.

Third, the future is built into this ethical vision. Once we apprehend that God intends a future, our task is to discern as best we can the direction of divine purpose and employ that as an ethical guide. When we invoke the apocalyptic symbol of the New Jerusalem, where "crying and pain will be no more," then this will inspire and guide the decisions we make today that will affect our progeny tomorrow.

Theologian Karl Rahner has emphasized that self-transcendence and the possibility for something new belong indelibly to human nature. Human existence is "open and indetermined."[25] That to which we are open is the infinite horizon; we are open to a fulfillment yet to be determined by the infinite and the ineffable mystery of God. If we try to draw any middle axioms that connect this sublime theological vision to an ethic appropriate to genetic engineering or other attempts to influence evolution, openness to the future translates into responsibility for the future, even our evolutionary future. Such a theological vision undercuts a conservative or reactionary proscription against intervening in the evolutionary process. The temptation to condemn genetic research and its application Rahner describes as "symptomatic of a cowardly and comfortable conservatism hiding behind misunderstood Christian ideals."[26] The concept of the created co-creator we invoke here is a cautious but creative Christian concept that begins with a vision of openness to God's future and responsibility for the human future.

The health and well-being of future generations not yet born is a matter of ethical concern when viewed within the scope of a theology of creation that emphasizes God's ongoing creative work and that pictures the human being as the created co-creator. A vision of future possibilities, not the present status quo, orients and directs ethical activity. When applied to the issue of germline intervention for the purpose of enhancing the quality of human life, the door must be kept open so that we can look through, squint, and focus our eyes to see just what possibilities loom before us. This will include a realistic review of the limits and risks of genetic technology. But realism about technological limits and risks is insufficient warrant for prematurely shutting the door on possibilities for an improved human future. Rather than playing God or taking God's place, seeking to actualize new possibilities means we are being truly human.

Conclusion

One characteristic of being truly human is becoming quite visible in our modern world, namely, the God-given curiosity to study nature through the eyes of science as well as tinker with nature through the tools of technology in order to make the world a better place. That curiosity about how nature came to be what it is has led to the theory of evolution. Scientists have been reading the Book of Nature and writing a book review to be read by students in our school systems.

We want our young people to learn from what our scientists are learning from the Book of Nature. We also want our young people to read the Book of Scripture. The Book of Nature reports on life; the Book of Scripture reports on eternal life. The younger Charles Darwin thought this, too. In the early editions of *Origin of Species*, Darwin opened with a quotation from Francis Bacon admonishing us to read "the book of God's word" and also "the book of God's works." This is sound advice.

NOTES

1. War? Really?

1. See Peter M. J. Hess, "God's Two Books: Special Revelation and Natural Science in the Christian West" in *Bridging Science and Religion*, ed. Ted Peters and Gaymon Bennett (London: SCM Press, 2002), 123-40.

2. The National Academy of Sciences, *Teaching about Evolution and the Nature of Science* (Washington D.C.: National Academy Press, 1998), 58. For updates on the controversy between evolutionary science and creationism, a most valuable resource is The National Center for Science Education, Inc., directed by Dr. Eugenie Scott at www.ncseweb.org.

3. Michael Ruse, "Evolution as Religion," unpublished essay, 13 May 2000. See Michael Ruse, "Is Evolution a Secular Religion?" *Science* 299 (7 March 2003): 1523-24. What contemporary American society appears to be experiencing is the oppressiveness of established evolutionary science in public education that presumes dogmatic authority and roots out heretics. Not only do creationists rebel, so do Native Americans. See Vine Deloria Jr., *Evolution, Creationism, and Other Modern Myths* (Golden, Colo.: Fulcrum Publishing, 2002).

4. Charles Darwin, *The Life and Letters of Charles Darwin, Including an Autobiographical Chapter*, ed. Francis Darwin, 2 vols. (New York: Basic Books, 1959), 2:312.

5. Huxley later disclaimed the word "equivocal." See http://www.oum.ox.ac.uk/debate4.htm.

6. Julian Huxley, "The Evolutionary Vision," in *Issues in Evolution*, vol. 3, *Evolution after Darwin*, ed. Sol Tax and Charles Callender (Chicago: University of Chicago Press, 1960), 260.

7. Stephen Jay Gould, *The Structure of Evolutionary Theory* (Cambridge, Mass.: Harvard University Press, 2002), 59.

8. Edward O. Wilson, *Consilience: The Unity of Knowledge* (New York: Alfred A. Knopf, 2000), 248.

9. Kenneth R. Miller, *Finding Darwin's God: A Scientist's Search for Common Ground Between God and Evolution* (New York: Cliff Street Books, 1999), 165.

10. Alister E. McGrath, *The Foundations of Dialogue in Science and Religion* (Oxford: Blackwell Publishers, 1998), 208.

11. Darwin, *Life and Letters*, 2:311.

12. Celia Deane-Drummond, *Biology and Theology Today: Exploring the Boundaries* (London: SCM Press, 2001), 16.

13. Pope John Paul II, "Evolution and the Living God," in *Science and Theology: The New Consonance*, ed. Ted Peters (Boulder, Colo.: Westview, 1998), 149-52.

14. Charles Darwin, *The Origin of Species by Means of Natural Selection*, vol. 49, *Great Books of the Western World*, ed. Robert Maynard Hutchins (Chicago: Encyclopedia Britannica, 1952), 243.

15. Darwin, *Life and Letters*, 2:312.

16. Michael Ruse, *Can a Darwinian Be a Christian? The Relationship Between Science and Religion* (Cambridge, U.K.: Cambridge University Press, 2001), 83.

17. Kirsten Birkett, *Unnatural Enemies: An Introduction to Science and Christianity* (Sydney and London: Matthias Media, 1997), 112.

2. Darwin, Darwinism, and the Neo-Darwinian Synthesis

1. Charles Darwin, *The Origin of Species by Means of Natural Selection*, vol. 49, *Great Books of the Western World*, ed. Robert Maynard Hutchins (Chicago: Encyclopedia Britannica, 1952).

2. Stephen Jay Gould, *The Structure of Evolutionary Theory* (Cambridge, Mass.: Harvard University Press, 2002), 96.

3. Thomas Kuhn, *The Structure of Scientific Revolutions*, 3rd ed. (Chicago: University of Chicago Press,, 1996).

4. See works by Aristotle such as "The History of Animals," "On the Parts of Animals," or "On the Generation of Animals."

5. Of note is the system proposed by Anaximander of Miletus, who argued that life originated in the primitive oceans. However, it is only with hindsight that his work can be argued to have ideas akin to Darwinian evolution.

6. Albert's biological works included *"De vegetabilibus et plantis," "De animalibus," "De motibus animalium," "De nutrimento et nutribili," "De aetate," "De morte et vita,"* and *"De spiritu et respiratione."*

7. Calling Lamarck a "biologist" is a necessary anachronism for clarity. He would have been known as a "naturalist." His major work was *Philosophie zoologique, ou exposition des considérations relatives à l'histoire naturelle des animaux* (Paris: Dentu, 1809).

8. William Paley, *Natural Theology: Or, Evidences for the Existence and Attributes of the Deity, Collected from the Appearances of Nature* (New York: American Tract Society, 1802).

9. Gould, *Structure of Evolutionary Theory*, 96.

10. Ibid., 192.

11. John Maynard Smith quoted in *Symbiosis As a Source of Evolutionary Innovation: Speciation and Morphogenesis*, ed. L. Margulis and R. Fester (Cambridge: MIT Press, 1991), 26-39.

12. For more details on and discussion of this correlation, see Kenneth Miller, *Finding Darwin's God: A Scientist's Search for Common Ground Between God and Evolution* (New York: Cliff Street Books, 1999), 44-45.

13. Darwin, *Origin of Species*, 87.

14. Charles Lyell, *The Principles of Geology: or, the Modern Changes of the Earth and Its Inhabitants As Illustrative of Geology* (London: Murray, 1833).

15. See, for instance, Michael Ruse, *Taking Darwin Seriously: A Naturalistic Approach to Philosophy* (Amherst, N.Y.: Prometheus Books, 1998) or Miller, *Finding Darwin's God*.

16. Quoted in Gould, *Structure of Evolutionary Theory*, 116.

17. Ibid., 117

18. Ibid., 119-21.

19. When it comes to theological responses, "two quite different meanings could therefore be attached to Darwin's *Origin*—that it was consistent with a biblical religion (as long as one did not take Genesis literally) and, conversely, that it undermined it. Because the prospect of evolutionary progress could become the basis of alternative religious creeds, the religious response to the Darwinian challenge is remarkable for its diversity" (John Hedley Brooke, *Science and Religion: Some Historical Perspectives* (Cambridge, U.K.: Cambridge University Press, 1991), 276).

20. This definition is taken from the glossary of terms on the Talk.Origins Archive website, located at http://www.talkorigins.org. This is a website devoted to the evolution/creation debate.

21. For instance, Phillip Johnson makes this crucial point in his anti-evolution argument published in *Darwin on Trial* (Washington D.C.: Regnery Gateway; Downers Grove Ill.: InterVarsity Press, 1991). We will discuss this text in more detail in chapter 5.

22. Ruse, *Taking Darwin Seriously*, 24.

23. Stephen Jay Gould and Richard Lewontin, "The Spandrels of San Marco and the Panglossian Paradigm: A Critique of the Adaptationist Paradigm," *Proceedings of the Royal Society of London* 205 B (1979): 205:581-98.

24. Stephen Jay Gould and Niles Eldredge, "Punctuated Equilibrium: The Tempos and Mode of Evolution Reconsidered," *Paleobiology* 3 (1977): 115-51.

25. Julian Huxley, *Evolution, the Modern Synthesis* (London: Allen & Unwin, 1942).

26. Julian Huxley, quoted in Gould, *Structure of Evolutionary Theory*, 503-4.

27. Gould, *Structure of Evolutionary Theory*, 1036.

28. Ibid.

29. See, for example, the list presented in the Talk.Origins website, "Observed Instances of Speciation" (http://www.talkorigins.org/faqs/faq-speciation.html).

30. Paul Davies, *The Fifth Miracle: The Search for the Origin and Meaning of Life* (New York: Simon & Schuster, 1999), 43.

31. Michael J. Behe, *Darwin's Black Box* (New York: Simon and Schuster, 1996); and William Dembski, *Intelligent Design* (Downer's Grove Ill.: InterVarsity Press, 1999).

32. Merriam-Webster Online Dictionary, found at http://www.m-w.com.

33. Richard Dawkins has written a number of excellent treatments that develop this theme, including *The Blind Watchmaker* (New York: W. W. Norton, 1986) and *Climbing Mount Improbable* (New York: W. W. Norton, 1996). The philosopher Daniel Dennett has written *Darwin's Dangerous Idea* (New York: Simon and Schuster, 1995), also in this vein.

34. Dawkins, *Blind Watchmaker*, 6. "What *is* arguably true . . . is that Darwin *should* have been an atheist. In this sense, those of his followers who try to portray him as an atheist are right" (David Ray Griffin, *Religion and Scientific Naturalism: Overcoming the Conflicts* [Albany, N.Y.: State University of New York Press, 1999], 259).

35. Michael Ruse, *Can a Darwinian Be a Christian?* (Cambridge: Cambridge University Press, 2001), 128.

36. Darwin, *Origin of Species*, 239.

3. Social Darwinism, Sociobiology, and Evolutionary Psychology

1. Herbert Spencer's essay, "The Developmental Hypothesis," was originally published anonymously in 1852 in *The Leader* and is now available on the Web at http://65.107.211.206/science/science_texts/spencer_dev_hypothesis.html

2. The reference can be found in Spencer's work in volume 1, on page 444, according to information found at http://educ.southern.edu/tour/who/pioneers/spencer.html. Darwin inserts this phrase into *Origin of Species* and credits Spencer with its origin. In chapter 3 ("Struggle for Existence") in the definitive 6th edition, Darwin writes, "I have called this principle, by which each slight variation, if useful, is preserved, by the term natural selection, in order to mark its relation to man's power of selection. But the expression often used by Mr. Herbert Spencer, of the Survival of the Fittest, is more accurate, and is sometimes equally convenient" (p. 32).

3. Herbert Spencer, *Social Statics: The Conditions Essential to Human Happiness Specified, and the First of Them Developed* (New York: D. Appleton, 1864), 414-15.

4. Thomas H. Huxley, *Evolution and Ethics* (London: Macmillan, 1893), viii, 44.

5. An interesting website devoted to the work of Francis Galton and a celebration of his achievements, including his hereditarianism and eugenics arguments, can be found at http://www.mugu.com/galton/.

6. Francis Galton, *Finger Prints* (London: Macmillan and Co., 1892).

7. Francis Galton, *Memories of My Life* (London: Methuen & Co., 1908), 322.

8. Francis Galton, *Hereditary Genius: An Inquiry into Its Laws and Consequences* (New York: St. Martin's Press, 1978).

9. Galton, *Memories of My Life*, 323.

10. Galton, *Hereditary Genius*, 338.

11. The Dolan DNA Learning Center at The Cold Spring Harbor Laboratory has mounted an impressive and important website devoted to the history of the eugenics movement in the United States. This is a must-visit for anyone interested in this topic. The site can be found at http://www.eugenicsarchive.org/eugenics/. An illuminating history can be found in Daniel J. Kevles, *In the Name of Eugenics* (Berkeley and Los Angeles: University of California Press, 1985).

12. See the report of the Buck case and the Supreme Court decision at http://www.dnalc.org/resources/buckvbell.html.

13. Ibid.

14. Joachim C. Fest, *Hitler*, trans. Richard and Clara Winston (New York: Harcourt Brace Jovanovich, 1973), 208; Hitler's words quoted in Fest, *Hitler*, 208.

15. An excellent website for information about the Holocaust can be found at the Simon Wiesenthal Center URL: http://www.wiesenthal.com/. We also recommend a physical visit to the United States Holocaust Memorial Museum in Washington, D.C. A day spent at that center will be challenging and ultimately transforming. The website for the museum is http://www.ushmm.org/.

16. See Robert N. Proctor, *Racial Hygiene: Medicine Under the Nazis* (Cambridge Mass.: Harvard University Press, 1988).

17. A wonderful collection of papers, published in honor of Max Delbrück, that describe this period is *Phage and the Origins of Molecular Biology* (Plainview, N.Y.: Cold Spring Harbor Laboratory Press, 1992). Another account of the beginnings of the disci-

pline can be found in *The Eighth Day of Creation* by Horace Judson (Plainview, N.Y.: Cold Spring Harbor Laboratory Press, 1996).

18. A new edition of Edward O. Wilson's book, *Sociobiology: The New Synthesis*, has recently been published by Harvard University Press (Cambridge, Mass.: Harvard University Press, 2000) in celebration of the twenty-fifth anniversary of the original edition (1975).

19. A recent account of the reaction to the publication of *Sociobiology* can be found in the online journal *First Things: The Journal of Religion and Public Life*. The article is called "Against Sociobiology" by Tom Bethell. It can be found at http://www.firstthings.com/ftissues/ft0101/articles/bethell.html.

20. Michael Ruse, *Sociobiology: Sense or Nonsense?* (Dordrecht; Boston: D. Reidel Publishing Co., 1985), 75.

21. Richard Herrnstein and Charles Murray, *The Bell Curve: Intelligence and Class Structure in American Life* (New York: The Free Press, 1994).

22. Edward O. Wilson, *Consilience: The Unity of Knowledge* (New York: Alfred A. Knopf, 2000).

23. Richard Dawkins, *The Selfish Gene* (New York: Oxford University Press, 1976), 2. Because genes are selfish, so also are organisms, including persons, selfish, contends Dawkins. Holmes Rolston III is reluctant to apply moral categories to natural phenomena. "Since genes are not moral agents," he writes, "they cannot be selfish, and, equally, they cannot be altruistic" (*Genes, Genesis, and God: Values and Their Origins in Natural and Human History* [Cambridge, U.K.: Cambridge University Press, 1999], 49).

24. Wilson, *Sociobiology*, 3.

25. R. D. Alexander, "The Search for an Evolutionary Philosophy," *Proceedings of the Royal Society, Victoria Australia* 24 (1971): 177. See R. L. Trivers, "The Evolution of Reciprocal Altruism," *Quarterly Review of Biology* 46 (1971): 35-57.

26. Patricia Williams, *Doing Without Adam and Eve* (Minneapolis, Minn.: Fortress Press, 2001), 134.

27. Ruse, *Sociobiology*, 61.

28. Ibid., 142. "In theory one can argue analogically from the primates to humans; but in practice I am far from convinced that the sociobiologists have yet provided enough evidence to do so" (p. 145).

29. Edward O. Wilson, *On Human Nature* (Cambridge, Mass.: Harvard University Press, 1978), 167.

30. Wilson, *Consilience*, 241.

31. Ibid., 253.

32. Edward O. Wilson, "Human Decency Is Animal," *New York Times Magazine* (12 October 1975): 50. Actually, Wilson gives two incompatible arguments for valuing universal human rights. On the one hand, he argues that such a valuing takes us beyond kin preference and, hence, beyond genetic influence. On the other hand, he also argues that valuing universal human rights is an extension of kin preference in mammals. See Wilson's *On Human Nature*, 198-99. For a critique of the latter argument, see Mikael Stenmark, *Scientism* (Aldershot, U.K.: Ashgate, 2001), 68-77.

33. Rolston, *Genes, Genesis, and God*, 267.

34. Stephen Jay Gould, "Darwinian Fundamentalism," *The New York Review of Books* (12 June 1997).

35. Wilson, *Consilience*, 265.

36. Ibid.

37. Arthur Peacocke, *God and the New Biology* (San Francisco, Harper, 1996), 110.

38. Ibid., 111.

39. Darwin, *Origin of Species*, 243.

40. Jerome Barkow, Leda Cosmides, and John Tooby, *The Adapted Mind: Evolutionary Psychology and the Generation of Culture* (New York: Oxford University Press, 1992).

41. The website for the "primer" is http://www.psych.ucsb.edu/research/cep/primer.html.

42. Taken from "Evolutionary Psychology: A Primer," http://www.psych.ucsb.edu/research/cep/primer.html.

43. Robert Wright, *The Moral Animal: Evolutionary Psychology and Everyday Life* (New York: Vintage Books, 1994), 204.

44. Ibid.

45. The interview with Richard Dawkins can be found at the website for "The Evolutionist," http://www.lse.ac.uk/Depts/cpnss/darwin/evo/dawkins.htm

46. Hilary Rose and Steven Rose, *Alas, Poor Darwin: Arguments Against Evolutionary Psychology* (New York: Harmony Books, 2000).

47. Ibid., 4.

48. Ibid., 150.

49. Ibid., 52.

50. "We, alone on earth, can rebel against the tyranny of the selfish replicators" (Dawkins, *Selfish Gene*, 201).

51. Wright, *Moral Animal*, 163.

52. Cited by Fest, *Hitler*, 209.

53. Dawkins, *Selfish Gene*, 3. David Ray Griffin objects to Thomas Huxley and Richard Dawkins for jumping to altruistic values based upon their evolutionary naturalism, which limits them to survival of the fittest or the selfish gene. They suppose "a magical emergence *ex nihilo*" (*Religion and Scientific Naturalism: Overcoming the Conflicts* (Albany, N.Y.: State University of New York Press, 2000), 295).

4. Scientific Creationism

1. Henry M. Morris, *History of Modern Creationism*, 2nd ed. (El Cajon, Calif.: Institute for Creation Research, 1993), 72-73.

2. Cited by Ronald L. Numbers, *The Creationists* (Berkeley: University of California Press, 1992), 43-44.

3. Cited in Numbers, *Creationists*, 38-39.

4. Morris, *History of Modern Creationism*, 67-68.

5. Benjamin B. Warfield, "The Real Problem of Inspiration," in *The Inspiration and Authority of the Bible*, ed. Samuel G. Craig (Philadelphia: The Presbyterian and Reformed Publishing Co., 1948), 173; cited by John C. Whitcomb and Henry M. Morris, *The Genesis Flood* (Philadelphia: The Presbyterian and Reformed Publishing Co., 1998), xx.

6. Numbers, *Creationists*, 74-75.

7. Morris, *History of Modern Creationism*, 206.

8. See Bill Cooper, *After the Flood* (West Sussex, England: New Wine Press, 1995), 165.

9. Morris, *History of Modern Creationism*, 134.

10. Ibid., 147.

11. Numbers, *Creationists*, 171-83. In the 1950s, J. Frank Cassel of ASA embraced what he called "evolutionary theism," which Numbers describes as "an elusive position somewhere on the spectrum of belief between progressive creationism and theistic evolution" (p. 173).

12. See Hugh Ross's "Reasons to Believe" ministry website: www.reasonstobelieve.org.

13. Creation Research Society (CRS) website, www.creationresearch.org.

14. See "Worldwide Directory of Creationist Organizations" by CRS, www.creationresearch.org/organizations.

15. Stephanie Simon, "T. Rex Meets Biblical Text at Museum," *Los Angeles Times* (Sunday, December 9, 2001). See Answers in Genesis website, www.answersingenesis.org.

16. Morris, *History of Modern Creationism*, 297.

17. Ken Ham, *The Lie: Evolution* (Green Forest, Ark.: Master Books, 1987), 89; see p. 114.

18. Henry M. Morris, *Scientific Creationism* (Green Forest, Ark.: Master Books, 1985), 219.

19. Ibid., 228.

20. See the summary by Roger E. Timm, "Scientific Creationism and Biblical Theology," in *Cosmos As Creation*, ed. Ted Peters (Nashville: Abingdon Press, 1989), 247-64.

21. Henry M. Morris and Gary E. Parker, *What Is Creation Science?* (San Diego: Creation-Life Publishers, 1982), 20.

22. Morris, *Scientific Creationism*, 209. Actually, creationists fall short of unanimity on the complete maturity of the world at the moment of creation, especially the contention that the earth appears to be old when it is believed to be young. See D. Russell Humphreys, *Starlight and Time* (Green Forest, Ark.: Master Books, 1994); and Barry Setterfield, "The Velocity of Light and the Age of the Universe, Part One," *Creation Magazine (Ex Nihilo)* 4, no. 1 (March 1981).

23. Morris and Parker, *What Is Creation Science?* 42.

24. *Kreatianismus* and *Kreationisms* in *Religion in Geschichte und Gegenwart*, 4th ed., ed. Hans Dieter Betz, et al., 8 vols. (Tubingen: Mohr Siebeck, 1998–2005), 4:1737-38.

25. Morris and Parker, *What Is Creation Science?* 108-23.

26. Ibid., 78-82. See H. B. D. Kettlewell, "Darwin's Missing Evidence," in *Evolution and the Fossil Record: Readings from Scientific American* (San Francisco: W. H. Freeman and Co., 1978), 23; D. R. Lees and E. R. Creed, "Industrial Melanism in *Biston betularia*: The Role of Selective Predation," *Journal of Animal Ecology* 44 (1975): 67-83; and J. A. Coyne, *Nature* 396 (5 November 1998): 35-36. Creationists excoriate Kettlewell and associates because they glued moths to the tree bark in order to take the pictures. The creationists then claim that the researchers supplied these photographs as evidence. This appears to assault the credibility of the scientific study. See Carl Wieland, "Goodbye, Peppered Moths," *Creation Ex Nihilo* 21, no. 3 (June-August 1999): 56; and www.answersingenesis.org/docs/4105.asp in 2003.

27. Morris, *Scientific Creationism*, 216-17. See Ham, *The Lie*, 159-60.

28. Duane Gish, *Evolution: The Fossils Still Say No!* (El Cajon, Calif.: Institute for Creation Research, 1995), 34.

29. Morris and Parker, *What Is Creation Science?* 110.

30. Ibid., 11; see p. 225.

31. Whitcomb and Morris, *Genesis Flood*, 66.

32. Gish, *Fossils Still Say No!* 226.

33. Ibid., 224. See: Morris, *Scientific Creationism*, chapter 7.

34. Whitcomb and Morris, *Genesis Flood*, 118. For Morris's employment of the Paluxy mantracks, see *Scientific Creationism*, 122. Not all agree with the creationist interpretation of the Paluxy mantracks. Some argue that the footprints in question could not have been made by humans, because the size of the prints is so much larger than normal human feet. See Robert T. Pennock, *Tower of Babel: The Evidence Against the New Creationism* (Cambridge, Mass.: MIT Press, 1999), 217-21.

35. Stephen Jay Gould, *The Structure of Evolutionary Theory* (Cambridge, Mass.: Harvard University Press, 2002), 44-45, 986-90.

36. Numbers, *Creationists*, 338-39.

37. Morris and Parker, *What Is Creation Science?* 253. Actually, creationists are not consistent on this point. On occasion they seem to allow for either an old earth or young earth; on other occasions they seem to require belief in a young earth. An argument by Henry Morris for the latter can be found in *Back to Genesis* 138a (June 2000) at www.icr.org/pubs/btg-a/btg-138a.htm.

38. Morris and Parker, *What Is Creation Science?* 50.

39. Morris, *Scientific Creationism*, 210.

40. Morris and Parker, *What Is Creation Science?* 307.

41. Morris, *History of Modern Creationism*, 50.

42. Ibid., 51.

43. Ken Ham, Carl Wiel, and Don Batten, *One Blood: The Biblical Answer to Racism* (Green Forest, Ark.: Master Books, 1999), 78-79.

44. Ibid., 53.

45. Ibid., 58.

46. Henry M. Morris and John D. Morris, *The Modern Creation Trilogy*, 3 vols. (Green Forest, Ark.: Master Books, 1996), 3:129; see Ham, *The Lie*, 18.

47. Whitcomb and Morris, *Genesis Flood*, xxvi.

48. Morris, *History of Modern Creationism*, 308.

49. Ibid.

50. Kenneth R. Miller, *Finding Darwin's God* (New York: Cliff Street Books, 1999), 61, 76.

51. Ibid., 124, 264. Additional support for transitional forms could be garnered from the recent fossil discovery in China of a four-winged bipedal dromaeosaur (*Microraptor gui*) that marks a transition from land dinosaurs to an ancestor (*Archaeopteryx*) to birds (Xing Xu, Zhonghe Zhou, Xiaolin Wang, Xuewen Kuang, Fucheng Zhang, and Xiangke Du, "Four-Winged Dinosaurs from China," *Nature* 421 [23 January 2003]: 335-40).

52. Miller, *Finding Darwin's God*, 80.

53. Ibid.

54. Howard J. van Till, *The Fourth Day* (Grand Rapids: Eerdmans, 1986), 246.

55. Ian Barbour, *Religion in an Age of Science*, vol. 1 of the Gifford Lectures 1898–1991 (San Francisco: Harper, 1990), 10.

56. Ted Peters, ed., *Science and Theology: The New Consonance* (Boulder: Westview, 1998), 15-17.

57. Morris and Parker, *What Is Creation Science?* 297.

58. Duane Gish, "Creation, Evolution, and the Historical Evidence," in *But Is It Science?* ed. Michael Ruse (Buffalo: Prometheus Books, 1996), 281.

59. Morris, *History of Modern Creationism*, 366.

60. Isaac Asimov, "Science Versus Creationism," in *Voices for Evolution*, ed. Molleen Matsumura (Berkeley, Calif.: The National Center for Science Education, 1995), ix-x.

61. Stephen Jay Gould, "Evolution As Fact and Theory," *Discover* 2, no. 5 (May 1982): 34; reprinted in *Hen's Teeth and Horses' Toes: Reflections in Natural History* (New York: W. W. Norton, 1983), 254.

62. Morris and Parker, *What Is Creation Science?* 297.

63. Wayne Frair and Gary D. Patterson, "Creationism: An Inerrant Bible and Effective Science," in *Science and Christianity: Four Views*, ed. Richard F. Carlson (Downers Grove, Ill.: InterVarsity Press, 2000), 46.

64. Morris, *History of Modern Creationism*, xv.

65. Langdon Gilkey, "The Creationist Issue: A Theologian's View," in *Cosmology and Theology*, ed. David Tracy and Nicholas Lash (New York: Seabury; Edinburgh: T. & T. Clark, 1983), 55-69.

66. Morris, *History of Modern Creationism*, 296.

67. Cited by Michael Ruse in *But Is It Science?* 17-18.

68. Ruse, *But Is It Science?* 28-29.

69. Langdon Gilkey, *Creationism on Trial: Evolution and God at Little Rock* (New York and San Francisco: Harper, 1985), 21.

70. Ibid., 137.

71. Ibid., 25.

5. Intelligent Design

1. See Ted Peters, *Playing God? Genetic Determinism and Human Freedom*, 2nd ed. (London: Routledge, 2002).

2. Francisco J. Ayala, "Teleological Explanations in Evolutionary Biology," *Philosophy of Science* 37 (1970): 1-15; and "Darwin's Devolution: Design Without the Designer," in *Evolutionary and Molecular Biology: Scientific Perspectives on Divine Action*, ed. R. J. Russell, W. Stoeger, and F. Ayala (Vatican Observatory Publications, 1998, distributed by University of Notre Dame Press), 101-16.

3. A good online source for information about Islam in the Middle Ages in Spain can be found at the Internet Medieval Sourcebook, http://www.fordham.edu/halsall/sbook1d.html

4. Thomas Aquinas, *Summa Theologica*, translated by the fathers of the English Dominican Province, revised by Daniel J. Sullivan (Chicago: University of Chicago Press, 1952).

5. Ibid.

6. Ibid.

7. William Paley, *Natural Theology: Or, Evidences for the Existence and Attributes of the Deity, Collected from the Appearances of Nature* (London: R. Faulder, 1802), 1.

8. Robert T. Pennock, ed., *Intelligent Design Creationism and Its Critics: Philosophical, Theological, and Scientific Perspectives* (Cambridge, Mass.: MIT Press, 2001) and Robert T. Pennock, *Tower of Babel: The Evidence Against the New Creationism* (Cambridge, Mass.: MIT Press, 1999).

9. Phillip E. Johnson, *Darwin on Trial* (Washington, D.C.: Regnery Gateway, 1991), 14.

10. Michael Behe, *Darwin's Black Box: The Biochemical Challenge to Evolution* (New York: Touchstone/Simon Schuster, 1996), 5.

11. William Dembski, *No Free Lunch: Why Specified Complexity Cannot Be Purchased without Intelligence* (Lanham, Md.: Rowman & Littlefield, 2002), 314.

12. Phillip E. Johnson, *The Wedge of Truth: Splitting the Foundations of Naturalism* (Downers Grove, Ill.: InterVarsity Press, 2000), 129.

13. Johnson, *Darwin on Trial*, 69.

14. Behe, *Darwin's Black Box*, 39.

15. Ibid., 196.

16. William A. Dembski, *Intelligent Design* (Downers Grove, Ill.: InterVarsity Press, 1999), 13.

17. William A. Dembski, *Design Inference: Eliminating Chance Through Small Probabilities* (Cambridge, U.K.: Cambridge University Press, 1998).

18. Dembski, *No Free Lunch*, 12.

19. Ibid., 22.

20. Ibid., 15.

21. Dembski, *Intelligent Design*, 17. Elsewhere, he argues that science can provide epistemic support for theological claims. William A. Dembski and Stephen C. Meyer, "Fruitful Interchange or Polite Chitchat? The Dialogue Between Science and Theology," in *Science and Evidence for Design in the Universe*, by Michael J. Behe, William A. Dembski, and Stephen C. Meyer (San Francisco: Ignatius Press, 2000), 213-32.

22. Johnson, *Darwin on Trial*, 14.

23. Ibid., 17.

24. Motoo Kimura, *The Neutral Theory of Molecular Evolution* (Cambridge, U.K.: Cambridge University Press, 1983).

25. Johnson, *Darwin on Trial*, 42.

26. "Understanding the crucial role of philosophy in Darwinism is the key to understanding why the theory is so controversial" (Phillip E. Johnson, *Defeating Darwinism by Opening Minds* [Downers Grove, Ill.: InterVarsity Press, 1997], 56). Despite Johnson's correct insight here, he confuses two questions: "One question is: How ought Christianity be related to evolutionary biology—the pure science? The other is: How ought Christianity be related to evolutionary metaphysics?" (Nancey Murphy, "Phillip Johnson on Trial: A Critique of His Critique of Darwin," in *Intelligent Design Creationism and Its Critics*, ed. Robert T. Pennock, 465-66). Robert Pennock puts it this way: "Johnson has conflated two varieties of Naturalism—Ontological Naturalism and Methodological Naturalism. If science assumed the former then Johnson's charge of scientific dogmatism might have some merit, but . . . science relies on the latter" ("Naturalism, Evidence, and Creationism: The Case of Phillip Johnson," in ibid., 78). Johnson replies to Pennock that Darwinists use "bait-and-switch"—that is, they confess methodological naturalism but then by claiming truth only for natural explanations they in effect commit themselves to ontological naturalism ("Response to Pennock," in ibid., 99).

27. Terry Gray, "The Mistrial of Evolution: A Review of Phillip E. Johnson's *Darwin On Trial*," online version at http://www.asa3.org/gray/evolution_trial/dotreview.html.

28. Phillip Johnson, *Darwin on Trial*, 20.

29. Michael Ruse, *Taking Darwin Seriously: A Naturalistic Approach to Philosophy* (Amherst, N.Y.: Prometheus Books, 1998), 24.

30. Kenneth R. Miller, *Finding Darwin's God: A Scientist's Search for Common Ground Between God and Evolution* (New York: Cliff Street Books, 1999), 160.

31. One of the more interesting exchanges of views has been between Dembski and Howard van Till, a professor of physics at Calvin College. This exchange can be followed on the Web. For instance, van Till's review of Dembski's most recent book is entitled "E. coli at the No Free Lunchroom: Bacterial Flagella and Dembski's Case for Intelligent Design" and can be downloaded at AAAS Evolution Resources page (http://www.aaas.org/spp/dser/evolution/perspectives/default.html). Dembski's lengthy and thoughtful reply is called "Naturalism's Argument from Invincible Ignorance: A Response to Howard van Till" (http://www-acs.ucsd.edu/~idea/dembskivanatill.htm).

32. Dembski, "Naturalisms Argument," xiii-xiv.

33. Francisco J. Ayala, "Intelligent Design: The Original Version," *Theology and Science* 1, no. 1 (2003).

34. See Dembski's response to van Till at http://www-acs.ucsd.edu/~idea/dembskivantill.htm.

35. Robert John Russell, "Divine Action and Quantum Mechanics: A Fresh Assessment," and William Stoeger, "Epistemological and Ontological Issues Arising from Quantum Mechanics," in *Quantum Mechanics: Scientific Perspectives on Divine Action*, (Vatican Observatory Press, distributed by University of Notre Dame Press, 2001).

36. Howard J. van Till, "Science and Theology as Partners," in *Science and Christianity: Four Views*, ed. Richard F. Carlson (Downers Grove, Ill.: InterVarsity Press, 2000), 229.

6. Theistic Evolution: A Survey

1. Ian G. Barbour, *Nature, Human Nature, and God* (Minneapolis: Fortress Press, 2002), 16.

2. Francisco J. Ayala, "Darwin's Devolution: Design Without Designer," in *Evolutionary and Molecular Biology: Scientific Perspectives on Divine Action*, ed. Robert John Russell, William R. Stoeger, S.J., and Francisco J. Ayala (Vatican City State: Vatican Observatory Publications; Berkeley: Center for Theology and the Natural Sciences, 1998), 101.

3. United Presbyterian Church in the USA, General Assembly 1982, "Evolution and Creationism," in *Voices for Evolution*, ed. Molleen Matsumura (Berkeley, Calif.: The National Council for Science Education, 1995), 107.

4. Passed by the 67th General Convention of the Episcopal Church, 1982, cited in *Voices for Evolution*, 92. The American Jewish Congress similarly opposes creationism in the name of the First Amendment, and this requires denying creationism its status as a science and confining it to the category of religion. "Despite attempts to describe scientific creationism as scientific theory, it is our position that scientific creationism is a religious theory and that, therefore, the First Amendment establishment clause prohibits its being taught as science in public school classes" (in ibid., 84).

5. Pope John Paul II, "Message to the Vatican Observatory Conference on Evolutionary and Molecular Biology," in *Evolutionary and Molecular Biology*, 1; see Pope John Paul II, "Evolution and the Living God," in *Science and Theology: The New Consonance*, ed. Ted Peters (Boulder, Colo.: Westview Press, 1998), 149-52.

6. B. B. Warfield, *Evolution, Scripture, and Science*, ed. Mark A. Noll and Daniel N. Livingstone (Grand Rapids: Baker Books, 2000), 165.

7. See David N. Livingstone, "Science, Region, and Religion: The Reception of Darwinism in Princeton, Belfast, and Edinburgh," in *Disseminating Darwinism*, ed. Ronald L. Numbers and John Stenhouse (Cambridge, U.K.: Cambridge University Press, 1999), 7-38. "Hodge was quite clear," comments Wentzel van Huyssteen of Princeton Theological Seminary, "to take design out of the process would be to take God out of the process, and precisely for that reason Darwinism was regarded by him as atheism" (*Duet or Duel: Theology and Science in a Postmodern World* [Harrisburg, Pa.: Trinity Press International, 1998], 102).

8. Warfield, *Evolution, Science, and Scripture*, 56-57.

9. Ibid., 168.

10. Ibid., 162.

11. Ibid., 279-80.

12. Ibid., 286-87.

13. Ibid., 309.

14. Huyssteen, *Duet or Duel?* 134-35.

15. R. Scott Appleby, "Exposing Darwin's 'Hidden Agenda': Roman Catholic Responses to Darwinism," in *Disseminating Darwinism*, 175-76.

16. Cited by Appleby, in ibid., 186.

17. Pierre Teilhard de Chardin, *The Phenomenon of Man* (New York: Harper, 1959), 218.

18. Ibid., 220; see p. 277.

19. Ibid., 248-49.

20. Ibid., 180-81.

21. Ibid., 297.

22. Ibid., 262.

23. Ibid., 294.

24. Pierre Teilhard de Chardin, *The Future of Man* (New York: Harper, 1964), 124-25.

25. Ibid., 323.

26. Teilhard, *Phenomenon of Man*, 288; see p. 310.

27. Teilhard, *Future of Man*, 149.

28. Ibid., 152.

29. Karl Barth, *Church Dogmatics*, 4 vols. (Edinburgh: T. & T. Clark, 1936–1962), III.3.150.

30. Kenneth R. Miller, *Finding Darwin's God: A Scientist's Search for Common Ground Between God and Evolution* (New York: Cliff Street Books, 1999), 253.

31. Ibid., 267.

32. Ibid., 197.

33. Ibid., 207.

34. Ibid., 213.

35. Ibid., 234.

36. Ibid., 221.

37. Ibid., 236.

38. Ibid., 239.

39. Ibid., 245.

40. Ibid., 246.

41. Ibid., 246, 248.

42. Ibid., 258.

43. Arthur Peacocke, *Creation and the World of Science* (Oxford: Clarendon Press, 1979), 197.

44. Arthur Peacocke, *God and the New Biology* (San Francisco: Harper, 1986), xx.

45. Arthur Peacocke, "Biological Evolution—A Positive Theological Appraisal," in *Evolutionary and Molecular Biology*, 359.

46. Ibid., 363.

47. Ibid., 364.

48. Ibid., 366-67. "There was no perfect past, no original, perfect, individual 'Adam' from whom all human beings have now declined, what *is* true is that humanity manifests aspirations to a perfection not yet attained" (ibid., 374).

49. Ibid., 370.

50. Arthur Peacocke, *Theology for a Scientific Age* (Minneapolis: Fortress Press, 1993), 123.

51. Ibid., 126.

52. Peacocke, "Biological Evolution," 368-69.

53. George L. Murphy, "Cosmology, Evolution, and Biotechnology," in *Bridging Science and Religion*, ed. Ted Peters and Gaymon Bennett (London: SCM Press, 2002), 211.

54. Denis Edwards, *The God of Evolution: A Trinitarian Theology* (New York: Paulist Press, 1999), 13.

55. Ibid., 15; see p. 126.

56. Ibid., 38.

57. Ibid., 41-42. Actually, to speak of God self-limiting is inconsistent with panentheism. According to panentheism, God is constitutionally limited by sharing existence with the world. Self-limitation is not a divine free choice. Edwards, *de facto*, does not embrace panentheism but rather a relational trinitarianism.

58. Ibid., 44.

59. Ibid., 31.

60. Ibid., 52; see p. 121.

61. John F. Haught, *God after Darwin: A Theology of Evolution* (Boulder, Colo.: Westview Press, 2000), 46.

62. Ibid., 110.

63. Ibid., 97. Haught has considerable sympathies with Whiteheadian process theology, as might be obvious by describing God in terms of a noncoercive lure. Yet his emphasis on eschatological transformation goes beyond what Whiteheadian metaphysics can accommodate, placing Haught more closely to the Theology of Hope school.

64. Ibid., 75.

65. Ibid., 87.

66. Ibid., 94.

67. Ibid., 190.

68. Ibid., 114, our italics.

69. Philip Hefner, *The Human Factor: Evolution, Culture, and Religion* (Minneapolis: Fortress Press, 1993), 45.

70. Ibid., 117.

71. Ibid., 121.

72. Ibid.

73. Philip Hefner, "Biocultural Evolution and the Created Co-Creator," in *Science and Theology*, 174-75.

74. Hefner, *Human Factor*, 199-200.

75. Philip Hefner, "Biocultural Evolution: A Clue to the Meaning of Nature," in *Evolutionary and Molecular Biology*, 329.

76. Ibid., 351.

77. Philip Hefner, "The Creation," in *Church Dogmatics*, ed. Carl E. Braaten and Robert W. Jenson, 2 vols. (Minneapolis: Fortress Press, 1984), 1:356.

78. The idea of an *Epic of Evolution* comes from the naturalist attempt to supplement, if not replace, a theological doctrine of creation. Edward O. Wilson writes, "The true evolutionary epic, retold as poetry, is as intrinsically ennobling as any religious epic" (*Consilience The Unity of Knowledge* [New York: Alfred A. Knopf, 2000], 265).

79. Ursula Goodenough, *The Sacred Depths of Nature* (Oxford and New York: Oxford University Press, 1998), 11; see Paul Tillich, *Systematic Theology*, 3 vols. (Chicago: University of Chicago Press, 1951–1963) 1:113.

80. Goodenough, *Sacred Depths of Nature*, 11-12.

81. Ibid., 174.

82. Ibid., 27-28.

83. Ibid., 29-30.

84. Ibid., 45-46.

85. Ibid., 102.

86. Ibid., 171.

87. Karl E. Peters, *Dancing with the Sacred: Evolution, Ecology, and God* (Harrisburg, Pa.: Trinity Press International, 2002), 47-48.

88. Robert John Russell, "Special Providence and Genetic Mutation: A New Defense of Theistic Evolution," in *Evolutionary and Molecular Biology*, 194.

89. Ibid., 203.

90. Ibid.

91. Nancey Murphy, "Divine Action in the Natural Order: Buridan's Ass and Schrödinger's Cat," in *Chaos and Complexity: Scientific Perspectives on Divine Action* (Vatican City State: Vatican Observatory and Berkeley, Calif.: Center for Theology and the Natural Sciences, 1995), 341.

92. Ibid., 342.

93. Russell, "Special Providence," 206.

94. Ian G. Barbour, "Five Models of God and Evolution," in *Evolutionary and Molecular Biology*, 433.

95. Russell, "Special Providence," 219.

96. Paul Davies, "Teleology Without Teleology: Purpose Through Emergent Complexity," in *Evolutionary and Molecular Biology*, 153.

97. Ibid., 159.

98. Ibid., 215.

99. Ibid., 221.

100. Ibid., 222.

101. Ibid., 223.

102. Our list of thinkers in the theistic evolution camps is by no means exhaustive. Numerous other scholars would deserve inclusion should we have room, especially Howard J. van Till, *The Fourth Day* (Grand Rapids: William B. Eerdmans, 1986); Keith Ward, *Divine Action* (London: Collins Religious Publishing, 1990); Holmes Rolston III, *Genes, Genesis, and God: Values and Their Origins in Natural and Human History* (Cambridge, U.K.: Cambridge University Press, 1999); and Vine Deloria Jr., *Evolution, Creationism, and Other Modern Myths* (Golden, Colo.: Fulcrum Publishing, 2002).

7. Theistic Evolution: A Constructive Proposal

1. See the discussion by Wolfhart Pannenberg, *Systematic Theology*, 3 vols. (Grand Rapids, Mich.: William B. Eerdmans, 1991–1998), 2:35-43.

2. Basil the Great, *The Hexaemeron*, Homily I:6.

3. "We believe in Genesis which by its very nature is epigenesis," wrote South African statesman and philosopher, Jan Smuts. *Holism and Evolution* (Capetown: N & S Press, 1926, 1987), 9. For Smuts, the drive towards holism in Evolution accounts for its creativity. "Evolution is not merely a process of change, or regrouping of the old into new forms; it is creative . . . it creates both new materials and new forms" (ibid., 89). Epigenesis is a key connector between evolution and theology. Wolfhart Pannenberg puts it this way: "The Bible conceives of God's relationship to the world in terms of free creative acts in the course of history as well as at the beginning of this world. . . . Consequently, a concept of evolution in terms of a purely mechanical process would not be easy to reconcile with the biblical idea of God's creative activity; yet the concept of an epigenetic process of evolution with something new to occur in virtually every single event is perfectly compatible with it" ("Human Life: Creation Versus Evolution?" in *Science and Theology: The New Consonance*, ed. Ted Peters [Boulder, Colo.: Westview Press, 1998], 141-42.

4. "*Holism* is both a rejection of ontological reductionism and a claim that the whole influences the parts. . . . The whole/part distinction is usually structural and spatial. . . . *Top-down causality* is a very similar concept, but it draws attention to a hierarchy of many levels characterized by qualitative differences in organization and activity" (Ian G. Barbour, *Nature, Human Nature, and God* [Minneapolis: Fortress Press, 2002], 22.

5. "The first creation was *ex nihilo* while the new creation will be *ex vetere*," writes John Polkinghorne. "The new creation represents the transformation of that universe when it enters freely into a new and closer relationship with its Creator, so that it becomes a totally sacramental world, suffused with the divine presence" (*The Faith of a Physicist* [Princeton: Princeton University Press, 1994], 167; or *Science and Christian Belief* [London: SPCK, 1994], 167).

6. Ibid.

7. Attempting to conceive of eschatological nature is the task of *Resurrection: Scientific and Theological Assessments*, ed. Ted Peters, Robert John Russell, and Michael Welker (Grand Rapids: William B. Eerdmans, 2002). Physical cosmology within science does not forecast eschatological redemption. Rather, it predicts one of two scenarios for the end of the universe: either dissipation into equilibrium, which will freeze it out of structured existence, or a collapse back into a singularity in which the rise in heat will destroy all structured form as we know it. Whether freeze or fry, science cannot predict the fulfillment theologians promise will arrive by divine action.

8. Augustine, *Confessions*, trans. Henry Chadwick (Oxford: Oxford University Press, 1991), XI:vii (9.), p. 226.

9. John Paul II, (1996) "Truth Cannot Contradict Truth," Address to the Pontifical Academy of Science, October 22, 1996; see "Evolution and the Living God," in *Science and Theology*, 150.

10. For a discussion of those aspects of the American Indian worldview that might be called "theology" in the Western definition, see C. S. Kidwell, H. Noley, and G. E. Tinker, *A Native American Theology* (New York: Orbis Books, 2001); and Vine Deloria Jr., *Evolution, Creationism, and Other Modern Myths* (Golden, Colo.: Fulcrum Publishing, 2002).

11. Thomas Aquinas, *Summa Theologica*, Part I, Q. II, Art. 3, Translated by the Fathers of the English Dominican Province, Revised by Daniel J. Sullivan (Chicago: Encyclopedia Britannica, 1952), 13.

12. David Hume, *An Enquiry Concerning Human Understanding*, Section XII, Part 3.

13. Timothy J. Wengert, "Peace, Peace . . . Cross, Cross: Reflections on How Martin Luther Relates the Theology of the Cross to Suffering," *Theology Today* 59, no. 2 (July 2002): 200.

14. Philip Hefner, *The Human Factor* (Minneapolis: Fortress Press, 1993).

15. "Man is condemned to be free," writes Jean-Paul Sartre (*Existentialism and Human Emotions* [New York: Philosophical Library, 1957], 23).

16. Plato, *Republic*, VI:505.

17. George Edward Moore, *Principia Ethica* (Cambridge: Cambridge University Press, 1966), 45.

18. Ibid., 58. Within the camp of those attempting to derive a social ethic from the precedents set by evolutionary biology we find division. Herbert Spencer's ethic based on survival of the fittest justified social emulation of nature's predatory brutality. Thomas Huxley, in contrast, appealed to progress within evolutionary development to support an ethic that lifts us beyond brute selfishness to social cooperation and humanistic values. This leads Mary Midgley to lodge our responsibility in inescapable choice. We must choose whether we will follow the ethic of predatory greed or carry a more high minded attitude. "The choice between these attitudes is a moral choice . . . so it cannot be determined by science" (Mary Midgley, "Criticizing the Cosmos," in *Is Nature Ever Evil?* ed. Willem B. Drees [London and New York: Routledge, 2003], 24).

19. See Ted Peters, *GOD—The World's Future*, rev. ed. (Minneapolis: Fortress Press, 2000), chap. 12.

20. John C. Fletcher and W. French Anderson, "Germ-Line Gene Therapy: A New Stage of Debate," *Law, Medicine, and Health Care* 20, nos. 1-2 (Spring/Summer 1992): 31.

21. "Virtually no ethicist, working within either a religious or a secular context, contests the principle that new genetic knowledge should be used to improve human health and relieve suffering" (Audrey R. Chapman, *Unprecedented Choices: Religious Ethics at the Frontiers of Genetic Science* [Minneapolis: Fortress Press, 1999], 68).

22. One aspect the changing character of information about genetic systems can be seen in the newly emerging science of networks as it is applied to biology. For a discussion of how this science can change the viewpoint, see Albert-László Barabási, *Linked: The New Science of Networks* (Cambridge, Mass.: Perseus Publishing, 2002). For a recent perspective on this, see also Zoltán Oltvai and Albert-László Barabási, "Life's Complexity Pyramid," *Science* 298 (2002): 763.

23. James C. Peterson, *Genetic Turning Points* (Grand Rapids: William B. Eerdmans, 2001), 321. See Ted Peters, ed., *Genetics: Issues of Social Justice* (Cleveland: Pilgrim Press, 1998).

24. Pope John Paul II, "The Human Person Must Be the Beginning, Subject and Goal of All Scientific Research," Address to the Pontifical Academy of Sciences, *L'Osservatore Romano*, N-45 (9 November 1994): 3.

25. Karl Rahner, *Foundations of Christian Faith* (New York: Seabury, 1978), 35.

26. Karl Rahner, *Theological Investigations*, 22 vols. (London: Darton, Longman, and Todd, 1961–1976; New York: Seabury, 1974–1976; New York: Crossroad, 1976–1988) IX:211.

GLOSSARY

Adaptationism. The concept in evolutionary theory that changes in a population represent adaptations to existing environmental conditions. Such adaptations result from the selection of variants in the population. These variants arise gradually over long periods of time by the random action of natural processes.

Altruism. In common parlance, altruism refers to our motive to seek the welfare of someone else, someone who is other to us. In sociobiology and evolutionary psychology, altruism refers to enhancing another organism's reproductive potential while diminishing one's own reproductive potential. Because the gene is always selfish, those whom the altruist serves will be kin—that is, those who share a large number of genes.

Archonic. From the Greek word *arche*, meaning both "beginning" and "governance." We find it in compound words such as "hierarchy" or "monarchy" or "archaeological." Archonic thinking presumes that the way something begins determines its being or essence or identity.

Aseity. Independence. God is a free being solely responsible for the divine being. God is not dependent upon anything else. Believed by theists and deists, but not pantheists or panentheists.

Atheism. A doctrine that says God does not exist.

Catastrophism. An explanation for the occurrence of features of the earth as a result of catastrophic events, such as floods or earthquakes. Although discredited with respect to the biblical flood of Noah, catastrophic events such as meteorite or comet impacts are invoked in the case of mass extinction.

Common Descent. The evolutionary principle that all life, including human life, shares a common descent from the beginning and shares a relationship on the evolutionary tree. Humans are not separately created.

Concursus. Cooperation of divine action with the action of finite creatures. Mediate *concursus* describes God's gift of the capacity of creatures to act contingently or independently; immediate *concursus* refers to the simultaneous exercise of divine action within human actions. B. B. Warfield applies immediate *concursus* to the cooperation of the Bible's writers with the inspiration of the Holy Spirit. Some theistic evolutionists apply mediate *concursus* to natural selection as divine activity in the world.

Contingency. The process by which events take place as a result of chance or random processes. The idea that such events are unpredictable.

Creatio ex nihilo. Creation out of nothing.

Creatio continua. Continuing creation.

Creationism. This term has three meanings. First, at the most abstract, it refers to the deistic or theistic belief that God created the entire natural world, that the natural world is not self-originating. Second, it refers to an ancient Christian belief still advocated by the Vatican that God creates each human soul *de novo*, brand new, either at birth or at conception. Third, it refers to the school of thought that denies Darwinian evolutionary theory by denying that natural selection can explain either the origin of life or the origin of new species. This anti-evolutionary creationism comes in two forms: (a) biblical creationism that relies upon the authority of the Bible, or (b) scientific creationism that relies upon scientific argumentation to establish the necessity for belief in God as creator of the natural world.

Day-age Theory. Theory within conservative biblical interpretation that assigns one thousand years or an indefinite period of time to each of the seven days of creation in Genesis 1:1–2:4a.

Descent with Modification. The way in which common descent leads to the observed diversity of species. Modifications, in this case, refer to variations in populations that increase the reproductive fitness of individuals.

Deism. The belief that a God with aseity created from nothing the world complete with its material content and the laws to govern it; then God absented the divine self to permit the world to undergo its own self-guided development. Deists usually deny miracles and other forms of divine intervention into nature's closed causal nexus.

Determinism. A mechanistic view of the natural world in which events are a predictable result of natural processes.

Divine Action. God acts as primary cause when creating the world *de novo*, when originating the natural world. God also acts within the created world, which ordinarily operates according to secondary causes or the laws of nature. Such divine action can be *interventionist*—that is, affecting or contravening the laws of nature—or *noninterventionist*—that is, in concurrence with the laws of nature.

Emergence. The principle that higher order structures are not explainable as the sum of the parts, but rather emerge from the complexity of the system.

Empiricism. The philosophical position that all knowledge arises from direct experience provided by the physical senses. When applied to the scientific enterprise, it includes the idea that direct experimental investigation is the proper way of gaining knowledge about the natural world.

Environment of Evolutionary Adaptedness (EEA). The environment in evolutionary history wherein a particular species adapted—that is, became reproductively successful.

Epigenesis. Literally, a second genesis. The emergence of new complex physical forms that transcend the constituent elements that make them up. Our use of "epigenesis" comes from Jan Smuts; it is not used here as E. O. Wilson does, where it refers to extra-genetic phenomena such as culture, which are constrained by genetic rules. Epigenesis is a sister concept to emergence and holism.

Epistemology. The branch of philosophy dealing with how one can have knowledge.

Eschatology. The doctrine of *last things*, which in Christian theology include: death, resurrection, consummation, kingdom of God, new creation, heaven, and hell.

Eugenics. The attempt to improve the human race by interventionist approaches. Positive eugenics involves the encouragement of breeding by certain desired types. Negative eugenics involves the culling of undesired types.

Evolutionary Psychology. The discipline that attempts to understand human behavior as a consequence of genetically determined traits that evolved during a specific period in human history, characterized as the environment of evolutionary adaptedness. Sometimes a synonym for sociobiology.

Explanatory Adequacy. A criterion for testing the relative value of a theory or model by measuring the scope of its power to illuminate data, experience, or other forms of existing knowledge. Applying to both theology and science, a conceptual model is explanatorily adequate if it is (1) applicable to what is known, (2) sufficiently comprehensive that all relevant knowledge is included, (3) logical or consistent, and (4) sufficiently coherent so that various components of the model imply other components and the whole.

Fitness. The relative ability of one species to be reproductively successful compared to another species under a given set of conditions. The larger the number of viable fertile offspring, the more fit.

Free-will Defense. Primarily within the tradition of Christian theism, free will is appealed to for explaining why the natural world operates independently of divine action and why evil in the form of sin, suffering, and death exists. Accordingly, God is free. Out of freedom God decides to restrict the scope of divine power so that creatures can become autonomous in the exercise of creaturely power. This results in human beings having a measure of freedom as well. Creaturely freedom becomes the condition whereby the created order can deviate from the divine will; and free creaturely action introduces evil into God's otherwise good creation. God is thereby defended from the charge of perpetrating evil. Sometimes, evil is considered a price worth paying for creatures to enjoy their God-given freedom.

Fundamentalism. A form of conservative Protestantism originating in America in 1910, which holds tenaciously to the "five fundamentals" of orthodox Christian belief: (1) verbal inspiration and inerrancy of Scripture; (2) deity of Jesus Christ; (3) substitutionary atonement; (4) physical resurrection of Jesus Christ; and (5) miracles. The energy of fundamentalism rises from its vehement opposition to the use of higher criticism in liberal protestantism when interpreting the Bible. Fundamentalism was not originally anti-science, nor anti-Darwinian. Its opposition to evolutionary theory developed as creationism developed.

Gap Theory. A theory within conservative biblical interpretation that places a temporal gap within Genesis 1:1-2 for an unidentified previous creation that was destroyed, accounting for the fossil evidence of ancient life-forms. Genesis 1:2 is translated "the earth *became* formless and void" rather than "the earth *was* formless and void." An original creation fell with Satan; so Genesis 1:3ff describes the present but second creation.

Gene, Genetics. The set of principles elucidated by Gregor Mendel that describe the quantitative laws by which traits are passed from one generation to the next. The gene itself can be defined as the unit of inheritance or as a specific set of base sequences in the DNA molecule that is the chemical structure of the genetic information.

Gradualism. The process whereby evolution proceeds by small, incremental changes. In the language of neo-Darwinian theory, gradualism presupposes that the small changes represent single base mutations in DNA, resulting in gradual variations that are subject to natural selection.

Group Selection. The effect of natural selection on a group of individuals not necessarily genetically related to one another.

Holism. The doctrine that the whole is greater than the sum of its parts. "Holism" is typically applied to the emergence of new life-forms, organisms that cannot be reduced to the chemical parts that make them up. A sister concept to emergence and epigenesis; the opposite of reductionism.

Human Evil. Sin, or the suffering caused by sin.

Imago Dei. "In the image of God," a reference to the statement of the creation of humankind as found in Genesis 1:26.

Intelligent Design. The theory that the observation of design in the natural world is an indicator of the action of an intelligence. Design, in this case, is defined as a kind of complexity that cannot be explained by appealing to natural processes (see **Irreducible Complexity**).

Interventionist Divine Action. Refers to God's action within the created world that affects or even contravenes the existing nexus of secondary causation. Miracles would be a traditional example. Leaps in evolutionary advance caused by Intelligent Design would be a contemporary example.

Irreducible Complexity. A single system composed of several interacting parts that contribute to the basic function, in which the removal of any one of the parts cripples the system. According to Intelligent Design advocates, such a structure is said to be irreducibly complex if one assumes that the structure could not have originated by natural processes, especially by gradualistic processes (see **Gradualism**).

Kin Preference. A correlate doctrine to the selfish gene within sociobiology, asserting that an organism will protect those who are genetically close to it in order to employ social organization in the service of perpetuating its own genetic code. Reciprocal altruism or mutual support usually engages other organisms that are genetically proximate—that is, kin. Xenophobia or fear of strangers applies to non-kin organisms that are genetically distant and hence not worth protecting until the age of reproduction.

Kind. The term "kind" as found in the first chapter of Genesis is employed by creationists as a near equivalent to "species." Creationists believe evolutionary change can occur within a kind (microevolution); but they oppose the contention that one kind can evolve into another kind (macroevolution). God fixed the kinds at creation (see **Preformitarianism**).

Logical Positivism. The philosophical position that science proceeds by the application of empirical methods and by the verification of theories.

Macroevolution. Natural selection applied to change as one species gives way to a subsequent species (see **Speciation**).

Materialism, Ontological Materialism. A form of naturalism that explicitly holds that the physical world of nature is self-explanatory, self-originating, and self-sufficient. Ontological materialism is usually associated with secular humanism and atheism.

Metaphysics. Literally, the philosophy beyond physics. In classical philosophy going back to Aristotle, metaphysics is the conceptual study of being *qua* being (see **Ontology**), utilizing the most comprehensive and inclusive descriptions of reality as a whole and the relations of its various parts. In the hermetic tradition and contemporary new age spirituality, "metaphysics" refers to supra-sensible or mystical realities. In this book, we use "metaphysics" in the classical philosophical sense.

Microevolution. Natural selection applied to change within a species.

Model. Conceptual models are produced in science when observations and data are incorporated into a testable structure that attempts to explain the observations and data. Models serve to approximate, to some extent, the real world situation.

Natural Evil, Physical Evil. Suffering caused to either human or nonhuman entities by natural forces other than sin. Disease, earthquakes, and bad weather are frequently described as natural evils because of the suffering they cause.

Natural Selection. The driving force of Darwinian evolution. Natural selection operates when a set of conditions differentiates between two variants in a population, based on their ability to reproduce successfully. As a result, the variant that can reproduce more successfully (or, is most fit) tends to be more represented in subsequent generations.

Natural Theology. An attempt to discern spiritual presence in nature or to arrive at proof for the existence of God through an appreciation of design and purpose in nature. In contrast to *Theology of Nature,* which relies on special revelation, *Natural Theology* relies on general revelation—that is, it presumes that God reveals divine presence within the natural realm in addition to any revelation that might take place in history or Scripture.

Naturalism. A philosophical position that presumes nature is self-sufficient and self-explanatory and the basis for human social and ethical values. Naturalism denies divine transcendence. In the context of the evolution controversy, naturalism provides the core commitments for ontological materialism, secular humanism, sociobiology, and related positions.

Naturalistic Fallacy. The logical fallacy of arguing that a moral *ought* can be based on the observation of what *is* the case in nature. Most often the fallacy is committed by evolutionary naturalists who want to provide a social ethic based upon what they observe in the nonhuman natural world. Some sociobiologists such as E. O. Wilson claim their ethical *ought* can be grounded in nature's *is* without committing a logical fallacy.

Noninterventionist Divine Action. God's action within the created world of natural processes without contravening or replacing secondary causation. Divine action at the level of quantum contingency as proposed by Robert John Russell would be an example of noninterventionist divine action. This contrasts with interventionist divine action, as we find it in miracles, and with the absence of divine action, as we find it described by deism.

Ontology. The philosophy of being.

Panentheism. Belief that the being of the world is in God and the being of God is in the world; but the world does not exhaust the being of God. God here has no aseity; rather, God is as dependent on nature as nature is dependent on God. Panentheism can be found among contemporary Whiteheadian process theologians and eco-feminists.

Pantheism. Literally the belief that all is divine, that the being of the divine is present within all living things and, in some cases, all physical things. The material world and God are coextensive. Pantheism can be found among American transcendentalists, Hindus, and new age spirituality.

Paradigm, Paradigm Shift. As defined by the philosopher and historian of science, Thomas Kuhn, a paradigm is a part of the underlying assumptions or working models in a discipline. When such paradigms no longer serve to elucidate problems in a discipline, they may be changed or altered. Kuhn argued that such paradigm shifts are how science progresses.

Preformitarianism. The pre-Darwinian idea that all of the observed diversity in nature had been created as it currently exists. Common to Aristotle and scientific creationism.

Primary Cause. In Aristotelian and Thomistic thought, a cause that has no prior cause (uncaused cause). God's action is the primary cause of creation, in complementary contrast to secondary causes operative within creation.

Providence. Divine care for—*providing* for—creatures through guidance of natural processes and events.

Punctuated Equilibrium. An evolutionary model proposed by Stephen J. Gould, Richard Lowentin, and others to explain gaps in the fossil record. According to this model, species are stable for long periods of time and then go through short (in geological terms) periods of rapid variation.

Reciprocal Altruism. Reciprocity ordinarily means mutual exchange. In sociobiology, reciprocal altruism is the service of an organism to enhance the reproductive fitness of another organism or of a community of organisms with shared genes.

Reductionism. The attempt to explain one level of organization by the principles at work at a lower level of organization. For instance, the attempt to explain all biology using the principles of chemistry and physics. When used as a protocol for experimental investigation, reductionism is a method. However, when taken as a theory of knowledge (epistemology) or a theory of being (ontology), reductionism is then a philosophical position.

Reproductive Fitness. The likelihood that one variant in a population will be more likely to reproduce and pass on its traits to the next generation, under a given set of circumstances.

Saltation. A sudden or abrupt change that brings about a new form of a thing.

Secondary Cause. In Aristotelian and Thomistic thought, a thing or event that proceeds from a prior cause. All secondary causes are the result of prior secondary causes or of the primary cause.

Selfish Gene. A term coined by Richard Dawkins, now common to sociobiology, referring to the inherent propensity of DNA nucleotide sequences to seek replication through reproduction of organisms.

Social Darwinism. Deriving from Herbert Spencer, various forms of social Darwinism employ natural selection, including reproductive fitness, to analyze human social behavior with moral approval of such principles as survival of the fittest.

Sociobiology. The study of social behavior in animals with implications for human social behavior based upon assumptions regarding genetic replication. E. O. Wilson and Richard Dawkins are considered leaders in sociobiology.

Speciation. The statement that new species arise by natural selection from preexisting species. Gradualism predicts that speciation occurred over a long period of time by slow changes. Punctuated equilibrium predicts that species arose during periods of increased variation, but that species were stable in between such periods.

Species. A distinct class of organisms or kind that share common characteristics. Members of a species can breed successfully within their species but not outside their species. The one word "species" is both singular and plural.

Survival of the Fittest. Although scientifically this refers to reproductive fitness in natural selection, sometimes it drifts toward a general moral approval of the strong eliminating the weak in society. Coined by Herbert Spencer and adopted by Charles Darwin as a synonym for natural selection.

Teleology. Theory of purpose.

Teleonomy. The appearance of design or purpose in natural functions that can actually be attributed to the operation of natural processes.

Telos. Purpose. *Telos* is the Greek word meaning *end* either as final state or goal.

Theism. Belief in a God with aseity who creates the world *ex nihilo* from the beginning and continues actively to engage the world with ongoing divine activity. Such engagement can take the form of interventionist divine action, such as miracles, or noninterventionist divine action, such as providence or *creation continua*. Trinitarian Christians tend to be theists.

Theistic Evolution. A family of theological positions that see a convergence between Darwinian evolutionary theory including natural selection with the doctrine of creation.

Theodicy. Literally, the justification of God in the face of a divinely created world that contains evil. In the philosophy of religion, the theodicy problem is the problem of evil formulated in terms of three premises: (1) God is omnipotent or all powerful; (2) God is omnibenevolent or all loving; (3) evil complete with suffering and death are present in the world God has created. This is an intellectual problem because only two of these premises can be affirmed, not all three, without introducing inconsistency.

Theology of Nature. Relying on special revelation, *Theology of Nature* interprets the natural world in light of understanding God as creator and redeemer. This contrasts with *Natural Theology*, which relies on general revelation to discern spiritual presence or to prove the existence of God.

Transcendence, Transcendentalism. A theological term designating reality beyond the material and social realm. God or spirit are usually considered transcendent to the physical world, beyond the physical while being present in the physical.

Two Books. Traditional Christian belief that revelation of God comes courtesy of two media, natural revelation and special revelation. Scientists study the first book and readers of the Bible, the second.

Uniformitarianism. The belief among scientists that the natural processes we witness today also operated in the past and will continue as they are into the future. Uniformitarianism usually opposes episodic jumps or punctuated leaps in evolutionary history; and it certainly opposes saltations or divine interventions.

Variation. Individuals within a population may exhibit slightly different inherited traits. Such differences or variations are acted on by natural selection. Some survive. Others don't. In the neo-Darwinian model, inherited variations are the result of genetic mutations.

Young Earth Creationism (YEC). Within creationism, the belief that the earth and the entire cosmos as we see it was created less than ten thousand years ago. YEC'ers presume that each of the seven days in Genesis 1:1–2:4*a* was twenty-four hours long.

INDEX

SCRIPTURE INDEX